*Drugs Alcohol and
Tobacco in Britain*

DRUGS ALCOHOL
AND TOBACCO
IN BRITAIN

Compiled

by

Jim Zacune and Celia Hensman

William Heinemann Medical Books Limited
London

First published 1971

© 1971 Jim Zacune and Celia Hensman

ISBN 0 433 39880 9

Printed by photo-lithography and made in Great Britain at
the Pitman Press, Bath

Contents

AUTHOR'S PREFACE

We have tried to gather, organise and focus a mass of data from many diverse sources in order to gain a perspective on the use and misuse of drugs, alcohol and tobacco and on the British response to these substances. Information we have found useful and relevant is set out with a minimum of comment.

There are two obvious limitations—one of place and one of time. The main focus throughout this volume is on problems and response in England and Wales, although wherever possible data have been included from Scotland and Northern Ireland. There are differences in administrative structure in these sections of Great Britain and no doubt problems and response differ to some extent. We have tried to make this clear wherever possible, but when this is not adequately interpreted the fault is entirely our own.

In terms of time, events overtake the writer—and his publisher—more rapidly than it is possible to predict. Decimalisation will have fully been implemented in Britain by the time this book is published and prices for earlier years are subsequently not exact. During the coming year the liquor licensing laws will be debated and if they are altered it may have enormous implications for the drinking habits of the country. Recently, the Secretary of the Department of Health (Sir Keith Joseph) has announced that two million pounds will be allocated for alcoholism treatment services over the next four years, and this expansion may considerably alter the existing arrangements for treating alcoholics. As regards drug use, the implementation of proposed legislation and the changing patterns of drug use in Britain are likely to alter the picture we have tried to assemble. We can only hope there will be later opportunities to assess these changes.

This book grew from a document called 'Problems of Alcohol and Drug Dependence in England and Wales—a Response to a World Health Organisation Enquiry' which was rapidly compiled for presentation at a series of consultations under the auspices of the World Health Organisation. All the members of the Addiction Research Unit in March, 1970 contributed to this preliminary document.

The earlier report was updated and expanded to form this book. Aside from the compilers, contributions were kindly provided by Dr. Griffith Edwards, Mrs. Stella Egert, Dr. Max Glatt, Miss Elspeth Kyle and Dr. Terry Spratley (Alcohol sections); Mrs. Julia Hancock, Dr. David Hawks, Miss Adele Kosviner, Dr. Martin Mitcheson and Mr. David Triesman (Drug sections); and Dr. M.A. Hamilton Russell contributed the Tobacco section. Information from Scotland was prepared by Dr. Chris Ross, Professor Henry Walton and Dr. John Warder, and information from Northern Ireland was provided by Dr. T. Baird, Mrs. Helen Hood and Professor L. Wade.

We have taken the liberty of substantially editing and re-arranging most of the contributions to this book and we hope the essence of these excellent writings have not been lost. Any errors, omissions or misinterpretations in the text are entirely our own responsibility. We have, by and large, used only British source material to be able to assess the strength and gaps of work in this country.

Comments, on the first draft of this document and later revisions, have proved enormously useful. Those kind enough to help us in this way include: Dr. T.H. Bewley, Dr. P.H. Connell, Dr. D.L. Davies, Mr. T. Cook, Dr. M. Glatt, Professor N. Kessel, Mrs. K. McDougall, Mr. C. Mellor, Mr. J. Orford, Dr. N. Rathod, Dr. B. Ritson, Dr. C. Salter, Dr. M. Sheppard and Dr. A. Wood.

Government Departments have provided us with a great deal of information and extremely good advice. These include: Department of Health and Social Security; Home Office; Scottish Home and Health Department; Department of Employment and Productivity; Board of Trade (especially H.M. Customs and Excise Department); Department of Education and Science; Health Education Council and Department of the Environment (especially Road Research Laboratory, Ministry of Transport).

Several organisations have contributed support and information services, including: British Medical Association; Institute for the Study of Drug Dependence; Institute of Criminology (Cambridge); Institute of Psychiatry; Medical Council on Alcoholism; National Association for Mental Health; National Council on Alcoholism and the Royal Society of Medicine.

Innumerable people have helped us, in one way or another, to complete this book; we are more grateful than any small acknowledgement can convey. There is no doubt, however, that without the never-ending patience of Christine Guest, who typed and creatively organised the manuscript, and the perpetual impatience of our colleagues in the Addiction Research Unit, this book would have never been conceived, nurtured or produced.

Jim Zacune
Celia Hensman

April Fools' Day, 1971.

FOREWORD

A World Health Organisation Expert Committee on Mental Health, meeting in October 1966, stated that 'Dependence on alcohol and dependence on other drugs create or contribute to major public health problems and should therefore be of concern to all public health organisations and administrations' and that 'The World Health Organisation should provide further leadership in the development of co-ordinated, multi-disciplinary, international research programmes and the stimulation of international co-operation and exchange of information on the problems under consideration'.

In 1967, Dr. Griffith Edwards was engaged as a consultant to assist in formulating a practical W.H.O. programme designed to foster improved services, research and exchange of information in this important field.

As a step in this direction, it was decided to undertake a series of W.H.O.-sponsored consultations on 'National Responses to Problems of Alcohol and Drug Dependence'. These consultations, it was hoped, would lead to the holding of one or more training courses or seminars that would 1) afford participants an opportunity to study and exchange views on several different types of programmes in at least three countries other than their own, 2) stimulate local and national compilation of information essential to sound programme planning, 3) stimulate research on the evaluation of preventive and treatment measures, and 4) stimulate further training in this area. Consultations were held in 1969 and 1970 and a travelling training course has been scheduled for the Autumn of 1971. In addition to Dr. Edwards and the undersigned, Dr. A. Bukowczyk (Poland), Dr. G. Jongsma (Netherlands) and Dr. J. Skala (Czechoslovakia) participated in both consultations. We were joined by several colleagues from these and other countries during the course of the 1969 and 1970 discussions.

Up-to-date, relevant information was needed as a basis for sound planning of action programmes dealing with alcohol and drug dependence. A means for gathering economically focused data that would yet allow for individual responses according to the national, cultural and economic context was essential. Consequently, the tabulation of major areas for inquiry were formulated as an 'Outline for National Inquiry on Problems of Alcohol and Drug Dependence'. This went through several revisions as a result of suggestions made by colleagues before and after field trials involving its use in Czechoslovakia, the Netherlands and Poland as well as in England. The final version of the Outline provided the framework around which members of the Addiction Research Unit, Institute of Psychiatry, London and many other professionals in Great Britain gathered and organised the data contained in this publication.

This review brings together a considerable amount of information that has never before been so extensively collated. A variety of agencies and individuals were approached for contributions. However the document cannot be expected to present a complete picture of the national situation. Hopefully, information will continue to be added or amended, so that the review may serve as a tool for surveillance. It should thus assist in present and future planning of local and national services to meet the problems related to the deviant use of alcohol and other drugs and should facilitate increased co-operation and co-ordination of effort between the various agencies and professions concerned. In the words of the W.H.O. Expert Committee: 'The etiology, prevention and control of dependence on alcohol and other drugs and the treatment of dependent persons involve multiple problems that extend beyond the competence of any single profession or group; it is therefore imperative that a multi-disciplinary approach be used'.

We take this opportunity of commending those who have contributed to this important document: it will serve as a valuable 'model' in future activities WHO's designed to encourage and assist the development of improved preventative, treatment and rehabilitation programmes and the pursuit of much needed knowledge in the field of dependence on alcohol and other drugs.

Mrs. Joy Moser, B.A., M.P.H.   Dale C. Cameron, M.D.
Scientist, Mental Health Unit.   Chief, Drug Dependence Unit.

World Health Organisation, Geneva, Switzerland.

INTRODUCTION

This book is profoundly unoriginal, at least in a certain sense. Its content is a mass of borrowings from the labours of other compilers, and nearly everything it contains could be otherwise picked up from a diligent reading of research reports and government publications. The generous agreement of all those many original compilers, collators and authors, to acts of piracy, is something to be very specially acknowledged.

Why then add another compendium to the library shelves? The intention is in part simply that of building up a useful box-file of snippets, tear-outs and reprints, so that instead of the reader having thereafter to walk once more all round the library, much data can be conveniently found in one place—a working tool.

But the larger intention of this volume was other than the mere accumulation of separate bits of data—and perpetuation of any sort of separateness. The intention was to attempt for the first time the portrait of a country's total response to the stark, but only fragmentally sensed and only particulately accepted fact of that country's inevitable and continuing co-existence with substances which act on the mind. One and the same country spends £2000 million a year on the alcohol it drinks, takes £900 million taxed revenue from those sales, and lays out over £20 million on advertising alcoholic drinks and the pleasures of the pub. Its liquor consumption climbs.

The same country—its left hand largely ignorant of its right hand—admits to hospital 7000 alcoholics each year, some of these to its 14 specialised alcoholism treatment units, makes over 80,000 arrests each year for public drunkenness, estimates that over 40% of its prison population and 60% of its vagrants have a serious drinking problem, makes 30,000 annual arrests for drunken driving. The country employs over 80,000 people in the brewing and distilling industry, and there are more than 125,000 licensed premises: as long ago as the 1930's Wilson reported that the cirrhosis death rate among publicans and barmen exceeded the national expectation by eleven times. Kessell and Grossman showed in 1961 that the suicide rate among a sample of alcoholics was 75% higher than the national average. The amount that the same country spends on educating the public as to the nature of safe and dangerous drinking is vestigial, and there appears to be only scant official concern directed toward prevention of alcoholic casualty. And so the story unfolds—the country smokes 365 million cigarettes a day, spends £12 million on tobacco advertising, derives £1000 million revenue, suffers 41,000 deaths as a result of its smoking habits, invests £100,000 in anti-smoking propaganda and finances one anti-smoking clinic. This same country makes 4685 convictions in a year on cannabis charges. It has set up 14 clinics in London to treat 2881 opiate addicts, and to these addicts it may give heroin. Its solid and ordinary citizenry consume each year 37.1 million prescriptions for sedative and tranquillising drugs and 3.9 million prescriptions for the amphetamines and stimulants.

The purpose of this compendium therefore is, with a minimum of comment or contention, to lay a range of facts side by side, and see then what sort of portrait emerges of a complex co-existence, of accidents and intentions, of implementations and inactions, of governmental and voluntary and commercial and criminal activities, which together go to make up a National Response.

The concept of a National Response needs clear definition—unless some framework for ordering all the mass of facts is available, their bulk and complexity can be overwhelming.

WHO 'RESPONDS'?

If there is to be talk of a 'National' response, what meaning is for present purposes to be given to the word 'Nation'? There are in fact many different elements within society which respond to one substance, and their response is at times opposed. Society is often ambivalent. The black market responds to a ready market for cannabis by supplying the need and reaping the profit; the official machinery responds by directing its energies to suppression; another element in society responds by campaigns for legislation. With alcohol the market is supplied by the response of licit enterprise, suppression is the aim of teetotal voluntary organisations, and tourist interests respond by pressing for easing of sales legislation; government takes some of the profit and treats or punishes some of the casualties. The same roles are there as for cannabis, but the players change. Departments of government, commercial investment, criminal interests, lobbies, charitable organisations, individuals, all have to be brought into the analysis of how the whole responding system works—sometimes the Government machine plays one role, sometimes another, and no single response or respondent can be understood in isolation. The activities of one influence the activities of another backwards and forwards in an inter-reacting system.

To designate only the government response as the national response would certainly be artificial.

WHAT ARE THE STIMULI WHICH EVOKE RESPONSE?

In terms of the behavioural model, a stimulus pre-supposes a response. What are the stimuli which evoke the responses of the system to a particular psycho-active substance?

a) The perceived possibility of profit. This, as outlined already above, at different times and with different drugs actuates government, commerce and crime.

b) The perceived threat to society. In the past this country has been urged to take action on alcohol because of the damage that drunkenness was supposedly causing to industry, the merchant marine, and the armed forces; the cost of alcoholism to industry is again today urged. Reaction to today's drug question seems to be partly in terms of perceived threat to 'the fabric of society'.

c) The perceived threat to the individual. To differentiate between danger to individual and to society is in the final analysis artificial, but certain responses seem more to be evoked by concern with the person than concern with the population. The individual alcoholic evokes concern, the individual drug addict, the person with carcinoma of the lung. The stimulus is often more effective when the individual casualty is seen as worthy rather than worthless, when he is seen as victim of disease.

WHAT DETERMINES 'PERCEPTION'?

Response is never to a stimulus but to a stimulus filtered through, accentuated, distorted or denied by, a process of perception. This country, and elements within this country, do not respond to its alcohol, drug and tobacco problems but only to the way they see these problems. What determines the nature of the perception?

a) The groundswell. A society reacts to and perceives problems of substance use and abuse in the general context of its prevalent value system. A society which has limited concern for the casualty can only have limited concern for the alcoholic. A society which is frightened of a new drug—entropy is always likely to result in less worried perception of the existing rather than the new problem.

b) The lobby. The organised lobby may be commercial, reformist, or medical and results when an influential group in society forces its perception on the larger society. The activities of the Royal College of Physicians in regard to smoking may provide a case in point. The health and helping professions in general, and increasingly too those concerned with the actual working of the penal system, likely to contribute to more or less diffuse or organised lobbying: the education of those professionals is therefore important.

c) The media. Press, radio, television, the cinema, the occasional play, the novel, all often perhaps without any conscious 'health education' motive, respond to society's perception and in turn share in the shaping of that perception. Professional journals play a specialised role.

WHAT CHOICE OF RESPONSE IS AVAILABLE?

For the whole range of psychoactive substances the following range of response choices are available:

a) Laissez faire. To do nothing is as much a response as to do something. Society can ignore lung cancer deaths, the policeman may often pass by the drunk on the street, cannabis at a Pop Festival may be smoked openly.

b) Take profit.

c) Seek to prevent or curtail substance use. Legislation, taxation, persuasion may be elements in such response.

d) Punish the user or particular manifestations of use. Cannabis use is automatically punishable, heroin use until such time as the doctor prescribes the drug, alcohol use when it leads to public but not private intoxication.

e) Treat the user or symptoms of his use. The person who consumes alcohol may be treated if he can establish necessary credentials for the sick-role: the criteria are not clearly stated, and he may rather easily find himself in the 'bad-role'. The cigarette dependent person may find it difficult to obtain treatment other than for his physical complications. The drug user will most easily be accepted in the sick role if he can display physical withdrawal symptoms, and opiate use is perhaps particularly likely to win him such recognition.

WHERE DOES THE POWER LIE?

Few would claim that society's response to problems of psychoactive substances is at present all for the best—co-existence probably implies a state of continuingly and intelligently revised imperfection, with the hope that someone has the power and ability to accept responsibility for the revision. Who initiates the decision to revise the national response—to put a new law on the statute books or take an old one off, to put a new class of people in prison or to transmute response from penal to therapeutic? The answer to this is difficult to determine. The civil servants may claim that the power in such complex matters lies with the politicians. The politicians may state that they can only respond to popular demand. The media may believe that they shape popular opinion but they admit the limit of their power. The answer seems to be that power in fact lies with no group but lies rather with the inter-reacting system: the system itself largely does not know how it works, but accidents may set off profound reactions within it, as also sometimes may skilled and intentional manipulation.

IS RATIONALITY A REASONABLE HOPE?

To suppose that national response to psychoactive substances will ever be entirely rational is unrealistic. Mind acting substances invite compassionate attack—the arguments relate to very basic values, to concepts of self and society which will never be other than value judgement. There will never be enough data to ensure that all actions are well grounded, and the variables are too many to suppose that the consequences of action will always be effectively monitored. The plea must however be that response should less often be only an immediate reflex answer to the immediate stimulus with neglect of wider implications and secondary consequences, and that the perception of the stimulus should more often be rather more accurate. Who determines the rationality of balance between prevention, treatment and research investment? What criteria differentiate the 'bad'- and the 'sick-role'? What logic determines the hierarchical ordering of the relevant danger of different substances? Total rationality may be impossible but the fair plea may be for more rationality than heretofore, a response which defines its premises and which makes goals explicit. The Standing Advisory Committee on Drugs may in some ways provide a model of how thinking may be aided toward rationality—is there room for a similar body with concern for alcohol or for tobacco, or should one control planning, integrating and reflecting body concern itself with all substances? Rationality is likely to be much aided by a sense of history, and an edited reprint of Dr. M.M. Glatt's classic paper on the history of alcoholism is to be found in Chapter 7.

WHO NEEDS WHAT DATA?

Data collecting as an end in itself is a purposeless game: data too easily becomes another sort of dust on the shelves. Data is only useful if it reaches the people who can and should consume it. We would hope that the present volume may contribute to the groundswell, may be useful to some lobbyists, and may even aid Power—wherever Power resides—in the planning of rational response.

SECTION 1

AVAILABILITY AND CONTROL OF
ALCOHOL AND DRUGS

This section discusses the total production of alcohol and other drugs in Great Britain and legislation which controls the use of these substances by the general population. Both alcohol and drugs are produced in a great quantity, but their distribution is controlled in very different ways.

Chapter 1 discusses the production of beer, wine and spirits and the structure of retail outlets from which the whole of the adult population in Great Britain can purchase alcohol. However, the purchase of alcohol is not entirely free of restriction and the licensing laws relating to these retail outlets are discussed in Chapter 2. This chapter reviews the taxation of alcohol and the duties levied on imported spirits, wines and beer. The revenues derived from taxation and import duties are a substantial source of income to the Government and these receipts are analysed. Finally, summaries of laws relating to the misuse of alcohol and drunkenness are given.

While less detailed data is available on the production of drugs, both manufacturers' figures for production and the cost of drugs to the National Health Service are outlined in Chapter 3. Chapter 4 reviews legislation concerning the general manufacture and control of drugs, as well as more detailed analysis of legislation relating to drugs which are illicitly misused.

CHAPTER 1
ALCOHOL PRODUCTION AND SALE

Production of beer is a major industry in England, as is the distillation of whisky in Scotland and—as will be described in Chapter 2—revenue derived from each contributes substantially to the national Exchequer. Questions of bulk and value of alcohol of all major types manufactured, exported and—of major importance in the case of wines—imported, are discussed in this chapter, as is the relatively small-sized problem of illicit spirit distillation. Some attention is also given to methods of retail distribution, which are however subject to the controls exercised by the Licensing Laws described in the following chapter.

MANUFACTURE

A total of approximately 139 million 'proof gallons' or 632 million litres of spirits were distilled, principally in Scotland, in 1969; 40 million bulk barrels or 6552 million litres of beer; and 11 million gallons, equivalent to 66 million bottles or 132 million litres, of wine; were produced in the United Kingdom, making a total equivalent to 23 gallons, or 105 litres of alcohol produced per head of the population. The trend in production over the past ten years can be seen in Table 1–1.

All three major categories of alcoholic beverage are imported to the United Kingdom also, a high proportion being retained for consumption; so that the total volume of spirits, beer and wine available in 1969 was approximately 25 gallons, or 114 litres, per head of a population of 55 million. For beer alone, United Kingdom consumption was 98.4 litres per head, which made her the eighth largest consumer by nation, in the world. (Brewers' Society, Personal Communication, 1971).

Production of beer accounts for the major proportion of the home production figures by bulk. Thus, in 1969, as can be seen from Table 1–1, 1148 million gallons of beer were brewed in Britain—nearly six times as much as the production figure for spirits—and a further 45 million gallons were imported from Denmark, the Netherlands, West Germany and the Irish Republic. Draught, bottled and canned beers are produced in six different basic types by the majority of the 103 brewery companies or groups active in the United Kingdom, making a probable total of almost 3000 brands.

In 1970 the Brewers' Society, the principal trade association concerned with the production, distribution and other activities of professional brewers within the United Kingdom, calculated that the industry had an invested capital of over £1700 million—more than three times that invested in the aircraft and aerospace industry, and not far short of the entire capital invested in the manufacture of foodstuffs: this investment totalled over 4.5% of the Gross National Product (Brewers' Society, 1970). Men and women employed in the brewing and malting industry in 1969 totalled 87,100, with a total of 33,400 engaged in spirit distilling and compounding or the making of British wine, cider and perry (Department of Employment and Productivity, Personal Communication, 1971).

Official United Kingdom production figures for 'ale' and 'beer' have been collected since the year 1684, although it is considered that less than 50% of actual production was recorded before 1800 (Monckton, 1966); domestic production from 1800 to 1950 was recorded in million bulk barrels, rising from an equivalent of 594 million gallons in 1800 to 1014 in 1950. (Wilson, 1940).

In recent years, production figures have been more reliably recorded by H.M. Customs and Excise, who are responsible for levying the tax. These figures are published annually, both by the Commissioners of H.M. Customs and Excise in their Annual Report, and in summary in the *Annual Abstract of Statistics* with reference to spirits, beers and wines separately (see Table 1—1).

OVERSEAS TRADE

The alcohol industry is a substantial export winner. The total value of United Kingdom exports of alcoholic liquor in 1969 was £186 million (see Table 1—2), over a third of the total national figure of £515 million for that year. Only a very small proportion of the beer produced in the United Kingdom is, however, exported—a total of 1.4% of home production in 1969, including re-exports of imported beer. (Central Statistical Office, 1970). In addition to direct exports, however, major United Kingdom breweries have been selling their beer overseas by acquisition of breweries and allied retail outlets on the Continent of Europe, in Africa and further afield during the past few years. One British company has been Belgium's third largest brewery concern since 1966, and this trend seems likely to develop further. In terms of money value, the import bill for drink was much smaller—some £69 million out of a total United Kingdom figure of £657 million; import duty is levied on all such trade. Account in both directions is kept by the Board of Trade and estimates published annually in the *Overseas Trade Accounts*, figures for such imports and exports over the past three years being as is shown in Table 1—2 overleaf.

Table 1–1. Home Production of Alcoholic Beverages in the United Kingdom. 1959–1969. (Converted to millions of gallons, see footnote).

	1959	1960	1961	1962	1963	1964	1965	1966	1967	1968	1969
SPIRITS (Converted from proof gallons)	94.9	109.3	112.7	123.0	142.9	172.4	200.0	207.3	186.1	178.0	199.1
BEER (Converted from bulk barrels)	914	954	997	1004	1019	1066	1066	1087	1105	1130	1148
WINE (Recorded in gallons)	6.3	8.0	7.2	7.6	8.1	9.2	9.3	9.4	9.5	11.0	11.0
Population of the United Kingdom (thousands)	51,956	52,372	52,816	53,341	53,678	54,066	54,436	54,744	55,068	55,283	55,471

Footnote: All figures estimated from total on which tax levied.
Spirits: measured in proof gallons where 1 proof gallon = 1.4 gallons spirits, 70° proof.
Beer: measured in bulk barrels where 1 bulk barrel = 36 gallons.

1 gallon = 4.55 litres.

Source: HM Customs and Excise. *Report for the Year 1970.* HMSO, London.

Table 1–2. United Kingdom Imports and Exports of Alcoholic Liquor. 1967–1969. (Converted to gallons. See note at Table 1–1. Imports calculated from total on which tax is levied).

		1967 Import	1967 Export	1968 Import	1968 Export	1969 Import	1969 Export
BEER	Value in £ thousand	11,636	2,653	12,618	3,235	13,065	3,946
	Quantity in thousand bulk barrels	1,533	297	1,617	340	1,607	377
	Quantity in thousand gallons	35,188	10,697	58,212	12,240	57,852	13,572
SPIRITS	Value in £ thousand	17,024	133,462	19,047	190,246	16,424	181,595
	Quantity in thousand proof gallons	Not	49,586	61,456	66,781	84,901	59,663
	Quantity in thousand gallons	known	70,837	87,794	95,401	121,287	85,233
WINES	(incl. fortified wine eg. Vermouth)						
	Value in £ thousand	35,655	447	41,146	545	39,528	770
	Quantity in thousand gallons	36,026	363	41,147	424	39,578	551
TOTAL	Import and Export value in £ thousand:	64,315	136,562	75,811	194,026	69,017	186,371

Source: *Overseas Trade Accounts*, 1970. H.M.S.O., London.

ILLICIT PRODUCTION OF ALCOHOLIC BEVERAGES

The only information available concerning the probable extent of illicit production of alcoholic beverages is provided by H.M. Customs and Excise, who report the number of persons convicted for 'illicit distillation' during the years 1966 to 1969 as follows:-

Table 1—3.   Illicit Distillation. 1966—1969.

	1966—67	1967—68	1968—69
Number of persons convicted in the United Kingdom	16	10	26

Source: H.M. Customs and Excise. H.M.S.O., London, 1970.

The quantity of spirits produced by those persons prosecuted for such offences is 'certainly insignificant in relation to the quantity of duty-paid spirits sold' (H.M. Customs and Excise, Personal communication, 1970). No information is available as to either the number of persons producing illicit spirits who remain undetected, or the amount of beer brewed privately at home for domestic consumption, which is a legal process encouraged by retail sales of the materials required. These are, however, believed to be of small dimensions in each case, 'of no social or revenue significance', and the quantity of beer brewed privately cannot be included in the official production figures.

Retail Outlets

The scale of manufacture of alcoholic drinks in the United Kingdom is matched by the increasing extent and variety of their retail outlets. Drink is on sale to the public on a take-away basis in supermarkets, grocery chains and 'Off-Licences' (authorised points of sale often associated with an inn or bar). It is also available for sale and consumption on the spot in public houses, hotels, restaurants and private clubs. (See Chapter 2). No figures are published relating to the number of people who are consequently employed.

The Tied-House System

The public house remains of major importance to the retail trade. According to the Brewers' Society (1970), over £1000 million of the capital invested in the brewing industry (60%) was represented by licensed property in 1969. An increasing number of the 115,000 premises licensed for sale of liquor in the United Kingdom, and a particularly high proportion in England and Wales, are currently owned by the Breweries; who have seen this form of vertical integration as a logical economic development. In a number of cases the Brewers have supply agreements which tie these premises, whether they are directly managed by the Breweries or let out to tenants, to their own brands of beer and, in a number of cases, to brands of spirits and wine which are themselves wholesaled by the Breweries concerned. By 1900 it seems probable that a majority of the 102,000 licensed premises then recorded for England and Wales were already owned by the Brewers, or tied to them by virtue of loan on mortgage. Since 1900 there has been a considerable diminution in the number of breweries and groups of breweries existing; there were 103 active brewery companies or groups at the end of 1968, and the trend towards smaller companies either going out of business or being bought up by larger groups has continued. Virtually all brewery companies or groups now own their own licensed premises, over 89% of beer supplied within the United Kingdom for retail sale such premises coming from brewers who own premises of their own. It was the possibility that the typing of retail outlets and of supplies to particular breweries was constituting a restrictive practice, which led to the referral of the entire beer retail system by the Board of Trade to the Monopolies' Commission in 1966, under the terms of the Monopolies and Mergers Acts of 1948 and 1965 (Monopolies Commission Report, 1969).

The tied house system has been energetically defended by the brewers, who emphasise the low rate of profit derived from retail sales alone, and the consequent necessity for investment in other spheres. This means however that it may prove impossible to purchase more than one brand of beer—or indeed of the wines and spirits which are supplied by the particular brewery involved—in many areas of England and Wales. Investment by the breweries in the hotel trade and in wider directions has increased, but it was admitted by the Monopolies' Commission that restrictive practice was in fact forced by existing Licensing Laws, which are consequently under review (see Chapter 2). It cannot be denied that the brewers frequently have a captive market; whether this is or is not in the public interest is the problem under debate. Allegations by the Monopolies' Commission were vigorously opposed by the Brewers' Society, who pleaded that brewers' activities and businesses should be examined and judged as a whole, not in relation only to profits in one sector. They complained this had not been effected by the National Board for Prices and Incomes, a body which is now (1971) extinct but had reported on the subject of prices in 1964 (National Board for Prices and Incomes. 1965).

As shown in Table 1—4 below, the net return on capital is a good deal lower in brewing than for instance in the food retailing and the leisure industries (11% as opposed to over 16%) and also lower than the industrial average across the board (14%). Additionally, the brewers plead, the cost of maintaining licensed premises is rising as a result of the average age of the buildings, and of sharply increasing labour costs in the building trade. The 206 public houses and hotels currently owned by the State have indeed suffered a relative decline in their profitability, although this stood at £249,689 net in 1969. They are to be denationalised during the course of 1971. None of this has deterred the brewers from launching a major publicity campaign for public houses, and devoting considerable ingenuity to the re-decoration and internal re-organisation of selected public houses in city centres and tourist spots (See also Chapter 5).

Table 1—4   Net Return on Capital by Industrial Sector.
(First nine months of 1970).

	%
Food retailing	16.7
Leisure	16.6
Chemicals	14.5
All industrials	14.2
Textiles	12.8
Food manufacturing	11.9
Aircraft	9.0
Breweries	11.1

Source: Brewers' Society.
Derived from Financial Times Analysis of
Industrial Profits, 1970.

Apart from the problem of brewery investment, the largest single expanding retail outlet over the past few years has proved to be the chain store and super-market. This development was encouraged by the abolition of Resale Price Maintenance, as a result of the Resale Prices Act of 1964. Thus, in August 1966, the distillers decided not to plead for retention of Resale Price Maintenance before the Restrictive Practices Court and in October, 1966 they abandoned it altogether; a move which was followed by the brewers during 1970. Supermarkets and discount houses which had off-licences immediately cut their prices extensively. Trade subsequently proved so brisk that by April, 1967, the number of large supermarkets (over 2,000 square feet in area) with off-licences in England and Wales had more than doubled. By the end of 1967 this figure was 264 (having risen from 102 in the autumn of 1966) and by 1969 the estimate was 473 (Board of Trade, 1970). On account of the changing price structure, proposals to change laws, and projected entry of Britain into the European Economic Community, it seems likely the entire pattern of distribution may be altered during 1971.

REFERENCES

BOARD OF TRADE, 1970. *Liquor Licensing Statistics.* H.M.S.O., London.
BREWERS' SOCIETY, 1970. *Problems behind the Pint of Beer.* Brewers' Society, London.
CENTRAL STATISTICAL OFFICE, 1970. *Annual Abstract of Statistics.* H.M.S.O., London.
CENTRAL STATISTICAL OFFICE, 1971. *Monthly Digest of Statistics.* H.M.S.O., London.
CENTRAL STATISTICAL OFFICE, 1970. *National Income and Expenditure.* H.M.S.O., London.
CUSTOMS AND EXCISE (HER MAJESTY'S), 1968–1970. *Annual Reports.* H.M.S.O., London.
MONCKTON H.A., 1966. *History of English Ale and Beer.* Bodley Head, London.
MONOPOLIES COMMISSION, 1969. *Beer: A Report on the Supply of Beer.* H.M.S.O., London.
NATIONAL BOARD FOR PRICES AND INCOMES, 1965. *Report on Prices of Alcoholic Liquor.* H.M.S.O., London.
WILSON G.B., 1940. *Alcohol and the Nation.* Nicholson and Watson, London.

CHAPTER 2
CONTROL OF ALCOHOL

INTRODUCTION

In the United Kingdom controls are placed on both the use and the abuse of alcoholic liquor. Alcohol is taxed and may be sold only in licensed places to people of a certain age, for a limited number of hours each day. Legislation exists to punish public drunkenness, to deal with offences which may be committed under the influence of drink, and to ascertain the culpability of those who may be intoxicated while in charge of a motor vehicle. By thus limiting misuse of alcohol, the State attempts to strike a balance between conflicting obligations; on the one hand permitting the majority of citizens for whom drink is no problem to drink when and where they would like, on the other hand dealing firmly with the minority who abuse alcohol and thereby become a threat to themselves and to others.

CONTROL OF NORMAL ALCOHOL CONSUMPTION

General

In the United Kingdom control is exerted by the State over the normal consumption of alcohol in two ways: first, by legislation governing the sale of drink (the Licensing Laws); second, by making liquor more expensive through taxation. The latter course, while presumably limiting the volume of liquor consumed, is not intentionally directed towards health.

The Licensing Laws

Legislation governing the sale of drink goes back to the 15th century, and descriptions of the historical evolution of the law have been provided by Sidney and Beatrice Webb (1902), more recently by Monckton (1966), and in the Monopolies Commission's Report on the Supply of Beer, (HMSO, 1969). Additionally, the implications of legal developments in licensing for abnormal consumption have been reviewed in the Home Office report on Habitual Drunken Offenders (HMSO, 1971).

The current law, which controls retail sale of all intoxicating liquor, is enacted separately for England and Wales, Scotland and Northern Ireland, and is of considerable complexity in all three countries. In England, for instance, law has evolved largely from the Alehouse Act of 1828 which was developed particularly by an Act of 1961, and enshrined in the Licensing Act of 1964 which consolidated all earlier enactments. In Scotland, licensing is governed by the Licensing (Scotland) Act of 1959, with some amendments which implemented recommendations made in a report of the Committee on the Scottish Licensing

Law in 1962 (Report of Guest Committee, HMSO, 1962). The authority to sell liquor in Scotland, granted by a licensing court, is termed a Certificate, there being separate Certificates available for hotels, public houses, 'off-sales' restaurants and 'restricted hotels'. Full details of current legislation and of the special situation relating to Scotland are provided in the Monopolies' Commission's Report (HMSO, 1969).

In Northern Ireland, the first licensing law to be enacted by its own Parliament was the Intoxicating Liquor Act (Northern Ireland) of 1923, amended in 1927 and in 1959; although some aspects of this law still derive from the Licensing (Ireland) Act, enacted at Westminster in 1833. Five types of retail licence apply: the publican's licence, hotel licence, off-licence, theatre or music hall licence and railway or airport refreshment room licence. Categories of liquor covered correspond to those for England and Wales; there being five possible categories, ranging from 'wine only' to 'intoxicating liquor of all descriptions' which can be granted.

Licensing Laws in England and Wales

Retail sale of intoxicating liquor in England and Wales requires a Justices' licence, issued by Justices of the Peace and by County or County Borough Councils. In granting such a licence, Justices have regard to the character of the applicant, the structural suitability of his premises, and the need for further licensed premises in the area. Registration certificates for clubs which permit the supply of liquor purchased by the club to members and their guests are issued on a different basis, since such premises are essentially private in nature and quite distinct. The four types of licence granted by Justices are for:-

On-licences, or premises with sale authorised for consumption either on or off the premises for which the licence is granted;

off-licences, with sale authorised for consumption off the premises only;

restaurant licences, which allow sale only to those taking 'table meals' to which the drink is ancillary;

residential licences, for premises 'habitually providing board and lodging, for reward'.

The five possible categories of licence, from 'wine only' to 'intoxicating liquor of all descriptions', is as for Northern Ireland.

In both licensed premises and registered clubs, liquor may be supplied and consumed during only a limited number of hours each day, which are generally from 11.00 a.m. to 3.00 p.m. and from 5.30 p.m. to 10.30 p.m. on weekdays; for 3½ hours less on Sundays and some Holidays. The exact hours are, however, subject to minor variations; and extension can be granted in circumstances where meals and/ or entertainment are provided to which the sale of drink is ancillary; that is for 'special occasions' and in other exceptional circumstances. An additional 10–30 minutes 'drinking up' period is allowed, in any case.

Children under 14 years of age are not allowed in the bar of licensed premises, and people under the age of 18 years are not allowed to buy or consume liquor in a bar, excepting those of 16 being allowed to take beer or cider with a meal. There are provisions in the law relating to the general conduct of licensed premises which cover such aspects as drunkenness (a licensee being forbidden to sell liquor to a drunken person), prostitution and gaming.

The total number of licensed premises, 'off-licensed' premises and of registered clubs (the members of which are deemed to be the owners of the stock of liquor held, so that their drinking is not considered as a sale in law; such clubs include social, political and sports gatherings), is recorded annually. The most recent figures for England and Wales are given with 1964 figures (for the purposes of comparison) below:-

Table 2—1.   Licensed Premises and Registered Clubs, in England and Wales. 1964—1969.

	1964	1969
Public Houses:		
Licensed to sell all liquors	65,483	64,448
Licensed to sell beer, wines and cider	1,448	600
Restaurants licensed to sell intoxicating liquor with meals	2,817	5,739
Residential establishments licensed to sell liquor to residents	837	1,504
Combined restaurant and residential licensed premises	1,358	2,055
Licensed (i.e. proprietary) clubs	2,040	2,488
TOTAL 'on-licensed' premises:	73,983	76,834
'Off-Licensed' premises	25,838	27,434
Registered clubs	21,872	23,176
Theatres where intoxicating liquor is sold to patrons	Not recorded	149

Source: Home Office Liquor Licensing Statistics. H.M.S.O., 1970.

The Monopolies Commission's Report on the Supply of Beer (1969) was convened by the Board of Trade to look into the whole question of retail supply and possible restrictive practices governing this; it recommended that, by way of remedy for the defects which had been found in the 'tied-house system', the licensing laws in England and Wales at least should be substantially relaxed (see Chapter 1). The general objective of such relaxation was to permit the sale of alcoholic drinks for consumption on or off the premises, by any retailer whose character and premises satisfied certain minimum standards. Greater flexibility than at present in opening hours was also suggested, and announcement was made by the Home Secretary on 8th December, 1970, of the setting up of an Independent Committee of Enquiry 'to review the liquor licensing laws in England and Wales in the light of the recommendations made by the Monpolies Commission, and of any other changes which have been made, and to make recommendations'. Lord Erroll of Hale has been appointed as Chairman of this Committee; its membership is still to be announced (January, 1971), and evidence will be taken during the coming year.

Table 2—2 shows the total number of premises for retail sale of intoxicating liquor licensed in England and Wales, Scotland and Northern Ireland for the last year for which comparable figures are available:-

Table 2—2.   Premises Licensed for Retail Sale of Liquor, and Registered Clubs, in United Kingdom. 1967.

Type of premises	England, Wales	Scotland	Northern Ireland	TOTAL
Full 'On-Licences' (mainly public houses)	65,916	6,634	2,451	75,001
Restaurant and Residential	7,550	405	–	7,955
Licensed Clubs	2,377	–	–	2,377
Registered Clubs	22,368	1,715	185	24,268
'Off-Licences'	26,702	3,555	108	30,365
TOTAL POPULATION	48,301	5,187	1,491	54,978

Source: Home Officer Liquor Licensing Statistics. Civil Judicial Statistics, Scotland. Ministry of Home Affairs, Northern Ireland. HMSO.

Excise licenses for the retail sale of liquor formerly required in parallel ιο Justices' licences had ceased to make a financial contribution to the Exechequer and were consequently abolished by the terms of the Finance Act, 1967. Control, as opposed to revenue collection, was seen to be exercised sufficiently by the Justices' licences; and excise licences for manufacture of beer and spirits, while retained are seen as a form of control also.

Taxation

Taxation of alcoholic liquor is a well-established governmental practice in the United Kingdom. The tax on imported wines is the oldest of British customs duties; the figures are available for duty on production of beer from the year 1643 (Wilson, 1940). Revenue from the liquor trade in the form of duties on home-produced spirits, wines and beers have been an important part of the national revenue ever since that time. The revenue from duties on manufactured products and imports in recent years is shown below.

Table 2—3.   Revenue Derived from Duty on Beer, Spirits and Wines. 1960—1969. (£ million).

YEAR April–March	SPIRITS (Home and imported)	BEER* (Home and imported)	WINE British	WINE Imported	TOTAL
1960–61	163	222	4	18	407
1961–62	172	247	4	20	443
1962–63	186	254	5	21	466
1963–64	206	263	6	24	499
1964–65	241	299	6	29	575

Table 2—3. (contd.)

YEAR April—March	SPIRITS (Home and imported)	BEER* (Home and imported)	WINE British	Imported	TOTAL
1965—66	245	340	8	34	627
1966—67	268	374	8	38	688
1967—68	301	390	10	47	748
1968—69	304	406	13	54	777
1969—70	332	450	16	65	863

Footnote: The major part of this revenue derives from beer produced in the United Kingdom. Some is, however, imported—chiefly Guinness from Dublin and lager from the Continent: £23 million of the total £450 million duty on beer in the year 1969—70 was derived from these importations.

Source: H.M. Customs and Excise Annual Reports. HMSO, London.

It may serve to indicate the relative importance of the above figures to the national exchequer if it is pointed out that the total revenue for 1969/70 represented 17.4% of the Government's revenue from both Customs and Excise duties, and 5.65% of their revenue from all sources. For comparison, the figures for 1963/4 were 18.0% and 6.8%, and for 1968/69 were 16.9% and 5.8% respectively (Annual Abstract of Statistics, 1970).

Home Brewing and Distilling

As judged by increasing sales reported of the ingredients required, there has been substantial increase in the volume of home brewing in recent years: this is, however, a legal activity, subject to no restraints. Home distillation of spirits is, on the other hand illegal, and control is exercised by H.M. Customs and Excise who record figures for the small number of successful prosecutions (see Chapter 1).

Total Taxation Levels

The continuous rise in the rate of duty levied on all types of alcohol in the United Kingdom over the past ten years, is shown in Table 2—4.

It should be noted that a proportion of the total price increases involves a rise in tax; a proportion only involves the manufacturers' price increase. A report of the Prices and Incomes Board in December, 1970 was followed by an immediate rise of 2d. per pint on beer at that time, and following the honouring of the Conservative Government's assurance to the brewers that they would no longer limit the retail price of beer in the public bars of public houses after the end of 1970, the rules of supply and demand have been working and a substantial rise in the price of beer, both in such bars and elsewhere, is expected during 1971.

The most recent changes in actual duty were effected by the Finance Act (1969) when, following the imposition of a surcharge of 10% on the duties on all alcoholic beverages the previous year (Revenue Duties Order 22/10/68), the crude rates on beer and spirits were consolidated. Basic rates of duty on imported heavy and light wine and British heavy and light wine were increased by 9s. 0d. (45p.) per gallon at the same time. No price increases were made by distillers for whisky from 1961 to 1970. Resale price maintenance was, however, abolished for whisky in .1966, and upper limits only could consequently be recorded after that date, for whisky as will now be the case for beer.

Table 2–4.   Government Taxation Levels for Beer, Spirit and Wines, United Kingdom. 1960–1970.
(In £.s.d.   1s.=5p.)

	1960	1961	1962	1963	1964	1965	1966	1967	1968	1969	1970
BEER											
Price per pint incl. tax(1)	1s. 4d.	1s. 6d.	1s. 6d.	1s. 7d.	1s. 9d.	1s. 10d.	1s. 11d.	1s. 11d.	2s. 0d.	2s. 0d.	2s. 2d.
Duty in (old) pence per pint (2)	6.7	7.4	7.4	7.4	8.4	9.4	10.3	10.3	11.3	11.3	11.3
Overall incidence of duty as % of consumer expenditure on beer	38.9	38.6	38.3	36.5	37.8	38.9	39.9	40.7	40.3	41.9	Not available
SPIRITS											
Retail price per bottle of proprietary Scotch whiskies (70% proof, on Sikes scale; 40° on Gay Lussac).	37s. 6d.	41s. 6d.	41s. 6d.	41s. 6d.	44s. 6d.	48s. 6d.	up to 51s. 11d.	up to 51s. 11d.	up to 54s. 5d.	up to 58s. 6d.	up to 61s. 6d.
Amount of tax per bottle	24s. 7d.	27s. 0d.	27s. 0d.	27s. 0d.	30s. 0d.	34s. 0d.	37s. 6d.	37s. 6d.	40s. 0d.	44s. 0d.	44s. 0d.
IMPORTED WINE Basic duty per gallon (= 6 bottles).											
(a) Lower rate not exceeding 27% proof	13s. 0d.	14s. 0d.	14s. 0d.	14s. 0d.	15s. 6d.	18s. 6d.	20s. 3d.	20s. 3d.	25s. 7d.	32s. 3d.	32s. 3d.
(b) Higher rate exceeding 27% proof	26s. 0d.	27s. 6d.	27s. 6d.	27s. 6d.	30s. 6d.	36s. 6d.	39s. 3d.	41s. 3d.	49s. 9d.	54s. 3d.	54s. 3d.

Footnote: (1) 1 pint = 0.57 litres; 1 bottle spirits $(26^2/_3$ fl. oz.) = 1.32 litres; 1 gallon = 4.55 litres.
(2) s.d. converted to NP–February, 1971. 1s. 4d. = 7p. approx.; 2s. 2d. = 11p. approx. 10s. = 50p.

Source: HM Customs and Excise. HMSO. 1970.

Detailed Incidence of Liquor Duties

The present coverage of taxation used is such that *spirits duty* is chargeable on all spirits consumed in the United Kingdom. However, spirits used for medical, scientific, certain domestic and industrial purposes are partly or entirely relieved of duty; and there are special reduced rates for imported perfumed spirits. The basis of charge is the content of alcohol, the unit being the proof per gallon. The basic rate of duty is the excise rate on spirits produced in the United Kingdom and warehoused for not less than three years, and stands currently at £18.85p. per proof gallon (January, 1971); spirits warehoused for less than three years are charged an additional duty of 7p. per proof gallon. *Imported spirits* are in general liable to an additional duty of 13p. per proof gallon; but since 1964 spirits from the Commonwealth Preference and European Free Trade Association areas have been charged rates equal to the home excise rates. Expressed as a proportion of retail prices, the duty burden on most spirits is currently in the range of 70% to nearly 90%. The total yield on the spirits duty in the 1969–70 financial year was £330 million (see Table 2–3, pages 14 and 15).

Because of this high rate of duty, manufacture and processing of spirits are hedged with severe restrictions. 'Distillers, rectifiers and compounders' are required to possess an annual licence issued by the Department of Customs and Excise, which must be satisfied on a large number of points of design and construction, before premises are approved. Traders who sell spirits by wholesale are also required to possess an Excise Licences, issued annually.

In the case of distilleries, much of the production process has to be carried out in closed or locked vessels and pipes to which the distiller has no access, except under the surveillance of an Excise Officer. Frequent 'spot checks' are made of premises, plant and raw materials used. When account has been taken of the quantity and strength of spirit produced, this is transferred to approved warehouses where it remains under stringent official control until it is released, either on payment of duty or for export. Some spirits, including whisky, have to be warehoused for at least three years before they are allowed to be sold in the United Kingdom.

'Rectifiers and compounders' (for instance, gin manufacturers) must use duty-paid spirits, and this permits some relaxation in official control of their processing. On completion of the manufacturing processes, they are entitled to a drawback of duty paid if they deposit their products in officially-controlled warehouses. The products then remain under official surveillance until they are withdrawn, either for home use (when duty is assessed and paid) or for export.

The use of duty-free plain spirits in manufacture and of spirits eligible for partial relief from duty for medical or scientific purposes, has to be controlled at the premises of the user. Methylated spirits have to be rendered non-potable under official control, before being released free of duty.

Imported spirits account for just over 20% of the total yield (see Table 2–3). Most imported spirits are entered into an officially-approved and controlled warehouse, and pay duty on subsequent removal.

The existing duty structure confines control to some 700 separate points (approximately 120 distillers, 160 rectifiers and compounders, and 420 spirits warehouses). Although official supervision is thus concentrated, the cost of collection of the duty is probably the highest amongst the Department of Customs and Excise's specified duties, in relation to its yield. This is due partly to the necessary strictness of the general controls, partly to the need to control spirits for industrial and other purposes, which are relieved of duty. More important, however, are the large stocks of spirits which have to be kept under official surveillance in bonded warehouses, a large proportion being destined eventually for export.

Beer duty is charged on all beer consumed in the United Kingdom, apart from that produced domestically for private consumption or that used for purposes of research or of experiments in brewing. The basic duty is the excise duty on beer brewed in the United Kingdom which produces over 97% of the total yield. The unit of charge is the 'bulk barrel' (equivalent to 36 gallons) and the duty rate varies according to the specific gravity of the beer, calculated on a scale in which water is 1000 degrees. The present rate of duty (1970) is £10. 37p. per barrel at 1030 degrees of specific gravity or less, plus approximately 3p.–4p. per additional degree. Duty is assessed on the 'worts' or liquid produced from the mash of malted barley and other materials before fermentation begins. A statutory deduction of 6% is made, however, from the assessment, to allow for wastage and loss during the subsequent preparation of beer for consumption. Beer imported from the Commonwealth preference or European Free Trade Association areas is charged with duty at a rate equal to the excise rate. Other imports of beer bear a surcharge of £1 per bulk barrel (36 gallons) and this is intended to give a measure of protection to the home industry. The incidence of duty on a pint of draught bitter sold in a public bar at, say, 10p. is about 5p. (see Table 2–4), but on more expensive beers the incidence of duty can be well below 50% of the retail price.

The yield of the beer duty in the 1969–70 financial year was £450 million. Beer produces just over half the total revenue from alcoholic drinks (see Table 2–3).

All brewers in the United Kingdom are required to be licensed annually by the Department of Customs and Excise; to give notice of their intention to brew and of the quantities of materials to be used in the brew; and to declare the quantity and strength of each brew of 'worts' produced. This declaration is subject to check by Excise Officers who, in the course of their frequent spot surveys of the brewery premises, measure the quantity and strength of the beer during the various stages of its production. The duty is payable in arrears. The relatively small quantity of imported beer (chiefly Guinness from Dublin and lager from Denmark) is required to be declared as to quantity and gravity by the importers.

The system of collection of the beer duty is thus centred almost entirely on the breweries, of which there are currently about 220, and the cost of collection is lower than that for distillers, described above.

As for *duties on wine,* about three-quarters of all wine consumed in the United Kingdom is imported. The charge to duty is based on the classification of the wine as either 'light' or 'heavy' according to its spirit content, the dividing line being 27 degrees proof for Commonwealth wine, and 25 degrees for other imported wine. This dividing line corresponds approximately to the upper limit of strength that can be achieved by natural fermentation alone; thus, the distinction is broadly between table wine, e.g. claret, and fortified wine, e.g. sherry. Corresponding to this division there are two basic rates of duty, currently (1970) £1. 61p. per gallon for light wine and £2. 71p. per gallon for heavy wine (which are equivalent to 27p. and 45p. per bottle, respectively). These basic rates apply to foreign still wine imported otherwise than in bottle; there are lower duty rates for wine from the 'Commonwealth Preference' area; higher rates are charged on still wine imported in bottles and on sparkling wine. Additional duties are charged on heavy wine exceeding 42 degrees in strength.

British wine is not normally made from the juice of fresh grapes, but from imported grape-pulp or from home-grown fruit. The term includes cider (from apples) and perry (from pears) of a strength exceeding 15 degrees proof spirit; cider and perry of a lower strength is chargeable with *purchase tax.* As for imported wine, there are separate rates for light and heavy British wine (the dividing line being 27 degrees proof as for wine from the Commonwealth); the current rates are £1.49p. per gallon (25p. per bottle) and £1.74p. per gallon (29p. per bottle) respectively. The British wine duty is charged only on wine commercially-produced for sale; there is no duty on home-made wine; and the yield of the wine duties in the 1969–70 financial year was £81 million (£65 million from imported and £16 million from British wine)—see Table 2–3

Most imported wine is taken direct to an officially-approved and controlled bonded warehouse (of which there are about 390) where, if imported in bulk, it may be bottled; duty is paid when the wine leaves the warehouse for home consumption. Other wine pays duty at importation and, if imported in bulk, is bottled duty-free.

British wine may be made only by licensed wineries surveilled by the Department of Customs and Excise of which there are currently (1970) about 60. Much British wine is fortified before duty payment by the addition of spirits, which may be delivered duty-free to wineries for this purpose; there is a statutory upper limit of 32 degrees proof spirit for the fortified wine so produced. Control is exercised through records kept by the manufacturer and through the Excise Officer's inspection visits. Duty is paid monthly in arrears, on the amount of wine despatched.

Approximately 80% of the receipts of wine duties are derived from imported wines. This preponderant proportion of the duty has to be assessed and collected on numerous consignments, either at the point of importation or on delivery from bonded warehouses. The wine duties overall are therefore relatively expensive to collect.

CONTROL OF ABNORMAL ALCOHOL CONSUMPTION

In addition to the sanctions outlined above concerning *production* and *retailing* of liquor, which are enshrined in over 100 separate pieces of legislation, penalties also exist for the punishment of abnormal *consumption* of alcohol. These penalties attach to being drunk (and a fortiori drunk and disorderly) in public places, and to drunken driving, the two broad categories of these offences being examined in detail below. In addition, there is a highly complicated literature with regard to the legal implications of intoxication during the committing of crimes of varying degree of seriousness, which has been reviewed by Napley (1969), who regards the laws as 'far from clear, and often contradictory'. Additional reference to the problem of criminal responsibility while a subject is intoxicated has been made both by Gibbens (1969) and by McClintock (1970); and the particular case of intoxication with alcohol (or other drugs) leading to amnesia has been discussed by Gibbens and Hall Williams (1966).

In general, self-induced drunkenness has not been seen as a defence to a criminal charge except when it amounts to insanity by the 'MacNaughton test'; if the accused was 'thought to be labouring under such defect of reason, as not to know the nature and quality of the act he was committing or—if he did know it—not to know that what he was doing was wrong', then the test would apply (Mannheim, 1965).

General Drunkenness

Legislation governing public drunkenness is complex and in part of long standing. Some of the laws on the Statute Book have fallen into total disuse, and the overall position has once more been described as 'unsatisfactory, illogical and confusing' (Napley, 1969). The following brief analysis of present legal practice is not intended to be exhaustive, but merely to give some idea of how the law actually works. A full account of the statutes relating to the drunkenness offence can be found in Stone's Justices' Manual, republished annually (1971) and in the Home Office Report on Habitual Drunken Offenders (HMSO, 1971).

The Statutes

The following are the laws which are most frequently infringed by the alcoholic and upheld by the Courts, at the present time:-

1. 'Being found drunk in any highway or other public place, whether a building or not, or any licensed premises—Penalty not exceeding £5'. *'Simple Drunkenness'*.
   (Licensing Act, 1872, S.12 as amended by Penalties for Drunkenness Act, 1962, S.1).
   If incapable of taking care of himself, the offender may be apprehended and dealt with according to law (Licensing Act, 1902, S.1).

2. 'Every person who in any highway or other public place, whether a building or not, is guilty while drunk of riotous or disorderly behaviour, or who is drunk while in charge on any highway or other public place of any carriage, horse, herd of cattle or steam engine; or who is drunk when in possession of any loaded firearm, may be apprehended—Penalty not exceeding £10 or imprisonment for a term not exceeding one month'.
   (Licensing Act, 1872, S.12 as amended by Penalties for Drunkenness Act, 1902, S.1). *'Drunkenness with Aggraviations'*.

   By S.91 of the Criminal Justice Act, 1967, this penalty will be increased to £50 and the power to sentence to imprisonment will be abolished; but not until the Secretary of State is satisfied that sufficient suitable accommodation is available for the care and treatment of persons convicted of being drunk and disorderly; which is not yet the case. (See Chapter 15)

Less frequent infringements of laws still upstanding include those appearing in breach of the Licensing Act, 1902 S.2 (1) as ordered by the Penalties for Drunkenness Act, 1962, S.1, namely:-

3. 'Any person found drunk in any highway or other public place, whether a building or not, or on any licensed premises while having the charge of a child apparently under the age of seven years may be apprehended.' Penalty, if the child is under the age of summary conviction, not exceeding £10, or imprisonment for a term not exceeding one month.

Still on the Statute Book, but fallen into disuse for lack of facilities, are the following provisions:

A. *The Habitual Drunkards Act, 1879,* authorises Justices to licence 'retreats' to which habitual drunkards may be admitted on their own application for a maximum of two years unless discharged on licence.

   A 'Retreat' is a house licensed for the reception, control, care and curative treatment of Habitual Drunkards. To date (1971) there are none.

   An 'Habitual Drunkard' is defined for the present as a person 'not being a mentally disordered person within the meaning of the Mental Health Act, 1959 (see Chapter 16), who is notwithstanding by reason of habitual intemperate drinking of intoxicating liquor (or drugs) at times dangerous to himself or others or incapable of managing his own affairs'.

B. By Section I of the *Inebriates Act of 1898*, any person convicted on indictment of an offence punishable by imprisonment, if the offence was committed when the defendant was under the influence of drink; or if drunkenness was a contributory cause, and the defendant either admits or is found by the jury to be an Habitual Drunkard, can be sentenced to be detained for up to three years in a State or certified Inebriate Reformatory. (There are none).

C. By the terms of Section II of the *Inebriates Act, 1898*, any person who commits any of the usual drunken offences and has three times in the immediately preceding twelve months been convicted of similar offences, and who is an Habitual Drunkard, shall be liable upon conviction on indictment (i.e. by a Higher Court); or if he consents to be dealt with in this way, on summary conviction; to be detained for a term not exceeding three years in any certified Inebriate Reformatory, the Managers of which are willing to receive him.

The Powers of the Courts

For the minor offences set out in (1)–(3), the Courts can fine and, if the defendant is of no fixed abode, can then and there fix an alternative of imprisonment up to 14 days in place of a £5 fine or 30 days in place of £10. For the offence of drunk and disorderly behaviour, the Courts can impose an immediate sentence of imprisonment up to one month, although this may have to be suspended. The other order available to the Courts is to remand in custody with a request for the Prison Medical Officer and/or Probation Officer to make enquiries and furnish a report to the Courts before the Courts finally dispose of the case. (See also Chapter 16).

Alternatively, the Court can make a Probation Order of from one to three years which has the advantage of involving an experienced social worker with the problems of the alcoholic, with the power given to the Court to recall the offender on any breach of the order, or on the commission of a further offence in the period specified. An Order of Conditional Discharge of any period up to three years has the advantage of a future penalty for the present offence, should the defendant offend again.

A somewhat comparable power is to bind over the defendant for a sum of money with or without a 'surety' for up to one year, a further offence enabling the Court to forfeit that sum or part of it. The Courts can also order the payment of a fine with the alternative of one day 'in the precincts of the Court', when the Court frequently remits the whole or part of the period.

The only form of medical treatments that a Court can order for minor drunkenness offences are:-

1. A *Probation Order* to contain a provision under S.4 of the Criminal Justice Act, 1948, that the defendant shall submit for up to 12 months to treatment by or under the direction of a duly qualified medical practitioner, either as a resident in certain hospitals, or non-resident at a place specified in the order; or for treatment under the direction of a specified doctor, who must so agree.

2. For offences which carry imprisonment, such as Drunk and Disorderly, an S.60 order under the Mental Health Act of 1959 can be made. The defendant must either be suffering from 'mental illness', 'psychopathic disorder',

'sub-normality' or 'severe subnormality' and the mental disorder must be such as warrants detention in hospital or 'reception into guardianship'; the Court must likewise be of the opinion that this is the most suitable method of disposing of the case. It can then authorise his admission to such detention which amounts to 'compulsory treatment'; but the evidence of two doctors as to the appropriateness is required; and this is infrequently used, in the case of drunkenness offenders.

Drunken Driving

The law relating to drunken driving is a good deal clearer and more up-to-date than that relating to drunkenness generally. Alcohol has an immediate, direct and certain action upon the central nervous system which can rapidly disable a driver from handling any vehicle with maximum efficiency. The arrival of powerful motor cars in large numbers on our roads, and the associated growth in the number of fatal accidents and serious injuries attributable in part or in whole to the influence of liquor, has therefore caused Parliament to pass a series of appropriate Acts. The law was first altered to take special account of drunken driving of motor vehicles in 1925. Today, it rests upon the provisions of the Road Traffic Acts of 1960 and 1962 and upon the Road Safety Act of 1967 (the 'Breathalyser Act'). The latter (for the first time) introduced compulsory medical tests to ascertain the degree to which offending drivers may have been under the influence of alcohol, making it an offence to drive or attempt to drive with a blood/alcohol level above the prescribed limit. A police officer may make a preliminary test of the breath of a driver whom he suspects of being drunk; if this test is positive, the driver is compelled to provide a specimen of blood or urine for analysis in a laboratory, and a penalty is also imposed for refusing the 'breath test' without reasonable excuse. It is on the basis of this second test that the driver is judged.

The Statues

The basic offences which it is possible for a driver to commit according to the above Acts, are as follows:-

1. Driving or attempting to drive a motor vehicle on a road or other public place having consumed alcohol in such a quantity that the proportion thereof in his blood, as ascertained by a laboratory test, exceeds the prescribed limit of 80 milligrammes of alcohol in 100 millilitres of blood (Road Safety Act, 1967).

2. Driving or attempting to drive a motor vehicle under the influence of drink or drugs within ten years of a previous conviction of driving a motor vehicle under the influence of drink or drugs (Road Traffic Act of 1960, amended by the Road Traffic Act of 1962).

3. Being incharge of a motor vehicle while unfit to drive through influence of drink or drugs as shown by the proportion of alcohol in the blood; and being in charge within ten years of a previous offence, while under the influence. (Road Traffic Act, 1960, amended by Road Traffic Act, 1962; Road Safety Act, 1967).

The penalties imposed for these offences are fines and/or imprisonment. Those prescribed under the 1967 Act are as follows:

a) On summary conviction: imprisonment for up to four months (six months for a second or subsequent conviction), or a fine of up to £100, or both.

b) On conviction 'on indictment': imprisonment for up to two years, or a fine, or both.

Under the 1967 Act, conviction entails virtually automatic disqualification from driving of not less than 12 months.

The recent increase in drunken driving convictions (see Chapter 8) is certainly considered attributable to the powers bestowed upon the police by this Act. Reduction in road accidents may be due however not only to the consequences of the Act, but also to other causes.

The Breakdown of Marriage

Final mention must be made of the civil law which relates to the breakdown of marriage. Under the Divorce Reform Act of 1969, which came into use on 1st January, 1971, the only grounds for divorce are a marriage having 'irretrievably broken down', or by mutual consent following a period of separation. There has been insufficient time for any substantial case-law to have grown up, but cruelty may still be brought in as evidence that a marriage has indeed broken down, and drunkenness can be said to amount to cruelty or 'constructive desertion' where it is persisted in in the knowledge that it is injuring the health of the spouse; or where the physical violence involved provides dangers so that 'continuance of matrimonial cohabitation is virtually impossible' (Samuels, 1963). In a Magistrates Court, the same grounds can be used for obtaining a separation order: but in neither case can drunkenness according mere 'inconvenience', theft of money from handbags or 'continuously disgusting behaviour' be regarded as sufficient.

There are no figures available on the proportion of the 12,000 odd divorces annually granted in England and Wales for cruelty (the figures ranging from 1–2,000 per annum in Scotland and approximately 300 in Northern Ireland) prior to the Divorce Reform Act, in which drunkenness was mentioned as a cause.

REFERENCES

CENTRAL STATISTICAL OFFICE, 1970. *Annual Abstract of Statistics.* HMSO, London.

CUSTOMS AND EXCISE. *Annual Reports.* HMSO, London.

GIBBENS T.C.N. Alcoholism and Personal Responsibility. Paper delivered at the 1st Summer School on Alcoholism, Birmingham, 1969.

GIBBENS T.C.N. and HALL WILLIAMS J.E. Medico-Legal Aspects of Amnesia. *Amnesia.* 1966, ed. WHITTY C.W.M. and ZANGWILL O.L. Butterworths, London.

HOME OFFICE, 1971. *Habitual Drunken Offenders* HMSO, London.

McCLINTOCK D. Alcoholism and Personal Responsibility. Paper delivered at the 2nd Summer School on Alcoholism, Brighton, 1970.

MANNHEIM H., 1965. Criminal Law and the Mentally Abnormal Offender. *Comparative Criminology.* Routledge and Kegan Paul, London.

MONCKTON H.A., 1966. *History of English Ale and Beer.* Bodley Head, London.

MONOPOLIES COMMISSION, 1969. *Beer—A Report on the Supply of Beer.* HMSO, London.

NAPLEY D, 1969. In Proceedings of International Symposium on The Drunkenness Offence. Pergamon, Oxford.

REPORT OF THE COMMITTEE ON SCOTTISH LICENSING LAW, 1962. Cmnd. 1217. HMSO, Edinburgh.

SAMUELS A., 1963. *Law for Social Workers.* Butterworths, London.

STONE: *Justices' Manual, 1971.* Butterworths, London.

WEBB S. and WEBB B., 1902. *History of Liquor Licensing in England principally from 1700 to 1830.*

WILSON G.B., 1940. *Alcohol and the Nation.* Nicholson and Watson, London.

CHAPTER 3

PRODUCTION OF DRUGS

The pharmaceutical industry in Great Britain produces and exports a wide range of products for the treatment of human and animal diseases. One section of the industry is comprised of large research-based companies producing medicines protected by patents and manufactures ethical preparations. The other section is smaller firms making household medicines that are publically advertised. There are some 286 enterprises manufacturing pharmaceutical preparations in the United Kingdom, but 90% of the sales are made by 79 firms, of which 41 are foreign subsidiaries (Central Office of Information, 1970). The Industry's output falls into five main categories:-

1. the production of synthetic organic chemicals, e.g. vitamins, antihistamines, etc.;
2. production of antibiotics;
3. the preparation of vaccine by the culture of micro-organisms;
4. production of drugs from naturally occurring substances, such as hormones or morphine;
5. the processing of bulk drugs into finished forms, such as tablets, capsules, etc. (Central Office of Information, 1970).

The industry is largely research-based with £14.5 million spent in 1967 (Association of British Pharmaceutical Industry, 1969–70).

In 1968 the industry sales were estimated at £292 million, which was more than double the figure ten years before. Sales to the National Health Service in that same year accounted for £127 million, exports were £97 million, household medicines available without prescription accounted for £45 million, and the remaining £23 million consisted of veterinary medicines.

Production data is not available for individual drug preparations or even for therapeutic groupings of drugs such as barbiturates. The only overall estimates of the extent of psychotropic drug use can be found in National Health Service prescription data in Chapter 6.

The largest buyer from the pharmaceutical companies is, of course, the National Health Service. The Medical Services were nationalised in July, 1948 under the provisions of the National Health Service (NHS) Act, 1946. Ethical preparations account for nearly three-quarters of the items on NHS prescriptions and over 90 per cent of the drug ingredient cost. The cost of pharmaceutical services in relation to total NHS expenditure is set out on Page 26.

Table 3–1. Estimated Value of Output and Sales of Drugs, 1959–1968.

Year	NHS (£m.)	Exports (£m.)	Household medicines (£m.)	Others (£m.)	Total (£m.)
1959	57	45	29	23	153
1960	60	48	32	27	168
1961	66	53	34	31	184
1962	72	55	37	24	188
1963	79	54	36	·22	190
1964	83	59	36	28	206
1965	98	67	42	24	230
1966	106	73	41	28	249
1967	116	78	44	24	262
1968	127	97	45	23	292

Where items do not sum to the total shown, this is due to rounding off figures.

Source: Association of British Pharmaceutical Industry, 1970. The Pharmaceutical Industry and the Nation's Health.

Table 3–2. NHS Total Expenditure and Expenditure on Pharmaceutical Services, United Kingdom, 1969–1968.

Year	Total NHS (£m.)	Pharmaceutical services (£m.)	% NHS	% National income
1958	828	88	10.6	0.45
1960	902	97	10.8	0.47
1961	981	100	10.2	0.45
1962	1,025	103	10.0	0.44
1963	1,092	115	10.5	0.47
1964	1,186	126	10.6	0.48
1965	1,308	151	11.5	0.53
1966	1,434	166	11.6	0.56
1967	1,594	177	11.1	0.56
1968	1,741	184	10.6	0.55

NHS Expenditure in the United Kingdom includes local authority expenditure and payments by patients (National Income and Expenditure 1969, Table 50. Annual Abstract of Statistics, 1969 Tables 53–55, Central Statistical Office).

The total number of prescriptions under the National Health Service and their average cost is set out below in Table 3—3.

Table 3—3.   NHS Prescriptions Average Cost, England and Wales. 1950—1968.

Year	Total prescription (millions)	Average total cost per prescription s.	d.	Year	Total prescription (millions)	Average total cost per prescription s.	d.
1950	217.2	3	3	1960	218.7	7	3
1951	227.7	3	8	1961	205.0	8	1
1952	216.0	4	1	1962	196.6	8	10
1953	219.8	4	1	1963	205.5	9	4
1954	218.7	4	2	1964	209.4	10	1
1955	226.1	4	5	1965	244.3	10	4
1956	228.9	5	0	1966	262.0	10	7
1957	207.2	5	11	1967	271.2	10	9
1958	203.4	6	5	1968	267.4	11	4
1959	214.0	6	10				

Department of Health and Social Security 1969 Annual Report for 1968.

The cost of drugs to the NHS is regulated by a Voluntary Price Regulation Scheme, which has been in operation since 1964 and recently re-negotiated in 1969. Negotiations between the Department of Health and Social Security and the representative organisation of the pharmaceutical industry came to the agreement that the price of medicines will not be based on production costs or on standard cost returns, but on the overall financial results of the company sales of NHS products. The drug companies show an above average profitability, but contend that this extra margin is necessary because of the high cost of research (Association of British Pharmaceutical Industry). The cost of pharmaceutical services was the subject of a Government committee of inquiry known as the Sainsbury Committee, which recommended that the Government should exercise more control over prices and drug sales promotion (Report of the Committee of Enquiry into the Relationship of the Pharmaceutical Industry with the National Health Service, 1967). The Committee questioned the expenditure on promotion, which amounted to £15.4 million in 1965 compared with £11.6 million spent on research in that same year. The relationship of a nationalised health service to a private pharmaceutical industry is extremely complex, and continuing debate on the role of the industry is inevitable.

Table 3—4.   The Cost of the National Health Service, 1968.

Total expenditure in 1968 was £1,741 million.

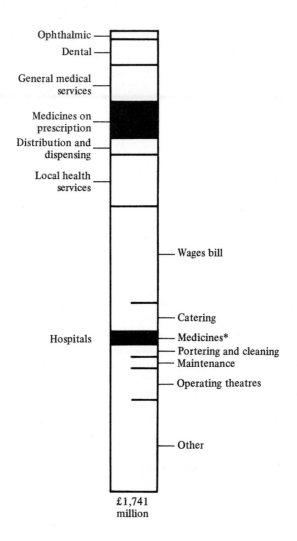

*Medicines used in hospitals are accounted separately from medicines on prescription from medical practitioners.

Source: Association of British Pharmaceutical Industry, 1970. The Pharmaceutical Industry and the Nation's Health.

REFERENCES

ASSOCIATION OF THE BRITISH PHARMACEUTICAL INDUSTRY. *Annual Report,*
   1969–1970.
ASSOCIATION OF THE BRITISH PHARMACEUTICAL INDUSTRY, 1970. *The Pharma-*
   ceutical Industry and the Nation's Health. A.B.P.I., London.
CENTRAL OFFICE OF INFORMATION, 1970. *Fact Sheets on British Industry—the*
   Pharmaceuticals Industry.
CENTRAL STATISTICAL OFFICE, 1969. *Annual Abstract of Statistics.* H.M.S.O., London.
DEPARTMENT OF HEALTH AND SOCIAL SECURITY, 1969. *Annual Report for the Year*
   1968. H.M.S.O., London.
NATIONAL HEALTH SERVICE (N.H.S.) ACT, 1946. H.M.S.O., London.
Report of the Committee of Enquiry into the Relationship of the Pharmaceutical Industry with
   the National Health Service (The Sainsbury Committee), 1967. H.M.S.O., London.

CHAPTER 4

CONTROL OF DRUGS

The laws relating to drug use are extremely complex and cover many different aspects of drug control. This chapter does not represent a comprehensive summary of the law, nor does it try to discuss the complex issues in the field of legislation. Three basic sections are set out. First, a brief view of general legislation relating to the sales, production and distribution of drugs with reference to poisons legislation and the Medicines Act, 1968. Secondly, the special legislation enacted for drugs which are considered to have serious addiction and social harm potential. This includes reference to the various Dangerous Drugs Acts as well as the Drugs (Prevention of Misuse) Act, 1964. There is new legislation before Parliament which will codify the existing laws into a more uniform way. Thirdly, a brief summary of the debate on powers of arrest with respect to drugs is set out. (Advisory Committee on Drug Dependence, 1970).

GENERAL CONTROL MEASURES

The general control of the production, distribution and availability of drugs is necessary to protect the public from unwarranted risk. The *Pharmacy and Poisons Act, 1933* regulates the sale and supply of listed poisons, but it does not regulate their possession by individuals. The Act established the Poisons Board as a statutory body. The Poisons Board is an independent body of experts representing the medical and pharmaceutical professions along with representatives from various Government departments. The Board prepares, for the approval of the Home Secretary, lists of substances which are classed according to the degree of control deemed necessary. This comprehensive list, with 16 schedules known as the *Poisons List,* is matched with appropriate controls in the *Poisons Rules.* The Rules lay down various requirements for manufacture, sale, storage, transport and labelling of poisons in the list. For instance, the drugs named in Schedule 4 of the Poisons List may be made available by pharmacists only to persons with a prescription from a qualified medical practitioner. (Pharmacy and Poisons Act, 1933; Poisons Rules, 1970; Poisons List, 1970; Cahal, 1970; Dawtry, 1968).

The Medicines Act, 1968

Aside from poisons, there are many drugs whose purity or potency are difficult to assay or which might be toxic (or ineffective) unless their production and testing is controlled. The general control of therapeutic substances has been incorporated under the Medicines Act, 1968. Comprehensive provision is made with respect to safety, quality and efficacy of human and veterinary medicines. The Act established a uniform inspection and licensing system to ensure the best conditions for manufacture, storage and distribution of drugs. It will be possible to enforce quality control on all products purporting to comply with British specifications and adequate standards will also be ensured for labelling, advertising and promoting drugs. All medicines other than those on the General Sales List in the Act will be available only from registered pharmacists.

The Act establishes a Medicines Commission with provision for expert advisory committees. Among its other duties will be responsibility for preparing future editions of the British Pharmacopoeia, which used to be compiled by the General Medical Council, and the distribution of supplementary independent information about medicines.

The Medicines Act will be brought into force over a period of time and is not yet fully operative. The most crucial task will be the change in the arrangements for the scrutiny of new drugs from the voluntary arrangement with the Committee on the Safety of Drugs to the statutory body provided in the Act (Medicines Act, 1968; Cahal, 1970; Priest, 1967; Department of Health and Social Security, 1969).

CONTROL OF SPECIFIC PSYCHO-ACTIVE DRUGS

International Control

Single Convention on Narcotic Drugs, 1961.

The United Kingdom is party to the Single Convention on Narcotic Drugs, 1961 which consolidated the various international treaties entered into since the First International Opium Convention held in the Hague in 1912. This convention controls the distribution, cultivation, export, import and labelling of the opiates, cocaine, cannabis and related narcotic drugs. It is obligatory under the convention to keep records of these drugs and control:

1) 'the establishments and premises in which trade or distribution may take place';

2) 'persons and enterprises carrying on or engaged in the trade or distribution of "the controlled drugs",'

3) 'the import and export of the drugs'.
   (The Single Convention on Narcotic Drugs, 1961).

The enforcement of the law is specified in part as follows:
'Subject to its constitutional limitations, each Party shall adopt such measures as will ensure that . . . action which in the opinion of such Party may be contrary to the provisions of this Convention shall be punishable offences when committed intentionally, and that serious offences shall be liable to adequate punishment, particularly by imprisonment or other penalties of deprivation of liberty...'
(Single Convention on Narcotics, 1961).

The history of international control with regard to cannabis is reviewed by the Wootton Report (Advisory Committee on Drugs Dependence, 1968) and the Convention is summarised by Dawtry (1968).

UNITED KINGDOM LAWS

Dangerous Drugs Act, 1965

This Act codifies earlier Dangerous Drugs legislation and implements the United Kingdom's obligation under the Single Convention on Narcotic Drugs. Among the more salient points of the Act are the following:

Part I of the Act prohibits, except under licence from the Home Office, the export and import of raw opium, coca leaves, poppy straw, cannabis and related substances. Power is given to control the production, possession, sale and distribution of these drugs. Section 5 makes it an offence for the occupier or manager to allow his premises to be used for smoking or dealing in cannabis substances.

Part II of the Act deals with the import, export, selling and possession of opium prepared for smoking.

Part III of the Act empowers the Home Secretary to make regulations controlling the manufacture, sale, possession or distribution of substances scheduled in the Act by means of Order in Council, that is, without the need for further legislation. Such regulations can only control substances scheduled in the Act or substances which the United Nations Commission on Narcotic Drugs may decide to add to the Single Convention.

Part IV of the Act defines other offences under the Act, such as contravention of the conditions in a licence. It provides for the granting of search warrants for premises where it is reasonably expected that a contravention of the Act may be found. Powers of arrests are granted to the police which allow arrest without warrant of persons suspected of committing an offence against the Act, if the name and address of the person are unknown, or if there are reasonable grounds to believe the person will abscond. Maximum penalties on summary convictions or indictment are specified (see Table 4–1.)
(Dangerous Drugs Act, 1965; Cahal, 1970; Dawtry, 1968).

Dangerous Drugs (No. 2) Regulations, 1964.

The regulations which control the manufacture, sale, possession and distribution of opiate drugs, cocaine and cannabis are contained in the Dangerous Drugs (No.2) Regulations, 1964.

These regulations specify the terms of licensing for manufacture and distribution as well as the general authority to possess and supply dangerous drugs. Among the persons given authority to possess these drugs are doctors, veterinary surgeons and veterinary practitioners, and persons in charge of laboratories for research and education. Persons are also able to legally possess dangerous drugs if they are 'lawfully supplied to them by a duly qualified medical practitioner or registered veterinary surgeon or registered veterinary practitioner', or given a lawful prescription for such drugs.

This regulation confirms the basis of the British legal approach to heroin addiction, that a practitioner had the discretion to legally prescribe heroin for any person. However, Rule 9 of the regulations added an important proviso. It was made unlawful to possess a dangerous drug even on the prescription of a medical practitioner, if the person was being supplied by another medical practitioner and did not disclose the fact, or if the person made a declaration or statement that was false in any particular. The latter proviso might refer to giving a false name or address for instance. (Dangerous Drugs (No.2) Regulations, 1964; Cahal, 1970; Dawtry, 1968).

Dangerous Drugs Act 1967 and subsequent Regulations

This Act made the first basic changes in the British legal approach to the problem of heroin addiction since the first Dangerous Drugs Act in 1920. It empowered the Secretary of State to require medical practitioners to notify to a central authority the particulars of any addicts using drugs covered by the Act, and to prohibit any doctor from administering, supplying or prescribing specified drugs except under licence.

Subsequent regulations made these restrictions explicit.

The Dangerous Drugs (Notification of Addicts) Regulations, 1968.

These Regulations came into force on 22nd February, 1968 and require for Dangerous Drugs that:

1) 'any medical practitioner who attends a person who he considers, or has reasonable grounds to suspect, is addicted to any drug shall, within seven days of the attendance, furnish in writing to the Chief Medical Officer at the Home Office such of the following particulars with respect to that person as are known to the medical practitioner, that is to say, the name, address, sex, date of birth and national health service number of that person, the date of the attendance and the name of the drug or drugs concerned'.

2) 'a person shall be regarded as addicted to a drug only if, as a result of repeated administration, he has become so dependent upon the drug that he has an overpowering desire for the administration of it to be continued'. (Dangerous Drugs (Notification of Addicts) Regulations, 1968).

The Dangerous Drugs (Supply to Addicts) Regulations, 1968

These Regulations came into force on 16th April, 1968 and prohibit a medical practitioner from administering, supplying or authorising the supply to drug addicts of *heroin* or *cocaine* except under licence, or for the purpose of relieving pain due to organic disease or injury.

The selective issue of licences under these regulations effectively prohibits the prescribing of heroin and cocaine to addicts by general practitioners and limits the treatment of heroin addiction to specialised clinics or hospitals. These regulations apply only to the specified drugs so that medical practitioners are not prohibited, at present, from the administration of other opiates, such as morphine or methadone. If necessary, other dangerous drugs could be restricted in this way by an Order in Council rather than further legislation.

In addition, administrative arrangements were made for advisory panels to be established all over the country by the Department of Health and Social Security to help medical practitioners in doubt about whether specific patients were addicted to opiate drugs. The Act establishes a medical tribunal to consider cases where a breach of the notification or supply regulations may have occurred.

The Act lays down circumstances and procedures by which the Home Secretary may withdraw a doctor's authority to administer or supply a dangerous drug or drugs. It also gives the police further powers to stop and search a person or vehicle and to seize evidence if they have reasonable grounds to suspect illegal possession of drugs. (Dangerous Drugs Act, 1967; Dangerous Drugs (Supply to Addicts) Regulations, 1968; Cahal, 1970; Dawtry, 1968).

Drugs (Prevention of Misuse) Act, 1964.

The Drugs (Prevention of Misuse) Act, 1964 makes it an offence to import or to possess without authority substances listed in the Schedule of the Act including amphetamines, amphetamine compounds, LSD, mescaline, psilocybin and related compounds. The Home Secretary is empowered to modify the drugs controlled after consultation with the Poisons Board. The Act gives the police power of arrest without warrant, a person committing offences under the Act, if his name and address is doubtful or unknown or if he is likely to abscond. (Drugs (Prevention of Misuse) Act, 1964; Cahal, 1970).

The present legislation is summarised below in Table 4—1 and the penalties compared. The opiates, cocaine and cannabis are covered under the Dangerous Drugs Acts and Regulations. Amphetamines and certain hallucinogenic drugs are controlled by the Drugs (Prevention of Misuse) Act. Both of these measures restrict possession as well as supply. The hypnotics, including barbiturates and tranquillisers, are largely controlled only under the Pharmacy and Poisons Act which regulates supply, but not possession by individuals.

FUTURE LEGISLATION (see page 42*)

A new Bill is at present before Parliament to replace the Dangerous Drugs Acts of 1965 and 1967 and the Drugs (Prevention of Misuse) Act, 1964. The previous drugs legislation was constructed on a piecemeal basis to meet new and previously unexperienced drug abuse. Taken as a whole the previous legislation is inconsistent, fragmentary and cumbersome. No drugs other than the opiates, cocaine and cannabis, are controlled under the Dangerous Drugs laws and the extent of control differed from that in the Drugs (Prevention of Misuse) Act. For drugs other than narcotics, control could be achieved only by voluntary means, such as with the methylamphetamine epidemic (see Chapter 11), or by the Pharmacy and Poisons Act if there was danger from inadvertant misuse (though possession is not regulated) and the Drugs (Prevention of Misuse) Act for social misuse. The abuse of drugs is now characterised by rapidly changing fashionability of many different types of substance which cut across the discrete categories of the old legislation. In some cases very different types of drug offences were subject to the same maximum penalties, such as possession of small quantities of cannabis and the possession of large quantities of heroin.

The proposed *Misuse of Drugs Bill* is designed to deal with new patterns of drug abuse as they arise and to provide penalties for drug offences according to relative harmfulness of different drugs. The Bill distinguishes between unlawful possession and trafficking, with several new trafficking offences created and the penalties for trafficking sharply increased. The general consequence of the new legislation will be to provide more flexible powers for the Home Secretary to control the availability and prescribing of a wider range of drugs without the need for new legislation.

The Bill has considered the problem of irresponsible prescribing of drugs by a small number of doctors. This problem was discussed in the second report of the Interdepartmental Committee on Drug Addiction (see Chapter 13), and by the Advisory Committee on Drug Dependence (1970). While it has been possible to discourage excessive prescription of drugs in the past, the procedures for withdrawing a doctor's authority to prescribe have been slow and cumbersome. The Bill provides powers to withhold the authority of a doctor to prescribe psycho-active

Table 4–1. Summary of Statutory Provisions for the Control of Drugs in the United Kingdom

	I	II	III
Acts	Dangerous Drugs Acts 1965 & 1967; Dangerous Drugs (No. 2) Regulations 1964. Dangerous Drugs (Notification of Addicts) Regulations 1968; Dangerous Drugs (Supply to Addicts) Regulations 1968.	Drugs (Prevention of Misuse) Act 1964.	Pharmacy & Poisons Act 1933; Poisons List 1970; Poisons Rules 1970.
Drugs controlled	Opiates, including Morphine Heroin* Synthetic analgesics Pethidine Methadone* etc. Cocaine* Cannabis*	Amphetamines* and some similar substances. Lysergic acid diethylamide (LSD 25)* and some similar substances, including mescaline.	All those named in the Poisons List including Barbiturates. *Note:* Barbiturate and other drugs are included in Part I of the Poisons List and Schedule IV of the Rules.
Main provisions	(a) Offence to possess without authority (b) Offence to import and export except under licence. (c) Persons authorised to possess have to keep records of drug movements. (d) Drugs to be kept under lock and key by persons authorised to possess.	(a) Offence to possess without authority (b) Offence to import except under licence.	(a) Offence for a poison in Part I of the Poisons List to be sold retail otherwise than by an authorised seller of poisons from registered premises. (b) Offence for substances named in Schedule IV to the Poisons Rules to be sold except on a prescription given by a duly qualified practitioner. (c) Records of sales of Schedule IV substances are not required, but private prescriptions must be retained for two years.

Table 4–1. (contd.)

	I	II	III
Main provisions	(e) Medical practitioners must notify all cases of persons addicted[x] to drugs controlled under the Act of 1965. (f) Heroin and cocaine may only be prescribed for an addict by a specially licensed medical practitioner.		
Penalties	Summary—£250 fine and/or 12 months imprisonment. Indictment—£1,000 fine and/or 10 years imprisonment.	Summary—£200 fine and/or 6 months imprisonment. Indictment—unlimited fine and/or 2 years imprisonment.	£50 fine.

*   Drugs commonly obtained illegally.

x   As defined in the Regulations.

Source: Advisory Committee on Drug Dependence, 1968. *Cannabis.* HMSO, London.

drugs restricted under the Bill if it is established that irresponsible prescribing has taken place. There is provision for three bodies to deal with this problem in the Bill, the Tribunal, the Advisory Body and the Professional Panel. All these bodies will have representatives of the respondents, professional organisation. The structure will allow over-prescribing to be stopped very quickly, but will have adequate safeguards for protecting medical practitioners from unfair action.

It is proposed that the Bill will create three classes of controlled drugs with different maximum penalties for trafficking and possession, in each case reflecting the relative harmfulness of the drugs. Some of the drugs included in the proposed classification are listed below. The Class A drugs will carry the most severe penalties, with classes B and C will be relatively less punitive.

Examples of drugs within the proposed classes are as follows:

Class A Drugs:
Almost 100 substances and products are listed, including:
>   Cannabinol, except where contained
>   in cannabis and cannabis resin
>   Cocaine
>   Diamorphine (heroin)
>   Injectable amphetamine
>   Lysergide and other N-alkyl
>   derivatives of lysergamide
>   (LSD and related compounds)
>   Mescaline
>   Methadone
>   Morphine
>   Opium, whether raw, prepared or medicinal
>   Pethidine.

Class B Drugs:
Included in the 12 listed substances and products are:
>   Amphetamine
>   Cannabis and cannabis resin
>   Codeine
>   Dexamphetamine
>   Methylamphetamine
>   Phenmetrazine.

Class C Drugs:
The 12 substances in this class are rarely abused, but include:
>   Benzphetamine
>   Mephentimine
>   Pipriadol.

(Misuse of Drugs Bill).

Arrangements are made in the Bill for adding or removing substances to be controlled by means of Order in Council, without the need for further legislation. The classification of drugs can be altered as necessary. Barbiturates and sedative drugs are not, at present, included in the Bill, but the Home Secretary has the power to control these drugs, if it appears necessary. The Bill provides for an Advisory Council on the Misuse of Drugs.

The proposed maximum penalties for offences under the Bill are set out below.

Table 4—2. Proposed Prosecution and Punishment of Offences (Misuse of Drugs Bill).

Section Creating Offence	General Nature of Offence	Mode of Prosecution	Punishment			
			Class A drug involved	Class B drug involved	Class C drug involved	General
Section 4(2)	Production, or being concerned in the production, of a controlled drug.	(a) Summary. .	12 months or £400, or both	12 months or £400, or both	6 months or £200, or both	
		(b) On indictment	14 years or a fine, or both	14 years or a fine, or both	5 years or a fine, or both	
Section 4(3)	Supplying or offering to supply a controlled drug or being concerned in the doing of either activity by another.	(a) Summary. .	12 months or £400, or both	12 months or £400, or both	6 months or £200, or both	
		(b) On indictment	14 years or a fine, or both	14 years or a fine, or both	5 years or a fine, or both	
Section 5(2)	Having possession of a controlled drug.	(a) Summary. .	12 months or £400, or both	6 months or £400, or both	6 months or £200, or both	
		(b) On indictment	7 years or a fine, or both	5 years or a fine, or both	2 years or a fine, or both	
Section 5(3)	Having possession of a controlled drug with intent to supply it to another.	(a) Summary. .	12 months or £400, or both	12 months or £400, or both	6 months or £200, or both	
		(b) On indictment	14 years or a fine, or both	14 years or a fine, or both	5 years or a fine, or both	
Section 6(2)	Cultivation of cannabis plant	(a) Summary. .	—	—	—	12 months or £400, or both
		(b) On indictment				14 years or a fine, or both
Section 8	Being the occupier, or concerned in the management, of premises and permitting or suffering certain activities to take place there.	(a) Summary. .	12 months or £400, or both	12 months or £400, or both	6 months or £200, or both	
		(b) On indictment	14 years or a fine, or both	14 years or a fine, or both	5 years or a fine, or both	

Table 4—2. (contd.)

Section Creating Offence	General Nature of Offence	Mode of Prosecution	Punishment Class A drug involved	Class B drug involved	Class C drug involved	General
Section 12(6)	Contravention of direction prohibiting practitioner etc. from possessing, supplying, etc. controlled drugs.	(a) Summary..	12 months or £400, or both	12 months or £400, or both	6 months or £200, or both	
		(b) On indictment	14 years or a fine, or both	14 years or a fine, or both	5 years or a fine, or both	
Section 13(3)	Contravention of direction prohibiting practitioner etc. from prescribing, supplying, etc. controlled drugs.	(a) Summary..	12 months or £400, or both	12 months or £400, or both	6 months or £200, or both	
		(b) On indictment	14 years or a fine, or both	14 years or a fine, or both	5 years or a fine, or both	

Source: Misuse of Drugs Bill. HMSO.

Under this structure the penalties for possession of an opiate would be somewhat reduced, while penalties for trafficking would be increased. Cannabis substances are now classified differently from the opiates with possession penalties decreased and trafficking penalties potentially more severe. Lysergide (LSD) and similar hallucinogens are proposed for inclusion in Class A which would considerably increase the maximum penalties in comparison with their present control under the Drugs (Prevention of Misuse) Act. Amphetamines are proposed for Class B which would allow greater control and punishment than currently possible under the Drugs (Prevention of Misuse) Act, 1964.

ARREST AND SEARCH IN RELATION TO DRUG OFFENCES

The powers of arrest and search available to the police under the drugs acts and general criminal legislation have given rise to some concern in the last five years (National Council on Civil Liberties, 1969; Coon and Harris, 1969). The Advisory Committee on Drug Dependence (1970) has reviewed these powers in relation to cannabis and other restricted drugs following a recommendation for the enquiry in the Wootton Report (Advisory Committee on Drug Dependence, 1968). The Committee examined the following areas:

(i)   the existing laws on arrest and search
(ii) procedures for bail
(iii) police operational practice
(iv) the procedures for complaints against the police.

The Committee was unable to reach unanimity in its findings or recommendations, but it was felt useful to publish the differing points of view so that informal public debate would be possible before the Misuse of Drugs Bill was enacted.

The Committee was divided on the issues of stop and search provisions in the law and the possibility of framing a legal definition of 'reasonable grounds' for searching individuals suspected of possessing illicit drugs. The grounds for granting bail, for communicating with a friend, relative, or solicitor following arrest and for the issue of granting search warrants were discussed in full. The essence of the debate involved with the enforcement of drug laws is that the balance between law and individual liberty is not easy to get right. This balance is the centre of the Committee's report.

REFERENCES

*The new legislation discussed in this section has now passed through parliament and received the Royal Assent. However, the Misuse of Drugs Act, 1971 has not yet come into force, and will not do so until the regulations are completed, probably in 1972.

ADVISORY COMMITTEE ON DRUG DEPENDENCE (Wootton Committee), 1968. *Cannabis.* H.M.S.O., London.

ADVISORY COMMITTEE ON DRUG DEPENDENCE, 1970. *Powers of Arrest and Search in Relation to Drug Offences.* H.M.S.O., London.

CAHAL D.A., 1970. Drug Addiction and the Law. *J. Roy. Coll. Gen. Practit.* 20, 32.

COON C. and HARRIS R., 1969. *The Release Report on Drug Offences and the Law.* Sphere, London.

DANGEROUS DRUGS (No.2) REGULATIONS, 1964. H.M.S.O., London.

DANGEROUS DRUGS ACT, 1965. H.M.S.O., London.

DANGEROUS DRUGS ACT, 1967. H.M.S.O., London.

DANGEROUS DRUGS (NOTIFICATION OF ADDICTS) REGULATIONS, 1968. H.M.S.O., London.

DANGEROUS DRUGS (SUPPLY TO ADDICTS) REGULATIONS, 1968. H.M.S.O., London.

DAWTRY, Frank (Ed.), 1968. *Social Problems of Drug Abuse.* Butterworths, London.

DEPARTMENT OF HEALTH AND SOCIAL SECURITY, 1969. *Annual Report for the Year 1968.* H.M.S.O., London.

DRUGS (PREVENTION OF MISUSE) ACT, 1964. H.M.S.O., London.

MEDICINES ACT, 1968. H.M.S.O., London.

MISUSE OF DRUGS BILL. H.M.S.O., London.

NATIONAL COUNCIL FOR CIVIL LIBERTIES, 1969. *Drugs and the Law.* N.C.C.L., London.

PHARMACY AND POISONS ACT, 1933. H.M.S.O., London.

POISONS RULES, 1970. H.M.S.O., London.

PRIEST, L. 1967. How does legislation protect the public from poisoning? in The Development and Use of Drugs. *The Advancement of Science.* (Special Issue).

SINGLE CONVENTION ON NARCOTIC DRUGS, 1961. H.M.S.O., London.

SECTION 2

NORMAL USE OF ALCOHOL
AND MEDICAL USE OF DRUGS

The 'normal' use of alcohol refers to the drinking behaviour of the great majority of the population in Great Britain. Chapter 5 discusses who drinks in Great Britain, what they are most likely to drink, the overall frequency of drinking and where most drinking takes place.

The medical use of drugs is taken to be the use of these substances for generally accepted medical reasons. For instance, the occasional use of an aspirin to control pain of an ordinary headache, or the use of a tranquilliser under medical supervision, is considered medical use; while the dependent use of a large quantity of barbiturates is not. Chapter 6 considers data on the prescription of psychotropic drugs in Britain and findings related to their use in medicine.

CHAPTER 5

THE "NORMAL" USE OF ALCOHOL

IN GREAT BRITAIN

The 'normal' use of alcohol refers to the drinking behaviour of the vast majority of the population in Great Britain, whereby alcohol is consumed for pleasure or sociability, its use leading to the social, mental or physical problems which are discussed in Chapter 8. This chapter examines the consumption of alcohol in Britain, national expenditure on alcoholic beverages, studies of 'normal' drinking behaviour and public houses.

ALCOHOL CONSUMPTION

The consumption of the three main types of alcoholic drink (beer, wines and spirits) has increased in the past ten years, both in absolute terms and in per capita consumption for the United Kingdom population. This increase is illustrated in Table 5–1.

EXPENDITURE ON ALCOHOL

Consumer expenditure on alcohol has risen over the past 10 years. For instance, expenditure on beer alone rose from £563 million in 1960 to £1058 million in 1969. The Department of Employment and Productivity (1970) publishes a national survey analysing consumer expenditure of representative households in Great Britain. The average weekly spending on alcoholic drinks is shown in Table 5–2.

Table 5–1.   Total Consumption of Alcoholic Drink in United Kingdom. 1960–1969.

	1960	1961	1962	1963	1964	1965	1966	1967	1968	1969
BEER:										
Total consumption (Litres–million)	4526	4734	4726	4747	4931	5026	5047	5218	5246	5512
Per capita–Total U.K. home population (litres)	85.5	87.8	87.4	89.2	90.5	91.0	92.3	92.3	94.6	98.7
Per capita–U.K. home population. Age 15+ (litres)	111.6	115.8	114.4	113.6	117.7	118.3	120.1	122.8	124.7	130.0
SPIRITS:										
Total consumption (Litres–million)	98	103	104	110	120	112	113	114	118	112
Per capita–Total U.K. home population (litres)	1.8	1.9	1.9	2.1	2.2	2.1	2.0	2.2	2.2	2.0
Per capita–Total U.K. home population. Age 15+ (litres)	2.4	2.5	2.5	2.7	2.9	2.7	2.7	2.7	2.9	2.6
WINE:										
Total consumption (Litres–million)	122	129	134	148	169	162	172	189	211	204
Per capita–Total U.K. home population (litres)	2.3	2.5	2.5	2.8	3.1	3.0	3.1	3.4	3.8	3.7
Per capita–U.K. home population. Age 15+ (litres)	3.0	3.2	3.3	3.6	4.0	3.9	4.1	4.5	5.0	4.8

Source: Adapted from H.M. Customs and Excise. *Annual Report.* H.M.S.O., London, 1970.

Table 5—2.   **Average Weekly Spending on Alcoholic Drinks by all Households in the United Kingdom. 1963—1969. (New Pence).**

	1963—65	1967—67	1967—69
Beer and cider	53	62	69½
Wine and Spirits	22½	27	33
All alcoholic drinks*	83	92	104½
Average Household Income	£22.42	£26.72	£30.24
All drinks as proportion of Income	3.39%	3.46%	3.46%

* Including alcoholic drinks other than beer, cider, wine and spirits.

Source: Department of Employment and Productivity. *Family Expenditure Survey.* H.M.S.O., London. 1970.

The average weekly spending within various income brackets is also reported in the *Family Expenditure Survey*. The table below indicates that the greater the income of a household, the higher the *proportion* of money spent on drink.

Table 5—3.   **Average Weekly Spending on Alcoholic Drinks by Household Income, 1969. (New Pence).**

Household Income Per Week	Weekly Spending			
	Beer and Cider	Wines and Spirits	All Alcohol (incl. other types of drinks)	All as proportion of total house-hold spending
Under £6	7½	3½	11.1	1.2%
£6—£10	22	10½	33	1.7%
£10—£20	68	27	98½	3.0%
£20—£30	125½	43	171½	3.9%
£30—£50	278½	113½	407½	4.5%
£50 and over	299½	188	507	5.2%
Average for all households	74.5	34½	113	4.3%
Proportion for all expenditure	2.8%	1.3%	4.3%	

Source: Department of Employment and Productivity. *Family Expenditure Survey.* H.M.S.O., London. 1970.

The relationship between expenditure and income, however, is complex, in that if average weekly expenditure on alcoholic drink is analysed by the occupation of the head of the household, manual workers spend proportionately more of their incomes on alcoholic drink than do people in other occupations. The picture is further complicated because the estimated average expenditure on alcoholic drink of all households in the survey is about one half of what might be estimated from returns by H.M. Customs and Excise (Department of Employment and Productivity, 1970). This is partly due to households under-estimating the amounts actually spent on alcoholic drink and partly because of the difficulty in distinguishing between household and non-household populations.

'NORMAL' DRINKING BEHAVIOUR

National Surveys

National surveys of drinking habits in Great Britain have been conducted by market research firms. Between 1947 and 1954, as part of an enquiry into press readership carried out by a consortium of advertising firms, the frequency of drinking was ascertained in a national, stratified quota sample based on 10,000 interviews (Hulton Readership Survey, 1947–54). The frequency of consumption of beer, wine and spirits was subsequently related to the sex, age groupings, social class, press readership and a limited number of other variables. By 1954, 84% of men and 55% of women were reported to drink beer at some time in that year with 51% of this group drinking regularly. A steady increase in the proportion of drinkers in the 16–24 year age group had been shown in each successive year of the survey.

As from 1968, the British Market Research Bureau has published reports on the drinking habits of a national sample of 25,000 picked randomly from the total adult population (aged 15 years and over) of Great Britain. The frequency of consumption of all alcoholic and soft drinks is recorded. While the survey assesses frequency of consumption, it does not assess quantity. Some results from the most recent survey (April, 1969–March, 1970) are shown below in Table 5–4.

Table 5–4.   Beer, Wine and Whisky Consumption in Great Britain by Social Class and Age Groupings, April 1969–March 1970. (N = 25,000)

	Social Classes A, B, C_1*		Social Classes C_2, D, E*		
	16–34 years	35+ years	16–34 years	35+ years	ALL
BEER:					
% of group drinking	55.6	34.4	49.6	35.2	43.7%
% of total consumption	16.0	18.8	27.7	37.5	100%
WINE:					
% of group drinking	63.8	52.4	24.1	17.5	39.4%
% of total consumption	23.2	36.1	17.1	23.6	100%
WHISKY:					
% of group drinking	50.2	58.1	39.5	48.6	49.1%
% of total consumption	12.4	26.2	18.2	43.2	100%

* Social class letter A to E represent a descending order of class from higher to lower social groups.

Source: British Market Research Bureau. *Target Group Index.* B.M.R.B., London. 1971.

The table above shows the percentage of persons drinking beer, wine and whisky—the most popular spirit—in age and social class groupings. The percentage of total consumption in each category by age group and class is also given. The figures indicate, for instance, that beer is more popular in the younger age groups of both the higher and lower social classes, that wine drinking is more popular amongst the higher social classes and that whisky drinking is fairly evenly spread across all social age groups and classes, although it is least popular in the younger age groups of the lower social classes. Although these surveys are conducted with a view to finding the actual brands of alcohol consumed within individual groupings, they are useful for the analysis of wider trends.

Surveys of Selected Populations

Wallace (1970) has examined drinking habits amongst a sample of 2,500 men and women aged between 21 and 65 years. This survey contained more detailed information on the frequency of drinking and differences of drinking behaviour in different regions of Britain. For example, Scottish men were reported to drink spirits to a greater extent than any other group, while Scottish women in this sample were shown to be less frequent drinkers than any other group (Wallace, 1970).

Edwards et al (1971) conducted a survey of drinking habits, motivation and drinking complications in a sample of adults (aged 18 and over) drawn from six housing estates in one South London borough. These housing areas were chosen to represent a wide range of social and economic status. There were 408 males and 520 females in the sample whose overall frequency of drinking is shown below in Table 5—5.

Table 5—5.   Frequency of Drinking in the Last Year in a London Borough

Frequency of Drinking	Males n = 408	Females n = 520
Every day	11%	4%
'Most days'	11	4
Weekends only	19	11
Once or twice a week	23	15
Once or twice a month	12	20
Once or twice in six months	7	14
Once or twice a year	10	22
Never	7	10
Total:	100%	100%

Source: Edwards G., Chandler J. and Hensman C. Correlates of drinking in a London suburb. *Quart. J. Stud. Alc.* In press. 1971.

The sample was also asked whether they drank 15 types of alcoholic beverage and the quantity of each type they usually drank on each occasion. Table 5—6 shows the 'usual' quantity of drink most frequently consumed. The category 'Number of Drinks' refers to the number of *singles* of whisky or other spirits, *glasses* of wine or Babycham, or *half pints* of beer or cider. These measures, as served in public houses, contain approximately equivalent quantities of absolute alcohol (9—10 grammes).

Drinking behaviour was then analysed in terms of quantity/frequency categories. Significant relationships were found between the quantity/frequency categories and sex, social class, age, religion, nationality, parental drinking, personality and choice of beverage. For example, older age groups showed a lower proportion of heavy drinkers than younger age groups among men. Men in the higher social classes

Table 5—6.   Usual Quantity of Most Frequently Consumed Drink in a London Borough.

Number of Drinks	Males n = 376	Females n = 465
1—2	27%	67%
3—4	24	22
5—6	19	7
7—8	10	2
9—10	6	1
11—12	6	*
13—14	1	—
15+	7	*
Total:	100%	99%

* Indicates percentage less than 0.5
— Indicates none.

Source: Edwards G., Chandler J. and Hensman C.
Correlates of normal drinking in a London suburb.
Quart. J. Stud. Alc. In press. 1971.

showed a pattern of frequent light drinking, while men in the middle and lower classes were more likely to be moderate and heavy drinkers. Men of Scottish and Irish ethnic background accounted for a disproportionately large number of heavy drinkers.

Edwards et al (1971) also showed that sex and class were related to weekly spending on alcohol, choice of usual place for drinking and influences of the weekend on drinking. Upper class males were more likely to be frequent light drinkers uninfluenced by the weekend, and prefer home for drinking. Spirits were the preferred beverage. On the other hand, lower class men were more often heavy drinkers who tended to drink more heavily at the weekend and usually in pubs. Beer was most frequently consumed.

Seventeen questions which bore on possible motivation for drinking were submitted to each respondent during the course of this same survey. Affirmative replies for male subjects who drank alcohol at all, are recorded below.

Table 5—7.   Proportion of Male Subjects answering affirmatively to 17 'Motivation for Drinking' questions, South London Survey.   (N = 304)

	Number	%
Job demands it	30	10
To forget worries	36	12
To sleep	40	13
'Revives me'	43	14
'When things get me down'	46	15
When restless or tense	49	16
For health reasons	49	16
By habit	61	20
'Difficult to refuse'	70	23
When dull and bored	98	32
At meals	101	33
To feel good	106	35
With other people	131	43

Table 5—7. (contd.)

	Number	%
To relax	140	46
When thirsty	143	47
For the taste	180	59
To celebrate	277	91

Source: Edwards G., Hensman C., Chandler J. and Peto J. Motivation for drinking among men: Survey of a London suburb. Unpublished report. 1971.

Student Drinking

It has been found that a majority of young persons develop regular patterns of alcohol consumption by the age of 17 or 18 years (Stacey and Davies, 1970), so that it is particularly important to establish what factors influence young people's drinking. In a survey of university students, Orford and Postoyan (1970) found that the drinking of peer groups, parents' drinking and the individual's own attitudes towards drinking were the most important factors determining the consumption of alcohol. 1,807 students at two London colleges were asked about their drinking habits in October, 1967 and a follow-up questionnaire was administered in October, 1969.

The survey found that 16—18% of male students had more than two drinks a day on average over the previous 12 months, while 64% had one drink a day or less in that same time. The largest group of male students (25—28%) had between 1 and 91 drinks in the previous year. The table below shows the alcohol consumption of students at these two colleges.

Table 5—8.   Quantity-Frequency Index of Alcohol Consumption among Under-Graduates at two Colleges of the University of London.

Estimated number of drinks in the last year	College A Males (%) n = 495	College B Males (%) n = 569
0 (Abstainers)	2%	4%
1—91 drinks	13	15
92—365 drinks	49	45
366 drinks +	35	35
Information not obtained	1	1
Total:	100%	100%

One drink equals *half pint* of beer, cider, shandy or Guinness;
or a *single* whisky, gin, vodka or other spirit;
or a *glass* of wine, sherry, etc.

Source: Orford J. and Postoyan S. Drinking behaviour and its determinants amongst university students in London. Paper presented at Third International Conference on Alcoholism and the Addictions. Cardiff, Wales. 1970.

The Public House in Britain

The traditional outlet for the consumption of alcohol in Britain is the public house (pub), which originated in Saxon times and has been the typical communal drinking centre for the majority of the population since thèn. The 19th century saw a large increase in the number of pubs and public houses began to move away from the traditional concept of a rest house with food and drink. (Monckton, 1969). (see Chapter 7)

In the 20th century, there has been a decline in the total number of public houses from over 90,000 in 1900 to approximately 70,000 in 1967 (Home Office, 1968). This decline probably results in part from the higher rate of tax on alcohol and also from the shortening of licensing hours (from 17½ hours per day at the beginning of the 20th century to 8 per day in 1970). Improvement in the material standards of living have also brought a number of counter attractions, such as comfortable homes, television and a greater motivation for saving.

The social function of the English pub has been examined (Mass Observation, 1943). More recently, an independent survey conducted on beer drinking habits established that 83% of 1,400 people who had drunk beer during the previous year had patronised a pub regularly.

MEDICAL USE OF ALCOHOL

Alcohol is occasionally recommended by general practitioners in small quantities for helping patients to sleep or as a cold remedy. However, prescription of alcohol is not allowable under the National Health Service.

A rum ration was originally introduced into the Royal Navy to allay scurvy and other such deficiences. Rum was issued at midday to all ratings over 18 years of age while at sea in Her Majesty's ships. This ration, equivalent to three tots of whisky, is now viewed as having been more harmful than helpful and has been abolished (Caldwell. Personal communication. 1971).

REFERENCES

BRITISH MARKET RESEARCH BUREAU, 1971. *Target Group Index.* B.M.R.B., London.

CUSTOMS AND EXCISE (H.M.), 1970. *Annual Report.* H.M.S.O., London.

DEPARTMENT OF EMPLOYMENT AND PRODUCTIVITY, 1970. *Family Expenditure Survey–Report for 1969.* H.M.S.O., London.

EDWARDS G., CHANDLER J. and HENSMAN C., 1971. Correlates of normal drinking in a London suburb. *Quart. J. Stud. Alc.*

HOME OFFICE, 1968. *Liquor Licensing Statistics.* H.M.S.O., London.

HULTON READERSHIP SURVEY, 1947–1954. Hulton Press, London.

MASS OBSERVATION, 1943. *The Pub and the People: A Worktown Study.* Gollancz, London. (Republished, Seven Dials Press, 1970).

MONCKTON H.A., 1969. *History of the English Public House.* Bodley Head, London.

ORFORD J. and POSTOYAN S., 1970. Drinking behaviour and its determinants amongst university students in London. Paper presented at Third International Conference on Alcoholism and the Addictions, Cardiff, Wales.

ROWNTREE B. and LAVERS G.R., 1951. *English Life and Leisure.* Longmans, London.

STACEY B. and DAVIES J., 1970. Drinking behaviour in childhood and adolescence: an evaluative review. *Brit. J. Addict.* 65, 203.

WALLACE J., 1970. Who drinks what in Britain? Paper presented at Third International Conference on Alcohol and the Addictions. Cardiff, Wales.

CHAPTER 6

MEDICAL USE OF DRUGS

PRESCRIPTION DATA

It has been suggested that the vast amount of medication being taken by large numbers of people in our society has made its own contribution towards the drug dependence problem, although the relative importance of this factor is not yet clear.

The attached tables and graphs show the trends between 1961 and 1968. The total number of prescriptions—just over 15 million for barbiturates—changed little between 1962 and 1968, except for a transient rise reaching a peak in 1965. Non-barbiturate hypnotics have risen from 2.6 million in 1962 to 5.8 million in 1968. Prescriptions for tranquillising drugs have risen over the same period from 6.6 to 16 million. As there has been an upward trend in the prescribing of all classes of drugs, it is possible that tranquillising substances are to some extent displacing barbiturates. There has been a reduction in the use of stimulants and appetite suppressants by 1.5 million prescriptions, while anti-depressants, which do not on the whole give rise to a dependency syndrome, have more than doubled from 2 to 5.2 million.

Table 6—1. Estimated Total Number of Prescriptions (Millions) in England and Wales—National Health Service. 1961—1968.

	1961	1962	1963	1964	1965	1966	1967	1968
Preparations acting on the nervous system:								
Addictive analgesics	0.9	0.9	0.9	0.9	0.9	1.0	1.0	1.0
Antipyretic analgesics	15.0	14.1	14.8	14.9	18.7	19.1	20.4	18.9
Specific analgesics	3.0	3.4	3.8	4.3	5.1	not given		
Barbiturates	15.2	15.8	15.9	16.1	17.2	16.8	16.1	15.3
Non-barbiturate hypnotics	3.4	2.6	2.5	2.6	2.7	3.5	4.8	5.8
Tranquillisers	6.2	6.6	7.1	9.0	10.9	12.5	14.7	16.0
Stimulants and appetite suppressants	6.0	5.4	4.9	5.1	5.3	5.2	4.8	3.9
Anti-depressives	1.4	2.0	2.4	2.8	3.5	3.9	4.9	5.3
Total prescriptions acting on the nervous system	51.1	50.8	52.3	55.7	64.3	62.0	66.7	66.2
Total prescription for all drugs	205.0	196.6	205.5	209.4	244.3	262.0	271.2	267.4

Table 6–2. Estimated Total Ingredient Cost (£ Million) in England & Wales. National Health Service. 1961–1968

	1961	1962	1963	1964	1965	1966	1967	1968
Preparations acting on the nervous system:								
Addictive analgesics	0.1	0.1	0.2	0.2	0.2	0.2	0.2	0.2
Antipyretic analgesics	2.1	2.2	2.3	2.6	4.0	3.6	3.9	3.8
Specific analgesics	1.5	1.7	1.9	2.3	2.6		not given	
Barbiturates	1.5	1.7	1.8	1.9	2.0	2.0	1.9	1.9
Non-barbiturate hypnotics	0.4	0.3	0.3	0.3	0.4	0.8	1.3	1.8
Tranquillisers	2.4	2.7	3.0	3.9	4.9	5.9	7.1	8.2
Stimulants and appetite suppressants	1.2	1.3	1.3	1.4	1.5	1.5	1.5	1.5
Anti-depressives	1.4	1.9	2.2	2.4	2.8	3.1	3.8	4.2
Total prescriptions acting on the nervous system	10.6	11.9	13.0	15.0	18.4	17.1	19.7	21.6
Total prescriptions for all drugs	55.4	59.0	64.1	72.0	86.4	95.8	102.1	108.6

Source of Tables 6–1 and 6–2:   Annual Reports of Ministry of Health (now Department of Health and Social Security). HMSO., London.

The data above takes into account all prescriptions dispensed by chemists, drug stores and appliance contractors, but does not include the relatively small number of private prescriptions issued or the prescription and cost of hospital medicines. The totals are for England and Wales, not for the United Kingdom. The total expenditure on medicines within the National Health Service for 1968, including all of the United Kingdom and the hospital and central supply comes to £210 million.

The number of prescriptions is only a crude index of the use of drugs in Great Britain. The quantity of the drug supplied and the exact pharmaceutical preparation prescribed within a therapeutic group are not given. The prescription may be intended for varying lengths of time so that an average quantity is difficult to calculate.

The proportion of preparations acting on the nervous system has remained fairly constant in relation to the total number of prescriptions. Those preparations accounted for 24.92% of all prescriptions in 1961, and 24.75% of all prescriptions in 1968, although the specific analgesics are not reported in the later date. The constancy of the percentage masks some of the changing characteristics within the grouping. Changes in the hypnotic, tranquillising and anti-depressive groups are set out in Table 6–4.

Figure 6—3.   Estimated Total Number of Prescriptions in Millions—England and Wales. 1961—1968.

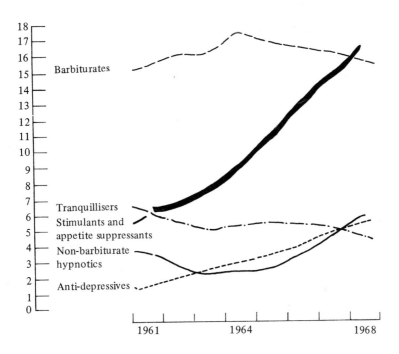

Source: Annual Reports of Ministry of Health (now Department of Health & Social Security). HMSO, London.

Table 6—4.   Number of Prescriptions for Hypnotics, Tranquillisers and Anti-Depressives. 1961 & 1968.

	1961		1968	
	Number of prescriptions (million)	Percentage of total prescriptions	Number of prescriptions (million)	Percentage of total prescriptions
Barbiturates	15.2	7.4%	15.3	5.7%
Non-barbiturate hypnotics	3.4	1.6%	5.8	2.2%
Tranquillisers	6.2	3.0%	16.0	5.9%
Anti-depressives	1.4	0.6%	5.3	2.0%
Total:	26.2 m.	12.6%	42.4 m.	15.8%

The total prescriptions in England and Wales have increased by just under one-third. The number of prescriptions for barbiturates has stayed the same, while prescriptions for tranquillisers have increased by two and a half times, prescriptions for non-barbiturate hypnotics by three quarters, and prescriptions for anti depressives by nearly four times. These three groups of drugs accounted for 26% of the rise in the total prescription figures.

In Northern Ireland the analysis of prescription data is more exact and detailed than in the rest of the United Kingdom. Every prescription is recorded on computer cards with the following information:

the code number of the pharmacy supplying the drug;
the code number of the prescribing doctor;
the code number of the pharmaceutical preparation prescribed;
the code number of the quantity supplied;
the prescription number: this allows the original prescription form to be traced (Wade).

The other administrative pricing bureaux in the United Kingdom use sampling methods to determine the cost of drugs. The relatively small size of Northern Ireland, with 756 doctors in general practice in 1962, compared to 21,006 doctors in England and Wales at that time, makes the detailed analysis more practicable. With these methods it is possible to analyse factors which may influence the prescribing of drugs, geographical differences in the prescription of drugs, the use of newly marketed preparations and, in the case of a new found danger with a specific drug, it would be possible to locate the patients who have received this preparation (Wade). The study of factors such as these are likely to reveal useful insights about diseases as well as the prescribing habits of doctors and drug consumption by patients.

MEDICAL USE OF CANNABIS

There has been very limited medical use of cannabis in the United Kingdom since World War II. In the 19th century cannabis was regarded as a remedy for pain, migraine, insomnia, dysmenorrhoea, difficult parturition and cramp (Department of Health and Social Security, 1970). It was considered an extremely valuable medicine by Reynolds (1890). It has not been used by doctors since the War except in an occasional experiment (Rolls and Stafford-Clark, 1954), although it is available in an alcoholic solution known as tincture of cannabis. It is considered as 'too unreliable in action to be of value in therapeutics as a cerebral sedative or narcotic, and its former use in mania and nervous disorders has been abandoned'. (British Pharmaceutical Codex, 1949). A listing for cannabis does not even appear in the 1968 Codex.

Within the past two years there have been reports of doctors prescribing tincture of cannabis to patients, but it is not known whether at the present time any doctors are issuing prescriptions for the drug.

MEDICAL USE OF LSD AND HALLUCINOGENIC DRUGS

Medical experimentation with LSD began in the United Kingdom in the middle 1950's and has continued on a small scale since then. A survey by Malleson (1971) indicates that over 80 doctors have used LSD clinically in the United Kingdom and that approximately 37 are still on occasions conducting clinical or experimental work. Most work in recent years has been the attempted therapeutic use with chronic alcoholics and people suffering from character disorders or psycho-sexual difficulties. Two principle approaches have been used, the first involving the administration of a very large dose (the psychlopetic approach), in which the patient is encouraged to have a major abreaction which may permit a radical restructuring of his own attitudes to life. The alternative use, generally described as psycho-therapeutic, involves the drug being given in a series of smaller doses, of about 200 microgrammes, with psycho-therapy taking place during sessions and between them. The value of LSD used in either of these manners remains a matter for debate and early, rather uncritical enthusiasm has become more temperate. There is no conclusive evidence that LSD therapy is superior to any of the other treatments currently used in psychiatry (Department of Health and Social Security, 1970).

There are risks with LSD therapy that have to be assessed. Acute adverse reactions to LSD in clinical and experimental use have been recorded (Malleson, 1971). Malleson reports some 5000 cases (including about 200 experimental subjects) have been treated with LSD clinically. These cases received a total of approximately 50,000 LSD doses. The survey disclosed three suicides which were around the time of such therapy, and 20 attempted suicides, although only in nine of these is there evidence that the intention of self-injury was a very serious one. There were 37 acute psychotic reactions lasting more than 48 hours, two-thirds of which had resolved within a few months, although usually much more quickly. It is not possible in this survey to ensure that there was a causal, rather than temporal, relationship to the use of LSD and these adverse reactions.

The Advisory Committee on Drug Dependence (1970) concluded:

'there is no proof that LSD is an effective agent in psychiatry. Equally, there is no proof that it is an exceptionally hazardous or a prohibitively dangerous treatment in clinical use, in the hands of responsible experts and subject to appropriate safeguards. We see no reason to recommend arrangements which would prohibit the continued careful and experimental use of LSD by approved and responsible practitioners'.

MEDICAL USE OF AMPHETAMINES

Amphetamine was first synthesised in 1887 and its pharmacology studied in 1927 (British Medical Assoc., 1968). The effects of a moderate dose are euphoria, wakefulness, increased initiative and a heightened sense of confidence and ability. These drugs were first used in the treatment of narcolepsy and for the treatment of depression (Guttman and Sargant, 1937). Other uses for amphetamine were claimed in certain severe behaviour problems in children, in epilepsy, in the treatment of aggressive psychopaths, abreaction in psychiatry, eneuresis, menstrual problems, pressor agents and barbiturate poisoning (British Medical Association, 1968). Amphetamines were issued to the armed forces of Great Britain during the war as stimulants for use in emergencies (Bett, 1947). Amphetamines have been most commonly used for the treatment of obesity or depression.

Between 1961 and 1968 (Table 6–1) there was a drop in the number of prescriptions for amphetamines and appetite suppressants. This reflects a declining use of amphetamine for the treatment of depression. Initial enthusiasm for amphetamine (Lancet, 1947) and the wide application of the drug to the conditions cited above have given way to the opinion that it is of limited value.

The British Medical Association (1968) established a Working Party on Amphetamine Preparations to consider both therapeutic and non-therapeutic usage of amphetamines in Great Britain. Some of their recommendations and conclusions were as follows:

1. 'In the view of the Working Party, amphetamines and amphetamine-like compounds are drugs with a limited use in modern therapeutics. They are valued by some individuals for their non-therapeutic usage, but this misuse can and does produce mental and physical deterioration....'

2. The Working Party therefore recommends:
   a)   'that amphetamine and amphetamine-like compounds should only be prescribed for those conditions for which no reasonable alternative exists, or as part of the therapy of those patients already dependent on these drugs; more specifically:'

   (i)   'these drugs should be avoided as far as possible in the treatment of obesity, but if in individual cases the doctors feel they must be employed, they should only be prescribed for a limited period....'

   (ii)   'the use of these drugs in the treatment of depression should be, in general, avoided as they appear to have no place in the modern treatment of this condition;'

   (iii) 'the use of these drugs in other conditions should be discouraged, with the possible exception of narcolepsy, as modern therapeutic methods have long since superseded the use of these compounds;'

   (iv)   'the treatment of patients already dependent upon small doses of these drugs should be considered individually. Patients dependent upon large doses will require special psychiatric treatment and support similar to that provided for heroin dependent cases and such treatment must readily be available for registered cases.'

   b)   'That in order to restrict the availability of amphetamines and amphetamine-like compounds or preparations containing these substances, manufacturers, pharmacists, nurses and doctors should voluntarily take the same precautions, and keep the same records as they do for those drugs covered by Part 1 of the schedule for the Dangerous Drugs Act, 1965....'

   c)   'That manufacturers should be encouraged to produce amphetamine compounds intended for oral use in a form from which the active ingredient could not easily be abstracted for intravenous use.'

3. 'The Working Party concludes that if the voluntary measures of control do not succeed, then restrictive legislation would seem inevitable. Such legislation would need to give powers to the General Medical Council to control unethical prescribing of drugs to dependent persons....'

MEDICAL USE OF HYPNOTICS AND TRANQUILLISERS

Barbiturates were introduced into clinical practice in 1903 and have since been very widely used. The therapeutic uses include the relief of anxiety and insomnia, the treatment of epilepsy, the introduction of anaesthesia, the maintenance of continuous narcoses and production of abreaction (Department of Health and Social Security, 1970). The number of prescriptions for barbiturates have risen only very slightly from 1961 to 1968 (Table 6–1) and the number has fallen as a proportion of total prescriptions. There have been rises in the prescription of non-barbiturate hypnotics which induce sleep without the same dangers of dependence and self-poisoning with barbiturates. Prescriptions for the tranquillisers (the phenothiazine drugs and the minor tranquillisers), and for the anti-depressive drugs (the MAO inhibitors and tri-cyclic anti-depressives) have risen as well (Table 6–1, 6–4). In spite of the increased use of other types of hypnotics and tranquillisers, the British Medical Journal (1968) stated 'In many cases the barbiturates are still unsurpassed in their ability to relieve anxiety, and they are far cheaper than tranquillisers'. The Journal commenting on their hypnotic effect states:

'The barbiturates have been in clinical use for about 50 years, and in that time they have become among the most used and probably also the most misused of the drugs of the twentieth century. According to Ministry of Health statistics about 10% of all prescriptions are for hypnotics and 66% of deaths from accidental overdosage of a drug are due to barbiturates. None the less, barbiturates must still take pride of place in any consideration of hypnotics because none of the other drugs, with the possible exception of chloral hydrate, has stood the test of time, and to date none has been proved to be convincingly superior'.

The wide use of barbiturates can be gauged from the following passage (Adams et al, 1966):

'In 1946, a rough estimate of the consumption of barbiturates in Great Britain suggested that enough was produced for "one sleeping tablet per head per day for a million of the population" (Locket, 1957). This calculation was based on the estimate of 71,500 lb. of barbituric acid and salts produced. Since then, the Interdepartmental Committee on Drug Addiction (1961) indicated that the estimated total quantity of barbiturate prescribed by general practitioners had increased from 90,000 to 162,000 lb. between 1951 and 1959. This occurred in spite of the introduction of other sedatives and "tranquillisers" during this period'.

In 1959 there were approximately 14.3 million prescriptions for barbiturates compared with 16.3 million in 1968.

Dunlop (1970) has presented a more detailed breakdown for prescription of drugs in the hypnotic, tranquilliser and anti-depressive groups. The figures refer to the whole of the United Kingdom and are therefore somewhat different from those in Table 6–1.

Dunlop (1970) has estimated that the prescriptions for phenothiazine tranquillisers would be 'roughly enough tablets to give a month's treatment . . . to every tenth person in the United Kingdom' and points out that in addition there are more than twice as many prescriptions for the minor tranquillisers (benzodiazepines).

The figure for barbiturates includes compound formulations that use a small amount for sedative effect. However, if only barbiturates principally used as hypnotics are considered (16.5 million prescriptions) along with the 5.5 million prescriptions for non-barbiturate hypnotics, Dunlop calculated 'very roughly that these represent sufficient tablets to make every tenth night's sleep in the United Kingdom hypnotic-induced'.

Table 6—5.   **Psychotrophic Drugs Prescribed in the United Kingdom in 1968 under the National Health Service.**

Drug Group	Prescriptions (millions)
Barbiturates*	24.7
Benzodiazepines	12.7
Phenothiazines	6.1
Non-barbiturate hypnotics	5.5
Tri-cyclic anti-depressants	5.0
Amphetamines	4.0 (approx.)
MAO inhibitors	0.4

* Including compound preparations containing them.

Source: Dunlop, D. 'The Use and Abuse of Psychotropic Drugs'. Proceedings of the Royal Society of Medicine, 63, 12. December, 1970.

MEDICAL USE OF OPIATES

Opiate preparations have been used in British medicine for hundreds of years. Opiate alkaloids such as morphine were not isolated until the 1800's and since that time hundreds of additional synthetic opiate-like substances have been produced (Laurence, 1966). All the opiate drugs are used principally for the relief of severe pain and are unsurpassed for this purpose. These powerful analgesics (pain-killing drugs) fall into three chemical familities typified respectively by morphine, methadone and pethidine (British Medical Journal, 1963).

The Interdepartmental Committees, which have considered the use of morphine and heroin in medical practice (see Chapter 13), have considered these drugs indispensible for the treatment of seiverely painful organic disease. Prescription figures for addictive analgesics (see Table 6—1) indicate that despite the rise in the non-medical use of opiates the overall use of opiates in medicine has remained virtually unchanged.

REFERENCES

ADAMS B.G. and HORDER E.J., HORDER J.P., MODELL M., STEEN C.A., WIGG J.W., 1966. Patients receiving barbiturates in an urban general practice. *J. Coll. Gen. Practit.* 12, 24.

ADVISORY COMMITTEE ON DRUG DEPENDENCE, 1970. *The Amphetamines and Lysergic Acid Diethylamide (LSD).* H.M.S.O., London.

BETT W.R., 1947. Editorial. *Brit. J. Addict.* 44, 94.

BRITISH MEDICAL ASSOCIATION, 1968. *Report of the Working Party on Amphetamine Preparations.* British Medical Association, London.

BRITISH MEDICAL JOURNAL, 1963, Current practice—Today's drugs. *Brit. Med. J.* 2, 409.

BRITISH MEDICAL JOURNAL, 1968. Current practice—Today's drugs. *Brit. Med. J.* i, 241.

BRITISH PHARMACEUTICAL CODEX, 1949. 'Cannabis' in *British Pharmaceutical Codex.* Pharmaceutical Press, London.

DEPARTMENT OF HEALTH AND SOCIAL SECURITY, 1970. *Amphetamines, Barbiturates, LSD and Cannabis: their Use and Misuse.* H.M.S.O., London.

DUNLOP D., 1970. The use and abuse of psychotropic drugs. *Proc. Royal Soc. Med.* 63, 1279.

GUTTMAN E. and SARGANT W., 1937. Observations on benezedrine. *Brit. Med. J.* 1, 1013.

INTERDEPARTMENTAL COMMITTEE ON DRUG ADDICTION, 1961. *Drug Addiction.* H.M.S.O., London.

LANCET, 1947. A versatile remedy. *Lancet.* i, 567.

LAURENCE D.R., 1966. *Clinical Pharmacology.* Churchill, London.

LOCKET S., 1957. The abuse of barbiturates. *Brit. J. Addict.* 53, 105.

MALLESON N., 1971. in press—*Brit. J. Psychiat.*

MINISTRY OF HEALTH (now Department of Health and Social Security), 1962—1969. *Annual Reports.* H.M.S.O., London.

REYNOLDS J.R., 1890. On the therapeutic uses and toxic effects of Cannabis Indica. *Lancet.* i, 637.

ROLLS E.J. and STAFFORD-CLARK D., 1954. Depersonalization treated by cannabis indica and psychotherapy. *Guy's Hosp. Rep.* 103, 330.

WADE O.L. (undated). The computer and drug prescribing. Reprint from Queen's University, Belfast.

SECTION 3
MISUSE OF ALCOHOL AND
NON-MEDICAL USE OF DRUGS

The misuse of alcohol involves excessive drinking to the point of physical, mental or social impairment. Chapter 7 is a historical review of alcohol misuse in Britain and Chapter 8 examines the current misuse of alcohol. The latter chapter gives classification of abnormal drinking patterns, alcoholism prevalence rates from a number of surveys and studies and social and physical complications which are attributable to the misuse of alcohol.

The non-medical use of psychotropic drugs is considered in the next six chapters (Chapter 9—14). Drug use which is not indicated by generally accepted medical grounds is considered to be non-medical use. Evidence about the non-medical use of cannabis, psychedelic drugs, amphetamines, hypnotics and tranquillisers, and opiates is considered in turn. The final chapter discusses the phenomena of concurrent multiple drug use and the debate about escalation from the illicit use of one drug to another.

CHAPTER 7

ABUSE OF ALCOHOL IN BRITAIN -
A HISTORIAL PERSPECTIVE

Adapted version of Dr. M.M. Glatt's article on 'The English Drink Problem: Its Rise and Decline through the Ages'. *Brit.J.Addict. 1958. 55, 51–65.*

From time immemorial, and probably as soon as alcoholic drink had been discovered, there were some who over-indulged in it and others who denounced such abuse. Drunkenness seems to have been known in all ancient civilisations; the drinking excesses of the Greeks and Romans were due to over-indulgence in wine, whereas the inhabitants of the northern parts of Europe used ale and beer. Wine was apparently unknown in Britain before the Roman conquest; at the beginning of the Christian era the inhabitants of the British Isles drank 'a kind of fermented liquor made of barley, honey and apples'. Thus ale, mead (from honey) and cider were probably the earliest intoxicants in Britain, and the festivals of the ancients were characterised by drinking orgies, drink being popular with Celts, Danes and Saxons. The favourite drink with the masses was ale prepared from malted grain, the use of wine being uncommon in the Anglo-Saxon period except among the rich. Excesses caused by wine consumption, however, did occur and a decree of Emperor Domitian in the year A.D.81 is described as having 'started the battle by regulation against the ravages of alcohol amongst Anglo-Saxon people': half the vineyards were to be destroyed, and no more to be planted without an imperial licence. This order remained in force for two centuries (French, 1884; Trevelyan, 1944; Woolley and Johnson, 1905).

Ale, however, was the main cause of drunkenness in the Middle Ages. The old open houses for 'dispensing hospitality' which had been kept by the inhabitants of ancient Britain had developed into Ale Houses which exercised a demoralizing influence. Wine taverns were apparently not much better: they were described as being '. . . a degree or, if you will, a pair of stairs above an alehouse, where men are drunk with more credit than apology' (Earle, 1628). Drunkenness became widespread among all sections of the population. 'Drinking and fires' were named in the 12th century as being 'the only plagues of London' (Nicholson, 1946). Ale was prepared in the main by monks in monasteries to which the majority of vineyards were attached and, along with university students, members of the clergy were the chief drunkenness offenders. Church authorities preached and wrote strongly against the prevalent intemperance and took measures against it. Thus a decree of Synod in A.D.569 ordered priests to do at least 15 days' penance for getting drunk, and in the tenth century the Archbishop of Canterbury's recommendation led to the suppression of many ale houses (Rolleston, 1933; Wilson, 1954).

Drunkenness was also strongly denounced by the great contemporary poets Chaucer, Langland and Gower, and the drunkard's fate was depicted in many woodcuts and in pamphlets sold freely to the public. Little notice, however, was taken of the subject in mediaeval medical writings, a finding that led one author to the conclusion that 'the notorious indifference to the alcohol problem among the great majority of the medical profession today dates back for many centuries'. One of the few positive findings he unearthed was the advice contained in a pre-Norman document to treat by abstinence loss of appetite due to strong drink and, in the summing up of his review of the problem of alcohol in mediaeval England, this observer remarked that:-

> 'This resembled the problem of the ancient Greeks and Romans in the absence of distilled liquors, and differed from it in its prevalence throughout all classes of society; and also by the fact that legislative measures were first taken in the Middle Ages'. (Rolleston, 1933).

Yet in general, in the Middle Ages, no restrictions were imposed on the number of ale houses or wine taverns, and their keepers required no special qualification. Not until late in the 15th and the middle of the 16th century were the beginnings laid of the present system of control of liquor by licensing. The first statute to that effect appeared in 1494, followed in 1552 by another that has become 'the foundation of all our legislation concerning the sale and consumption of intoxicating liquor' (Royal Commission on Licensing, 1932; see also Chapter 2).

In spite of the prevalence of drunkenness for many centuries, it was not until spirits came into common use that the results of excess drinking required more stringent legislative measures. Climatic conditions in Northern Europe may have contributed to the popularity of spirits which Boswell described as 'a means to supply by art the want of that genial warmth of blood which the sun produces' (Bailey, 1951). Insobriety increased in England in the 16th century—'guzzling' then taking on the meaning of drinking to excess—without reaching, however, the degree of intemperance of other contemporary Europeans: according to Jellinek 'the phantastic excess' of the 16th century German scene 'was hardly ever approached at any other time or by any other nation'.

Though made punishable earlier by Church authorities, drunkenness did not legally become an offence until the beginning of the 17th century. By then 'the loathsome and odious sin of drunkenness' had seemingly taken root and consequently an Act of 1606 imposed a fine of five shillings for each conviction of drunkenness; alternatively, the offender was committed to the stocks for six hours. By that time he was presumed to '. . . have regained his senses, and not be liable to do mischief to his neighbours' any more. Such regulations may have been the precursors of the present-day practice of fining the 'drunk and disorderly' 10 or 20 shillings on each court appearance, and of assuming that once a drunken alcoholic had been sobered up his treatment was finished, paying no regard to the need for a long term policy of rehabilitation. (Second Royal Commission on Licensing, 1932).

Uphopped ale, which had been for more than a thousand years the national alcoholic drink, found a new rival in the 15th century, after the continental habit of adding hops had been introduced. Although there had been at first strong opposition against 'bere', this newcomer soon began to outgrow the old 'ale' in popularity. The 17th century witnessed the emergence of spirits, however, as fiercer and more dangerous competitors to ale and beer for the favour of the masses. From 1660 onwards all intoxicating liquor became a fruitful source of revenue to the State (East, 1940).

In order to reduce the import of foreign brandies the State, during the 18th century, encouraged the manufacture of cheap 'gin' from English corn. The yearly production of British distilled spirits rose from half a million gallons in

1684 to over three and a half million in 1727. In 1700 the selling of distilled
liquors was licensed, as had already been the practice for ale. But whereas ale houses
continued to require licensing by the justices, restrictions on the sale of gin were
removed in the 1720's, in order to boost its consumption; the consequences were
appalling. Drunkenness caused by ale and beer had been bad enough, but paled into
insignificance once gin superseded beer in popularity with the working classes; so
much so that William Hogarth contrasted the 'healthy, well nourished inhabitants of
Beer Street' with the 'sick, emaciated citizens of Gin Lane'. That was the time when
doctors declared that 'in excessive gin drinking a new and terrible cause of mortality
has been opened for the poor'; when the death rate in English towns exceeded the
birth rate; when much the greater part of poverty, murder and robbery in London
was attributed by juries to this single cause when retailers of gin attracted customs
by the promise that they could 'get drunk for a penny, dead drunk for twopence
and have straw for nothing' (George, 1953; Renner, 1944).

Naturally, many voices were raised against this epidemic of excessive gin drinking,
which was at its height between 1720 and 1750. John Wesley, denouncing 'that
liquid fire, commonly called drams or spiritous liquors', admonished Methodists in
1743 to 'avoid buying or selling spiritous liquors, or drinking them unless in cases
of extreme necessity' (Carter, 1933). Doctors, magistrates and the press joined in
an effort to get Parliament to act, and several legislative attempts were in fact
made during the first half of the 18th century to stem this orgy of gin drinking.
As 'the licentious use of these pernicious liquors' was held to be encouraged by
their cheapness, an extra five shillings a gallon was placed on spirit manufacture in
1729. Other measures followed, among them an Act of 1736, aimed practically
at prohibition, which did not appeal to the masses (Hammond & Hammond, 1933;
East, 1940).

Prohibition attempts were therefore abandoned in favour of measures directed
towards control: Acts of 1743 and 1751 aimed at an increase in price of spirits and
a better control of its sale. In fact, the Act of 1751—the same year in which Hogarth
so vividly depicted the evils of excessive gin drinking—was described as 'a turning
point in the social history of London.' There was a definite improvement of
conditions in the second half of the 18th century. The emergence of another new
popular drink, tea, used by 'the meanest families, even of labouring people', may
have been one of the factors contributing to the lessening of gin consumption
(Trevelyan, 1944).

Having lost its hold on the masses in the second half of the 18th century, gin
drinking once more became universal in the 19th century, in particular in its third
decade. It was said that gin interfered with the consumption of beer and, in the hope
of setting up beer as a rival to gin, the Duke of Wellington's Beerhouse Act of 1830
abolished beer tax and permitted everybody to sell beer by retail after taking out a
licence. The hope thereby to reduce spirit drinking was, however, dashed almost
immediately. Not only did thousands of new ale houses begin to sprout like
mushrooms all over the country but, in order to compete with these, new and
more glamorous 'gin palaces' vied with the ale houses in attracting customers.
Wages were low, work hard, the price of bread high, housing conditions appalling.
Yet drinking facilities were cheap and plentiful, so the temptation was great to
take 'the quickest way out of Manchester' (where in 1837 one tenth of the
population is said to have lived in cellars), and escape from poor and sordid living
conditions to the warmth, light and companionship of beerhouses and gin palaces.
Acting as allies rather than rivals, beer and gin drinking combined to cause a
National Plague of Intemperance.

'Everybody is drunk. Those who are not singing are sprawling.
The sovereign people are in a beastly state'. (Carter, 1933).

Like Hogarth almost 100 years before him, George Cruikshank now had occasion to start a new campaign against the evils resulting from abuse of 'The Bottle', which once again had come to the fore. However, in spite of many protests, the period of Free Trade in Beer did not come to its end until 1869, when a Wine and Beerhouse Act placed the control of beer sale back into the hands of the Licensing Justices. A few years later, the Licensing Act of 1872 started a period of modern licensing legislation, involving additional licensing restrictions in the Acts of later years.

The era of Free Trade in Beer which saw the recrudescence of the horrors of widespread drunkenness, also witnessed the emergence and growth of the organised 'English Temperance Movement'. The first temperance societies had sprung up in America early in the 19th century, followed in the late 1820's by similar associations in Ireland and Scotland. From 1830 onwards temperance reformers became active in England. At first they were satisfied with a 'partial pledge' affecting only the drinking of spirits, but very soon the failure of the Beerhouse Act's prescription for more beer and less spirits led to the foundation of the Total Abstinence Movement by Joseph Livesey and his 'Preston Friends' in 1832. They initiated 'The Reform', and soon the Teetotallers' Movement spread all over the country. More spectacular still was its progress in Ireland. The number of abstainers in England and Wales at the time of Queen Victoria's accession to the throne was said to be about 150,000 (Carter, 1933; Woolley & Johnson, 1905).

Within the English Temperance Movement, Livesey's approach by 'Moral Suasion' was, in the second half of the 19th century, challenged and later superseded in influence by the claim for 'Legislative Suppression', put forward by the United Kingdom Alliance. The latter was founded in 1853, shortly after prohibition had been introduced in the State of Maine in the United States. From 'ending the drink evil', the emphasis was shifted to that of 'finishing the drink traffic!' The Moral Suasionists' claims for personal abstinence and for step-by-step legislative reforms, came to be overshadowed by the Suppressionists' demands for total prohibition; a divergence of opinion which was to come to the fore again in 1932, when the proposals made by the second Royal Commission on Licensing were welcomed by the Suasionists, the Suppressionists keeping aloof (Urwin, 1955).

At the turn of the 20th century conditions in general had improved, and drunkenness appeared less prevalent than it had been at the beginning of the Victorian era. When the first Royal Commission on Licensing' published its report (1899) it did not find much ground for satisfaction concerning the drink problem, however. There had been some improvement in the last quarter of the century, and the Report stated that 'the zealous labours of countless workers in the Temperance movement count for much'. Nevertheless, when compared with conditions 40 years earlier, the consumption of intoxicating liquors particularly of beer and whisky, which by then had far outstripped gin in popularity; the number of prosecutions for drunkenness; and the mortality from alcoholism; had all much increased. Among the legacies which the 20th century received from its predecessor, there was still the unsolved drink problem constituting, in the words of the Royal Commission '. . . a gigantic evil that remains to be remedied'. (Royal Commission on Liquor Licensing Laws, 1899).

This report recommended further licensing restrictions, and several Acts within the next few years strengthened the licensing legislation. However, convictions for drunkenness remained high, fluctuating from 200,000 at the turn of the century to 207,000 in 1905, falling to 160,000 by 1910 but rising to 190,000 in 1913. (See also Chapter 8).

Thus, at the outbreak of the First World War, the drink problem was still very acute; Lloyd George regarding drink as the 'greatest of three deadly foes, Germany, Austria and drink' (Urwin, 1955). The war acted as a spur for drastic action in the

form of heavy taxation of alcoholic drink and the establishment of the Liquor
Traffic Control Board. In 1915 the Board heavily cut down the facilities for drinking,
by departing from the old system of a short period of closing hours and putting in
its place the principle of permitted hours for the sale of alcoholic drink, with the
further provision of a mid-day break to prevent continuous drinking. Up to the war
there were practically no 'closing hours', public houses remaining open on weekdays
for 19½ hours in London, 17 hours in the provinces. In 1915 the Board reduced
these times to 5½ hours, ordering a break of two hours at mid-day. The combination
of all these restrictive measures (reduction of hours of sale, limited supplies and
increased costs) soon began to show results, described some years later by the
Chairman of the Board, Lord D'Abernon:-

'There is nothing in English history more dramatic than the story of drink
control. For 300 years statesmen and reformers devised remedies for the abuse
of alcoholic liquor which marred English efficiency and gave this country a bad
pre-eminence'. Most remedies proved so ineffective '. . . that regulation came
generally to be regarded as impossible'. Failure to regulate the drink traffic was
so marked that '. . . in the first year of the Great War, national efficiency was
seriously impaired and defeat threatened through absence of munitions; the
supply being impaired by drunkenness among munition workers'. As a result
of the Central Control Board's activities '. . . within 18 months, drunkenness
had diminished by one half; within three years . . . by more than 80 per cent
on the pre-war convictions . . . Inefficiency, . . . bad time keeping, cases of
Delirium Tremens and illness proceeding from drunkenness, all diminished
rapidly'. (Vernon, 1942).

The remarkable improvement during these years was probably brought about
by the administrative restriction on hours of sale, by dilution of beer and spirits
and, 'as the controlling factor', by direct restrictions on the supply of liquor
(Wilson, 1941).

The experiences of the Control Board provided the basis of the licensing laws
in the 1921 Act which maintained the system of permitted hours (9 hours in
London, 8 hours in the provinces). Convictions for drunkenness, which had
fallen from 189,000 in 1913 to an all-time low figure of 29,000 in 1918, rose
again temporarily with increased alcohol supplies to 96,000 in 1920; only to go
down to 75,000 in 1925, 53,000 in 1930 and 30,000 in 1932; these climbed
afterwards to 53,000 in 1939. Figures for the consumption of liquor—which were
usually highest at times of national prosperity as in 1875 and 1900—corresponded
in the main with those for convictions of drunkenness. The same trend was shown
by the yearly number of deaths from alcoholism and liver cirrhosis (Shadwell,
1929; Wilson, 1941).

The limited number of 'permitted hours' and the hastened pace of living leaves
the modern drinker less time for drinking than his counterpart of an earlier, more
leisured age, who could enjoy his drink without having to keep an eye on the clock.
However, the fact that they were 'genuinely leisured' and 'drank without haste'
may have saved the great, leisurely drinkers of the 18th century. Unlike them the
modern drinker often has to make do with a few 'quick-ones' gulped down in haste,
but the balance sheet as regards the consequences of intemperance has become
more satisfactory since the 'permitted hours' system put a brake on the practice
of continual 'soaking'.

The question of a reform of the Licensing Laws led to the appointment of the
Second Royal Commission (1929–1931). Its report (1932) found '. . . excessive
drinking in this country . . . greatly, even spectacularly, diminished'. The drink

problem was 'no longer the gigantic evil' which it had been at the turn of the century (in the time of the first Royal Commission) but it was found still of a certain magnitude in that

'excessive drinking still exists in large measures and, apart from actual intemperance, expenditure on intoxicants still reaches a figure which we believe definitely uneconomic'.

The Report recommended several legislative proposals and the encouragement of specific education on alcohol. Commenting on these suggestions a temperance reformer wrote in 1955 that '... for more than 20 years the legislative harvest has been almost negligible; ... the increase of sobriety in this land hangs uncertainly on the continuance of shortened hours for supply and sale of intoxicants, high taxation and the development of other resources for the use of leisure.' (Urwin, 1955).

In his review of the Liquor Problem in England and Wales from 1860 to 1935, Wilson (1941) ascribed the general decline in alcohol consumption, drunkenness proceedings and alcoholic mortality to the operation of three main factors '... arising from legislation and taxation, conditions of trade and employment, and from competing interests'. Some of these factors had influenced the problem directly, others indirectly by producing changes in the general habits of the people. The three factors influencing consumption levels of alcohol are, in Wilson's view:-

(1)   Increase or decrease of opportunity; depending for example on a worker's pay or the price of liquor.

(2)   Social changes: for instance those diverting expenditure away from the public house, and increasing social responsibility or competitive luxuries.

(3)   Educational and moral cause: including temperance propaganda, counteracted more recently by an increasing propaganda campaign by the Trade.

'Wider sociological factors such as the general progressive tendencies of the age' were added to Wilson's third category of important factors by Levy (1951).

Among his third set of influences, Wilson included also the change in medical opinion and practice which had taken place in regard to the medicinal value of alcohol. In ancient Britain ale had formed a part of prescriptions for diverse ailments and, later on, spirits were for a long time credited with all kinds of medicinal properties. For hundreds of years the generous prescription of liquor was regarded as an essential tool in the doctor's equipment, so much so that dissenters were 'looked upon askance by ... colleagues and ostracized from practice among higher society'. (Rolleston, 1942). However, in the course of time individual doctors and medical society began to stress the ill effects resulting from intemperance. Thomas Trotter of Edinburgh was one of the first to restate in his doctoral thesis (1804) the long forgotten concept of alcoholism as a disease. Nearly a century later, in 1884, the Society for the Study of Inebriety (now the Society for the Study of Addiction, see Chapter 17) was founded by Norman Kerr. At first, this had more lay members than medical ones, but it was the first society to investigate alcoholic and drug addiction in a medico-scientific manner. A little earlier, in 1873, a medical journal had warned doctors that 'the rash attempt to treat disease without alcohol might result in conviction for manslaughter '(Wilson, 1941). Approximately 60 years later, however, Lord Moynihan stated that medical science regarded alcohol, 'while it has its uses as unnecessary and often harmful in the routine treatment of disease', and the Medical Research Council considered that 'alcoholic beverages are in no way necessary for a healthy life, and may be definitely injurious for . . . most persons of unstable nervous system' (Medical Research Council, 1938).

As regards the treatment of inebriates, homes had been established for this purpose under the Habitual Drunkards' Act of 1879. Nearly 40 years later the Inebriates Act of 1918 provided for compulsory detention and treatment of alcohol addicts. After three years this method was abandoned and the Inebriates Act became defunct, as therapy of the unwilling inebriate had in general proved unsuccessful (see Chapter 2).

At the beginning of the Second World War drunkenness was no longer the menace it had been in 1914. These war years brought with them reduced supplies of liquor and increasing taxation of beer as an 'easy revenue collector'; at the same time the duty on wines and spirits was also raised 'in order to preclude criticism that the poor man's drink was being made more expensive while the rich man's drink was left untouched' (Sayers, 1956). Convictions for drunkenness fell steadily to reach their lowest figure, just over 20,000 in 1946. Beer consumption, however, did not decrease and the total personal expenditure on drink rose considerably at the same time.

The twentieth century's first half which was by now drawing to its close had certainly witnessed a revolutionary change. The consumption of spirits had shown a marked decline over these 50 years, the actual consumption of alcohol having fallen by more than one-half; although the National Drink Bill had risen from £185 million in 1900 to £727 million in 1950 due to the great increase in price. The numbers of abstainers and of very moderate drinkers had risen, those of excessive drinkers diminished; drunkenness convictions had fallen considerably. A tentative estimate by the World Health Organisation showed England and Wales in 1948 to have the lowest proportional number of alcoholics among various countries listed. By 1954, the death rate attributed to alcoholism in England and Wales had fallen to 0.1 per 100,000 for both sexes (whereas in Scotland it amounted to 0.6 for men and 0.2 for women), the actual number of such deaths reported having decreased from 3,000 in 1901 to 34 in 1954. In the same period, the number of deaths from liver cirrhosis fell from more than 4,000 (in 1901) to about 800 in the years 1944—1948; all this in spite of a population increase of almost 25 per cent. The nation had certainly seemed to become more sober when the mid-century was reached, so much so that a medical journal in an annotation at the end of 1949 talked of a 'general recognition that alcohol was no longer the pressing social problem that it had been in former years' and mentioned 'the waning of alcoholism'. (Lancet, 1949).

THE 1950's AND 1960's

Justification for the relative complacency reported above was provided by the seeming absence of drunken men in the streets, and by a real decline in figures for incidence of delirium tremens, liver cirrhosis and mental disorder 'ascribed to alcohol' around 1950. Despite this, however, the number of convictions for drunkenness offences rose from the abnormally low post-war figure of 20,000 in 1945, to 48,000 in 1950, 65,000 in 1958, 84,000 in 1962 and—despite a gradual fall to 70,000 in 1966—back to 80,500 in 1969 (see Chapter 8). The special increase in juvenile drunkenness becoming apparent during the 1950's continued throughout the 1960's, convictions for drunkenness of those under 21 in England having almost doubled during that period (from 6,600 in 1959 to 12,000 in 1968), the increase affecting both the age groups 'under 18' and, to a larger extent, those between 18 and 20. While the absolute numbers in the younger age group remain small, nevertheless, it is known that only a proportion of drunken people come under observation at all, still fewer being convicted.

The number of deaths from liver cirrhosis has risen steadily since 1948, particularly amongst women (see Chapter 8); the number of road accidents committed under the influence of alcohol has steadily risen, as has the 'National Drink Bill' itself (as shown in Chapter 5).

Naturally, many pitfalls beset attempts to interpret such statistics. The Buckmaster Report, describing the results of an investigation into 'The Social and Economic Aspects of the Drink Problem' in 1931, warned that the problem was '. . . so complicated in its reactions and inter-relations as to require the utmost caution in exposition and inference'. (Buckmaster, 1931). Taking these figures as a whole, they do not show any evidence that the downward trend of the drink problem which started in the first half of this century has continued into the present time. There does not seem to have been much permanent change in the 25 years that have elapsed since the 1932 Royal Commission stated that 'The Drink Problem was still of a certain magnitude'. (1932).

In the past, drunkenness was the most striking expression of the drink problem. But it is no more than one aspect of the whole question. Drunkenness is no more synonymous with the drink problem that it is with heavy drinking or with alcoholism. For example, there are some writers who hold 'the regular but moderate drinker' responsible for causing today's drinking problem, which is said to manifest itself 'not . . . in excessive drunkenness but in the high total consumption of a large number of mainly moderate drinkers' (Rowntree and Lavers, 1951).

Of all people taking alcoholic drink only a minority became alcoholics, probably not more than five to six per cent (WHO, 1951). Yet the modern quest for statistics and the 'obsession for the typical' should not blind one to the difficulties confronting the individual. More important in the phenomenon of alcoholism than dry figures is the human element, the broken homes and marriages. The sufferings of unhappy wives, husbands and children are not less real today than they were a hundred or two hundred years ago, even though they were then witnessed in public by the whole street, while nowadays they are more likely to be borne at home.

In the past, doctors were in general not interested in the alcoholic's plight unless he developed complications. Rather than deal with the long-drawn-out developmental process of alcoholism itself, they concentrated on its end results, leaving the task of coping with the earlier phases of the illness to social reformers, private societies and the Churches.

Whereas, formerly, an interest in alcoholism was evinced only by a few medical men, nowadays many more doctors and other professional workers are active in the field, and quite a few also playing an active part on the international scene.

Scotland and Ireland have in recent years showed signs of taking active steps to cope with the problem. London, Cardiff, Edinburgh, Glasgow, and Belfast have all been venues of international conferences on Alcoholism over the past ten years.

For many centuries the 'loathsome and odious sin of drunkenness' held this country in a firm grip, tightening it even closer on a number of occasions Numerous unco-ordinated efforts made by social reformers, the Churches, Legislators and at times also by doctors to loosen the tight hold were of no lasting avail. It was chiefly the campaign against drunkenness during the 1914—18 War which extricated the country from this grip, and since then a number of factors acting in combination have prevented drunkenness from becoming a menace once more.

Even if nowadays drunken people are not sprawling on the streets any more, there is urgent need for research, vigilance and public education in the complex phenomenon of alcoholism.

REFERENCES

BAILEY M., 1951. *Boswell's Column*. Wm. Kimber, London
BUCKMASTER E.F., 1931. *Social and Economic Effects of the Drink Problem*. H.M.S.O., London.
CARTER H., 1933. *The English Temperance Movement*. Epworth Press, London.
EARLE J., 1928. *Micro-Cosmogrcμ.:ie* from WILSON J.D., 1944. *Life in Shakespeare's England: A Book of Elizabethan Prose*. Penguin, England.
EAST, W. NORWOOD, 1940. Alcoholism and crime in relation to manic depressive disorder. *Brit.J.Inebr.* 38, 1.
ECCLES W. McA., 1942. Alcohol and efficiency in war. *Brit.J.Inebr.* 40, 22.
FRENCH R.V., 1884. *Nineteen Centuries of Drink in England*. Longmans, London.
GEORGE D., 1953. *England in Transition*. Penguin, London.
HAMMOND J.L. and HAMMOND B., 1934. *The Age of the Chartists*. Longmans, London.
JELLINEK E.M., 1945. A specimen of the 16th century German drink literature. Obsopens' art of drinking. *Quart.J.Stud.Alc.* 5, 647.
LANCET, 1949. Editorial. *Lancet*. i, 310.
LEVY H., 1951. *Drink: An Economic and Social Study*. Routledge, Kegan Paul, London.
MEDICAL RESEARCH COUNCIL, 1938. *Alcohol: Its Action on the Human Organism*. H.M.S.O., London.
NICHOLSON B., 1946. *Drink, a London Survey*. London Diocesan Church of England Temperance Society, London.
RENNER H.D., 1944. *The Origin of Food Habits*. Faber, London.
ROLLESTON J.D., 1933. *Brit.J.Inebr.* 31, 33.
ROLLESTON J.D., 1942. Some aspects of the alcohol problem. *Brit.J.Inebr.* 39, 45.
ROWNTREE B.S. and LAVERS G.R., 1951. *English Life and Leisure*. Longmans, London.
ROYAL COMMISSION ON LIQUOR LICENSING LAWS, 1899. *Report*. H.M.S.O., London.
SAYERS P.S., 1956. *History of the Second World War*.
SECOND ROYAL COMMISSION ON LICENSING (ENGLAND AND WALES) 1932. *Report*. H.M.S.O., London.
SHADWELL A., 1929. Temperance in *Encyclopaedia Britannica*, 14th Ed. 21, 915. London.
SOCIAL AND ECONOMIC ASPECTS OF THE DRINK PROBLEM, 1932. *Report*. H.M.S.O., London.
TREVELYAN G.M., 1944. *English Social History*. Longmans Green & Co., London.
TROTTER T., 1804. *An Essay Medical, Philosophical and Chemical on Drunkenness*. Longmans Green & Co., London.
URWIN E.C., 1955. *Henry Carter*. Epworth Press, London.
VERNON H.M., 1942. Lord d'Abernon and his work for the Central Control Board. *Brit.J.Inebr.* 39, 76.
WILSON G.B., 1941. The Liquor problem in England and Wales: A survey from 1860–1935. *Brit.J.Inebr.* 38.
WILSON J.D., 1944. *Life in Shakespeare's England: A Book of Elizabethan Prose*. Penguin, London.
WOOLLEY J.G. and JOHNSON W.E., 1905. *Temperance Progress of the Century*. Chambers, London.
WORLD HEALTH ORGANISATION, EXPERT COMMITTEE ON MENTAL HEALTH, 1951. *Alcoholism Sub-Committee, 2nd Renort*. World Health Org. Tech. Rep. Ser. 42, 20.

CHAPTER 8
THE MISUSE OF ALCOHOL
IN GREAT BRITAIN

In the first half of this century, the misuse of alcohol decreased in relation to the 19th century. In the last 20 years there has been an overall increase per capita in money spent on alcohol, and fluctuating rates for drunkenness convictions, hospital admissions for alcoholism and convictions for drunken driving. The fluctuation in these indicators makes it impossible to assess whether there has been a real increase in the misuse of alcohol. This chapter presents definitions of alcoholism and problem drinking currently used in Britain. Varying prevalence rates provided by different methods of estimation, both direct and indirect, are examined. Finally, the demographic characteristics of selected alcohol-dependent populations are reported along with some of the social and physical consequences of alcohol misuse.

CLASSIFICATION OF PROBLEM DRINKERS

A review of 25 separate systems of classification for abnormal drinkers in the world literature led Bowman and Jellinek (1942) to enumerate 14 types of abnormal drinking. This classification was later revised by Jellinek (1960). Although Jellinek did not consider his five-part system as exhaustive of all possible types of drinking it is the classification that has been most widely used in Great Britain. The five categories are as follows:

Alpha Alcoholism—is purely psychological 'continual dependence, or reliance on the effect of alcohol to relieve bodily or emotional pain'. Such drinkers do not show a progressive alcohol involvement and certainly have no great difficulty in abstaining, but certain social effects may be present, such as loss of time from work or family discord.

Beta Alcoholism—designates those drinkers who are causing themselves physical damage without signs of dependence on alcohol. This type of alcoholism is virtually unreported in Great Britain.

Gamma Alcoholism—involves loss-of-control drinking with craving for alcohol present and the symptoms of alcohol withdrawal, such as morning drinks, morning shakes, etc. present. This type of alcoholism creates a stereotype for people receiving help from Alcoholics Anonymous.

Delta Alcoholism—is a type of alcohol dependence in which drinkers have an inability to abstain from alcohol. This pattern may be characteristic of a heavy drinking executive, whose addiction only comes to light when he goes into hospital for an unrelated condition and alcohol withdrawal symptoms become apparent.

Epsilon Alcoholism—is periodic or bout drinking and is sometimes known as 'dipsomania'.

These five types of drinking can be further reduced to those which indicate evidence of pathological changes leading to craving or alcohol addiction (Gamma, Delta and Epsilon types) and those which do not show these characteristics (Alpha and Beta types).

Horn and Wanberg (1969) have suggested that individual variations within any drinking system are so great as to make classification impossible. There has, however, been continuous debate in Britain centred on the applicability of the Jellinek types and the extent to which these different patterns of drinking might present different basic syndromes of alcoholism. Personality and social factors are both likely to hinge upon clinical presentation and a patient's drinking pattern may change over a period of time from one Jellinek type to another. Evidence of a return to 'normal drinking' by former alcohol addicts (Davies, 1962; Kendell, 1965) indicate that various types of alcoholism may not be irreversible. Walton (1968) and Mellor (1969) have produced evidence suggesting that Gamma and Delta type alcoholics differ from one and other on certain personality variables.

Various alternative classifications of alcohol misuse have been evolved. White (1937), for instance, suggested three ways of classifying alcoholics:

'The essential type who shows maladjustment in adolescence and early misuse of alcohol; those who make achievements early on and drink in response to over-stress later; and those whose drinking is symptomatic of some other psychiatric condition'.

Kessell and Walton (1965) have suggested three stages in the development of alcohol dependence:

Excessive drinking—which is characterised by increased tolerance, the feeling of a need to drink in order to perform adequately socially or at work, and increased guilt feelings.

Alcohol addiction—characterised by increase frequency of amnesia, social disruption and lowering of self-esteem.

Chronic alcoholism—when physical and mental disturbance dominate, tolerance increases further and delirium tremens may set in.

Williams (1960) divided alcoholics that he had seen in his own experience into the basically psychopathic ('bad'), the basically neurotic ('sad'), those with underlying psychosis ('mad'), and those reacting to situational stress.

No single classification has been accepted by all clinicians or research workers and it seems likely that the debate about classification will continue.

PREVALENCE ESTIMATES OF ALCOHOLISM AND PROBLEM DRINKING IN THE GENERAL POPULATION

The most frequently used indirect method of estimating the prevalence of alcoholism in the United Kingdom has been the Jellinek formula. This formula is based on the relationships between the total number of alcoholics existing in a given area at a given time, the number of liver cirrhosis deaths recorded, the proportion of these attributable to alcoholism and the proportion of all alcoholics with complications who die of cirrhosis of the liver. These measures are obtained from hospital records and from autopsy. The ratio of 'all alcoholics' to alcoholics 'with complications' is also included (W.H.O., 1951). This method of assessing the prevalence of alcoholism yielded an estimate of 11 alcoholics of all types per thousand of the adult population in England and Wales in 1948. Among all alcoholics it was estimated that 2.78 per thousand had 'complications' (World Health Organisation, 1951). The total alcoholic population was therefore 'in the region of 350,000 persons in England and Wales', including some 86,000 'chronic alcoholics' in that year.

Since this estimate there have been an increasing number of direct surveys which are discussed below.

General Practitioners' Surveys

Parr (1957) attempted to estimate the prevalence of alcoholism in general medical practices throughout Britain. He used as his defining criterion the World Health Organisation's definition of an alcoholic which is:

Excessive drinkers whose dependence upon alcohol has attained such a degree that they show a noticeable mental disturbance or an interference with bodily or mental health, interpersonal relations, smooth economic and social functioning; or the prodromal signs of such development; they therefore require treatment'. (World Health Organisation, 1952).

The larger part of the population in Britain is on a general practitioner's 'list' and Parr chose a sample of general practitioners from the Royal College of General Practitioners' register. He asked how many of their patients they regarded as alcoholic according to the definition above. Only single-handed, as opposed to group practices, among the sample were analysed because these single-handed practices were more likely to be aware of the problem. This was particularly true when the list size was close to 500 patients (minimal) rather than 4,500. Parr estimated a total of approximately 40,000 alcoholics in England which represented an average of two and a half to three alcoholics per practice. Regional differences in the rate of reported alcoholism were found with southern England, east and west Yorkshire and the Midlands having the highest rates, and northern England the lowest (Parr, 1957).

A later survey in South London (Hensman et al, 1968) also found that general practitioners with smaller lists reported higher rates of alcoholism in their practices. Rathod (1967) has also conducted surveys amongst general practitioners, but these studies have been primarily directed towards the assessment of attitudes to alcoholism.

General Practitioners', Health Visitors' and Probation Officers' Surveys.

A survey using information supplied by health visitors and probation officers in five geographical areas revised the estimate of alcoholism prevalence in Parr's survey (Prys-Williams, 1965). Prys-Williams felt that the pressure of time on general practitioners with larger lists resulted in their failing to identify patients with drinking problems. By considering the rate of alcoholism reported only in the smaller practices (between 500 and 2,500 patients), Parr's estimate of 40,000 alcoholics was adjusted to 60,000 in England and Wales. This revised estimate was confirmed by reports of health visitors who were interviewed. Further it was concluded that Parr's figures had excluded those alcoholics who did not consult general practitioners, and by interviewing probation officers in selected areas, Prys-Williams again revised the estimate of chronic alcoholics. He concluded that there were 70,000 chronic alcoholics with complications in England and Wales. While there are many drawbacks to this calculation these results do approximate estimates found by use of the Jellinek formula.

The Survey of an English County

The prevalence of alcoholism and problem drinking in the county of Cambridgeshire was estimated in a survey carried out by Moss and Davies (1968). Thirteen social agencies were asked to report all clients known to them who had experienced:

'Admission to hospital because of a drinking problem;
A consultation for a medical or psychiatric condition attributable to excessive drinking over a prolonged period of time;
Two or more prosecutions for drunkenness, drinking of crude spirits or more than one of these.'

Also included were all reported cases who had experienced at least two of the 'consequences of drinking' which included:

'Serious loss of functioning in employment;
Suicide attempt; injury while under the influence of alcohol;
Help sought from Alcoholics Anonymous;
Family difficulties as a result of drinking;
Causing a disturbance in the community, for example,
public drunkenness, debt or eviction'.
(Moss and Davies, 1968).

The result of this survey, which was the most intensive so far conducted in Great Britain, was an estimated alcoholism prevalence rate for the population 15 years and over of 6.2 per thousand males and 1.4 per thousand females in England and Wales.

The Prevalence of Alcohol Misuse in a
Survey of a London Borough

A survey of 'normal drinking habits' conducted in a South London suburb in 1965–1966 (see Chapter 5) did not aim to detect abnormal drinkers. However, it did, in the course of the survey, inquire into 25 possible 'troubles connected with drinking' items. Twenty-five of the 404 males interviewed in this survey were judged on the basis of replies to these items to have drinking problems of various intensities at some time. This might indicate a very much higher prevalence than has been deduced from other surveys (Edwards, G., Chandler J., Hensman C and Peto J., 1971b).

PREVALENCE ESTIMATES AMONG SELECTED POPULATIONS

Surveys have been conducted among selected sections of the general population in an attempt to assess prevalence of abnormal drinking in groups that are better defined. These groups include young people, general hospital populations, the homeless, and offenders appearing before the courts or in prisons.

Table 8—1.   Estimates of the Number of Alcoholics, England and Wales, Selected
Surveys.

Survey	Date	Population	Informants	Area	Rate per 1,000	Number estimated for 1968*
WHO Expert Committee on Mental Health	1948	Adults 20 and over	Jellinek formula	England & Wales	11	370,000
College of General Practitioners	1955 −56	All	G.P.s	England & Wales	0.2	10,000**
Parr	1956	Adults 15 and over	G.P.s	England & Wales	1.1	40,000
Prys- Williams	1960 −63	All	G.P.s, Health visitors & probation officers	5 towns	—	280,000
Moss and Davies	1961 −64	Adults 15 and over	13 sources	Cam- bridge- shire	6.2 (males) 1.4 (females)	220,000***

* The rate per 1,000 found for each survey has been applied to the 1968 England and Wales
population.
** Excludes diagnosis of alcoholic psychosis.
*** An OHE estimate devised by weighting the Cambridgeshire figures according to Parr's
regional differentials.

Source: Office of Health Economics. *Alcohol Abuse*. O.H.E., London. 1970.

Misuse of Alcohol among Young People and Students

A marked increase in juvenile drunkenness is reported in the drunkenness
offence statistics during the first half of this century and drunkenness convictions
of people under 21 years in England and Wales has almost doubled from 6,600
convictions in 1959 to 12,000 in 1968 (Home Office, 1970). West (1967) has
shown that the number of convictions for drunkenness amongst 14—16 year olds
trebled between 1955 and 1962. However, there is still little evidence to show that
adolescent drinking presents a large problem in Great Britain. Work has been
carried out by Glatt and Hills (1968) and by Hassall (1968, 1969) on the particular
problems of young drinkers and a report by Gibbens (1963) noted evidence of
'excessive drinking' in 9% of 200 Borstal boys.

A survey of the total first year population of one college at a British university
investigated 'complications' as a result of their drinking. From a total of 495 male
students, 53% reported breaking the law (without however becoming involved with
the police) at least once as a result of drinking; 19% missed a day at school or
university following drinking; 11% lost a friend or damaged a friendship as a result
of drinking; and 10% feared that they might become dependent upon alcohol in the
future. While these are not serious complications of drinking, they may be early
pointers to trouble in the future. Nineteen per cent of these students said they were
'unable to recall the next morning anything that had happened over a lengthy period

of time during the previous evening after drinking alcohol' and 8% had suffered the next morning from 'uncontrollable shaking of hands or other parts of the body'. It is uncertain whether these symptoms reported are evidence of experimentation and learning or evidence of early pathology (Orford and Postoyan, 1970).

Homeless Persons

The National Assistance Board (now within the Department of Health and Social Security) carried out a survey of homeless single persons between October, 1965 and March, 1966 to collect information concerning 'the increasing problem of misfits and drifters in society, particularly those who habitually live in lodging houses and hostels, or sleep rough' (National Assistance Board, 1966). Within this survey the drinking habits of men surveyed who were in reception centres was as follows:

Table 8−2.   Drinking Habits of 837 Residents in Government Reception Centres, March 1966.

	No.	%
Non-drinkers	125	15.0
Moderate drinkers	479	57.0
Heavy drinkers	178	21.0
Suspected alcoholics	55	7.0
Total:	837	100%

Source: National Assistance Board. *Homeless Single Persons.* H.M.S.O., London. 1966.

The label of 'heavy drinkers' was slightly more common amongst the younger men in the sample, with no man either under 30 or over 60 recorded as an alcoholic.

Edwards et al (1968) surveyed 279 men resident for one night at the Camberwell Reception Centre in London. Forty-nine per cent of that population admitted to drinking problems and the rates for symptoms of abnormal drinking are shown below.

Table 8−3.   Occurrence Rate of Symptoms of Abnormal Drinking and Mean Age at First Occurrence: Camberwell Reception Centre, 1966.

Symptom	Percentage				Age in years at first occurrence	
	Never	'Once or twice'	'Quite often'	'Unsure'	Mean	S.D.*
Morning amnesias	62	12	24	2	30.8	9.5
Morning shakes	61	10	25	4	31.8	10.8
'Morning livener'	60	9	28	3	30.7	11.5
Arrest for drunkenness	53	'Ever' 45		2	34.5	11.5

* Standard deviation.

Source: Edwards G., Williamson V., Hawker A., Hensman C. and Postoyan S. Census of a reception centre. *Brit. J. Psychiat.* 114, 1031, 1968.

Other studies examining excessive alcohol use amongst homeless persons include Edwards et al (1966), Glatt and Whiteley (1965), Priest (1970), and Lodge-Patch (1970, 1971). The most recent survey of the problem of homelessness in London has been compiled by Brandon (1971) who has traced the history of the problem.

Drunkenness Offenders and Prison Populations

Gath (1969) surveyed 151 men arrested for drunkenness in two London courts during 1968. Of the total, 24% were considered not to have serious drinking problems, 26% were assessed to have serious drinking problems but to not be chemically dependent, and 50% of the sample were thought to have serious drinking problems with clear evidence of alcohol dependence.

Hensman (1969) surveyed a sample of 188 short-term recidivist prisoners in a London prison. The relation between the number of arrests for drunkenness offences and alcohol dependence in this sample is shown in the table below.

Table 8—4. Symptoms of Chemical Dependence in Relation to Previous Drunkenness Offences

	Number of drunk arrests				
Symptoms	0 n = 67 (%)	1-5 n = 53 (%)	6+ n = 75 (%)	x^2	Probability level
Amnesias ever	16	49	79	54.9	.001
Morning shakes ever	12	40	73	54.7	.001
Crude spirits ever	0	7	29	29.9	.001
Morning drinking ever	6	42	85	90.1	.001

Source: Hensman C. Problems of drunkenness amongst male recidivists. In Cook T., Gath D. and Hensman C. (Ed.) *The Drunkenness Offence.* Pergamon, Oxford. 1969.

General Hospital Patients

A pilot study of 107 consecutive admissions to a medical unit in a South London general hospital has shown that 18 patients (17%) had a primary or secondary diagnosis of alcoholism (Gaind, Personal Communication, 1971).

DEMOGRAPHIC CHARACTERISTICS OF ALCOHOLICS

Certain consistent demographic characteristics have been found among alcoholics in Great Britain. These include sex, age, nationality, socio-economic groups, marital status and place of residence.

Sex

The rate of alcoholism in men has consistently been found to be higher than in females. Table 8—5 compares the ratios of male to female 'alcoholics' in five separate surveys made between 1956 and 1971.

Table 8—5.   Comparison of Sex Ratio of Male to Female Alcoholics Identified in Five Surveys, 1956—1971.

Survey	Population Surveyed	Reporting Services	Male/Female Ratio
Parr (1957)	NHS-registered patients in England and Wales (from selected practices)	Sample of G.P.s	2.2:1
Hensman et al. (1968)	NHS patients registered in one South London borough	All G.P.s in Borough	3:1
Moss & Davies (1968)	County of Cambridgeshire	13 Agencies	4:1
Edwards et al. (1967)	Alcoholism Information Centres	4 Centres in England and Scotland	7:1
Hensman et al. Personal communication	Sample population of South London Borough	All social and medical agencies	8:1

Source: Derived from surveys in table.

The differences in the ratios above can probably be accounted for by the comparative readiness of female alcoholics to consult their general practitioners and the low proportion of female alcoholics who consult social agencies for help.

Age

The mean age of male alcoholics in any sample in Great Britain is likely to be in the mid-forties. The mean age of male clients at three alcohol information centres in Glasgow, Liverpool and Gloucester was found to be 43.6 years (Edwards et al, 1967), 306 male members of London's Alcoholics Anonymous had a mean age of 45.7 years (Edwards et al, 1966b) and the mean age of Skid Row alcoholics was found to be 44.7 years (Edwards et al 1966a). Women alcoholics have generally been found to be slightly older on average. Moss and Davies (1968) found the average age of male alcoholics in their sample to be 44.3 years and that of women to be 47.0 years. Moss and Davies also report that more than half their sample were between the ages of 35 and 54 whereas this age group constitutes only a third of Britain's total population.

Nationality and Religion

In many studies of alcoholics, particularly in urban areas, Irish and Scottish men appear to have more trouble from alcohol dependence than would be expected by their representation in the population. There are also relatively more alcoholics who were brought up Roman Catholic than those who were brought up in the Church of England than would be expected. While religion and ethnicity undoubtedly inter-react, there is some evidence that ethnic origin is the more important of the two factors (Edwards et al, 1971). However, it cannot be ascertained whether it is ethnicity or immigrant status which is more important and this is unlikely to be resolved until there is further cross-cultural research. Higher rates of prevalence for alcoholism in Scotland (Ross et al, 1970) may be due to factors other than simply the use of alcohol, such as relatively more treatment facilities or better data-gathering organisations.

Socio-Economic Status

The socio-economic status of alcoholics varies depending on the sample that is being studied. In the Cambridgeshire work (Moss and Davies, 1968), women alcoholics from professional and managerial groups were the most prevalent (54.4%) and this is undoubtedly higher than the proportion of women in those socio-economic groups in Cambridgeshire. For men, alcoholism was more common among unskilled workers (90 per 10,000), semi-skilled workers (82 per 10,000), employers and managers (81 per 10,000) and professional men (76 per 10,000); and less common among skilled workers (37 per 10,000) and non-manual workers (42 per 10,000).

In a survey of a South London borough (Edwards et al, 1971) there was no difference in trouble from drinking among all social classes and, indeed, the prevalence of problem drinkers was identical in three grouped class categories. However, in samples of Alcoholics Anonymous' clients or Skid Row alcoholics, social class distribution would differ.

Marital Status

Virtually all studies have revealed that a significantly high proportion of individuals are single, widowed or divorced. The table below illustrates the comparison between the marital status of alcoholics and that of the general population in Cambridgeshire (Moss and Davies, 1968).

Table 8–6. Marital Status of Alcoholics in the Cambridgeshire Survey (Percentage)

	Single	Married	Widowed	Divorced	Total
Male alcoholics	28.7	61.7	3.6	5.9	99.9
Male Cambridge population	26.3	69.9	3.8	0.5	100
Female alcoholics	12.5	71.1	10.6	5.8	100
Female Cambridge population	23.3	63.3	12.5	0.9	100

Source: Moss M. and Davies E.B. *A Survey of Alcoholism in an English County.* Geigy, London. 1968.

Rural and Urban Factors in Alcoholism

Despite the expectation that prevalence of alcoholism will be higher in urban than in rural areas, surveys including Parr (1957) and Moss and Davies (1968) have found a higher proportion of alcoholics reported in rural areas. This may be, however, that social agencies and doctors in rural areas tend to have smaller numbers of clients and are therefore more aware of individual's social problems. In urban areas a higher proportion of the population is mobile and may evade recognition.

In Scotland, the incidence of alcoholism is higher in the northern region, which is the most rural part of Scotland, than in all other regions (Morrison, 1964)

SOCIAL CONSEQUENCES

This section will examine the effect of alcoholic misuse on unemployment, drunkenness offenders in court and prisons, the relationship of alcohol and crime and data on drunken driving.

Alcohol Dependence and Employment

While the employment history of some alcoholics is erratic, there are a large number of currently employed alcoholics. Fifty-four per cent of a series of male Alcoholics Anonymous members in London claimed that their employers did not know of their drinking problem (Edwards et al, 1966a). Of 300 male alcoholics consecutively consulting the National Council on Alcoholism's three information centres during 1967, 50% were in full-time employment. Half of the alcoholics who were working had been with their current employers for more than two years, 13% for one to two years, 15% for six to twelve months and 23% for less than six months. However, these same individuals reported losing time from work, Monday morning absenteeism, loss of prospective promotions and suffering accidents (Edwards et al, 1967).

In a South London borough, 279 firms employing from 2 to 200 people were asked to report the total number of problem drinking employees by noting individuals who kept bad time, were often away on Mondays, took prolonged lunch-hours, requested 'subs' often or were thought to be heavy drinkers. Replies from 247 questionnaires returned indiciated a prevalence of 'visible' problem drinking among current male employees ranging from 6.8 per thousand in firms employing less than ten people (52 firms), to 2.0 per thousand in firms having over 200 employees (9 firms). The overall prevalence rate was reported at 3.5 per thousand. On the basis of information supplied by the firms and a knowledge of the borough, the authors concluded that the majority of problem drinking in industry was going unrecognised. The low rates reported could not be satisfactorily explained simply on the basis of a lower rate of alcoholism amongst the employed population (Hawker et al, 1967).

Drunkenness Offenders in Court and in Prison

The official statistics of the Prison Department report the total number of persons imprisoned each year for drunkenness 'with aggravations'. An analysis of the legal framework for drunkenness offences and alternative forms of control now proposed is given in Chapter 2.

In 1969, 2,772 men—representing 5.9% of all men in prison in that year—served sentences for drunkenness offences.

211 women—13.4% of all women in prison—were also imprisoned for drunkenness. While the number of persons in prison for non-payment of a drunkenness fine or for drink-related motoring offences are not available from official statistics, an important study by Sparks (1971) has estimated that number to be approximately 2,511 persons in 1968. The table 8—7 illustrates a sharp rise between 1950 and 1962 in the number of persons convicted of drunkenness in England and Wales and the more recent levelling out of these figures.

Concern over the number of drunkenness arrests and the different rates of arrest reported from different areas of the country led to a survey on drunkenness offenders in England and Wales by the Government Social Survey. This survey has not yet been published, but it deals largely with the attitudes of the police, and contrasts characteristics of offenders found in the London metropolitan police district with those in the rest of England and Wales.

In Scotland, the number of convictions for drunkenness 'with or without aggravation' rose from 1960 to 1963 and then levelled out in a similar manner to England and Wales (see Tables 8—7 and 8—8).

Table 8—7.   Offences of Drunkenness Proved in England and Wales, 1950—1969.

Year	Total Number of convictions	Number per 10,000 of male population aged 15 years and over	Number per 10,000 of female population aged 15 years and over	Number per 10,000 of total population aged 15 years and over	Variation compared with previous year in number of offences proved
1950	47,700	26.24	2.83	13.95	+11,984 +33.54%
1961	74,700	41.50	2.51	20.99	+ 6,585 + 9.67%
1962	84,000	45.95	2.54	23.26	+ 9,298 +12.45%
1963	83,000	45.07	2.51	22.83	− 985 − 1.17%
1964	76,800	41.31	2.32	20.97	− 6,165 − 7.43%
1965	73,000	39.17	2.02	19.80	− 3,862 − 5.03%
1966	70,500	37.50	2.09	19.04	− 2,481 − 3.40%
1967	75,500	39.94	2.26	20.32	+ 5,045 + 7.16%
1968	79,000	41.69	2.19	21.24	+ 3,526 + 4.67%
1969	80,500	42.27	2.58	21.56	+ 1,432 + 1.81%

Source: Home Office. *Offences of Drunkenness, 1969.* H.M.S.O., London. 1970.

Table 8—8.   Convictions or Findings of Guilt for Drunkenness Offences in Scotland, 1960—1968.

Nature of Offence	1960	1961	1962	1963	1964	1965	1966	1967	1968
Simple drunkenness, Drunk and incapable	7,931	9,174	9,667	10,464	10,449	10,060	10,236	10,010	10,435
Drunk and Disorderly	432	379	174	148	152	128	227	317	326
Other drunkenness offences	157	160	155	197	177	192	157	163	176
Total:	8,520	9,713	9,996	10,809	10,778	10,380	10,620	10,490	10,937

Source: Scottish Home and Health Department. *Personal Communication.* 1970.

A number of studies of chronic drunkenness offenders have shown that a high proportion of drunkenness arrests in any one year are made on the same men. Parr (1954) estimated that of 67,000 drunkenness offenders in England and Wales, 54,000 were arrested once only during the year but 4,500 'habitual' offenders were estimated to have had at least one previous conviction. A survey of drunkenness offenders appearing in two London courts (Gath et al, 1968) revealed that in the preceding 12 months 51% of the 151 men interviewed had been arrested for drunkenness on at least one other occasion and 30% had been arrested three times or more. A study of 188 short time recidivist prisoners interviewed in London, found that 40% had been arrested for drunkenness six times or more in the past, although not necessarily in the same year (Hensman, 1969).

The Relationship of Alcohol and Crime

Glatt (1965), in a broad review of the relationship between alcohol and criminal activity, pointed at the need to distinguish between the 'alcoholic criminal' who sometimes drank to excess and may in time develop into an alcoholic, and the 'criminal alcoholic' who, after many years of drinking, is driven to break the law as a consequence of his alcohlism. The age at which drinking became a problem and a person's first criminal conviction was examined by Hensman (1969). Fifty-four per cent of the men interviewed in this survey stated that they had no problem with drink at all, 29% admitted criminal involvement before drink became a problem and 17% claimed that they had a drinking problem before becoming involved with crime.

The overall incidence of problem drinking among prisoners has been much debated in Britain. Hopwood and Milner (1940) identified excessive drinking in 12.1% of 1,000 men admitted to Broadmoor, a special institution now under the direction of the Department of Health. Norris (1941) suggested that abnormal drinking was apparent in 10% of admissions to a local English prison and McGeorge (1963) felt that 40% of all English prisoners were addicted to alcohol. In a northern Irish prison, Robinson et al (1965) reported 65% of prisoners had a history of alcoholism.

Gibbens and Silberman (1970) have conducted a large survey amongst prisoners. They found that 50% of 400 men interviewed admitted a 'serious drinking problem'. The men admitting a serious drinking problem included 17% of 35 men in an 'open prison' which theoretically excludes alcoholics, 27% of first offenders and 47% of the recidivist prisoners in the survey. They also differentiated prisoners serving their first or second sentences. Twenty-five per cent of the men serving their first sentence and 32% serving second sentences claimed they had committed their first offences under the influence of drink or drugs. Edwards et al (1970) reported that 68% of 188 men claimed to have been drinking immediately before committing the offence for which they were imprisoned. Fifty-five per cent were 'drunk' at the time of the offence, 12% reported a 'black-out' related to the offence and 6% were stealing money for drink.

Comparatively few research workers have examined the role of alcohol involvement in female offences. Woodside (1961) found that 13—18% of all receptions to Holloway Prison in London were considered alcoholic and Prince (1969) reported that 8% of 500 admissions for remand or imprisonment at that same institution were drunkenness offenders.

The Relationship Between Drinking and Specific Types of Crime

Homicide

Morris and Blom-Cooper (1969) have studied criminal homicide offenders and their victims in England and Wales. In 1968, 42% of all murder defendants were known to have had some alcohol in their bodies at the time of the offence. Scott (1968) has reviewed the relationship between drinking and murder.

Other Crimes of Violence

McClintock et al (1963) studying crimes of violence, revealed that 20% of such crimes during the years 1957—1960 had occurred in pubs or cafes where alcohol was served and the violence was 'supposedly' committed under the influence of alcohol. Further research work has been completed (McClintock and Avison, 1968).

Arson and Sexual Offences

Hurley and Monahan (1969) studied 50 arsonists in prison at Grendon Underwood in Buckinghamshire. This sample included 22 alcoholics, but the relationship of alcoholism to arson is difficult to establish. Odgers and McClintock (1957) surveyed a sample of sexual offenders and noted that 20% of the men had been drinking at the time of their offence.

Drunken Driving

Willet (1964) clearly outlined the difficulties involved in interpreting the statistics of alcohol-related motoring offences. His examination of the records of 653 serious motoring offenders in one police district in the Home Counties revealed that 15% were charged with driving while unfit through drink or drugs. He also found, however, that alcohol was a contributing factor in just over 8% of all other serious motoring offences and felt this might be an under-estimate.

The difficulties of obtaining evidence for a drunken driving prosecution were to some extent obviated by the Road Safety Act, 1967 which authorised the use of breath tests for proof of alcohol consumption. Data on convictions for driving, or being in charge of, a motor vehicle while under the influence of alcohol or drugs in England and Wales can be derived from *Offences Relating to Motor Vehicles,* which is published annually by the Home Office and annual summaries of Chief Constable's reports published by the Christian Economic and Social Research Foundation.

In 1968, the year following the introduction of the 'breathalyser' for detecting alcohol, 51,414 'breath tests' were administered, of which 26,429 were positive. The total number of prosecutions for drink or drug related motoring offences in that same year was 22,746. The total number of prosecutions for these same offences in 1967 (during the course of which the breathalyser was introduced) was 10,792. This very large increase does not of course, necessarily reflect any increase in the incidence of drunken driving as it may well be wholly, or in part, attributable to the introduction of improved methods of detection. Motorists under the age of 30 years now account for 47% of drunken motoring offences compared with 33% in 1966 (Christian Economic and Social Research Foundation, 1970).

The Road Safety Act, 1967, has probably contributed largely to a decrease of persons killed or injured on the roads in Great Britain. This reduction of fatal and serious casualties is especially noticeable in the late night hours from 10 p.m. to 4 a.m. Other factors aside from the Act may be recent improved legislation covering the use of safety belts and tyres. The table below shows the number of road casualties in the month of September from 1967 to 1970.

Table 8—9.   Road Casualties in Month of September 1967—70 in Great Britain

	1967 (pre-Breath test)	1968	1969	1970
Fatal casualties	706	620	666	600
Serious casualties	8,457	7,966	7,759	8,063
Slight casualties	24,397	22,642	21,507	22,418
Total casualties	33,560	31,928	29,932	31,081

Source: Department of the Environment. *Three Years of Breath Tests—Still Saving Lives.* (Press Notice). 23rd December, 1970.

PHYSICAL CONSEQUENCES OF ALCOHOL MISUSE

Many forms of physical damage have been associated with alcohol misuse, including peptic ulceration and gastritis, alcoholic cirrhosis and hepatitis, alcoholic carditis, tuberculosis, damage to the peripheral and central nervous system including peripheral neuritis and dementia, accidents and suicide (Edwards, 1967). Of all these possible disorders, relatively few have been adequately described amongst alcoholic populations in Great Britain, and in some cases the relationship with drinking has not been clearly defined.

Peptic Disorders

Prevalence figures for peptic ulceration have been collected in a number of studies. During the course of a survey which investigated the association between alcohol and gastrectomy records of 138 male patients admitted to the Maudsley hospital with a primary or secondary diagnosis of alcoholism and a control series of 130 patients' case notes were examined. The samples were matched for age and social class. Alcoholic patients had a significantly higher rate of peptic disorder (Dixon, 1960).

Cirrhosis, Alcoholic Psychosis and Death

The total number of deaths recorded from cirrhosis with alcohol mentioned, alcoholism and alcoholic psychosis have risen from 1962 to 1968 (see Table 8–10). It is possible that there is an inter-change between alcoholism and cirrhosis in terms of diagnosis and death certificate classification, but in fact, only a small proportion of cirrhosis deaths are alcohol-related. Nonetheless, the World Health Organisation (1967) considered that 'the relationship between alcoholism and cirrhosis of the liver is so definite that changes in the death rate from this cause do indicate changes in the rate of alcoholism'. Wilson (1940) examined the mortality rates of persons working in the liquor trade and found a consistently higher mortality rate from alcohol-related disease amongst publicans and bar-men compared with the general population. In the early 1950's, death rates from cirrhosis of the liver amongst publicans were nine times higher than for all men of comparable age (Registrar General, 1957).

Table 8–10. Deaths from Alcohol Cirrhosis, Alcoholism and Alcoholic Psychosis in England, Wales and Scotland. 1962–1968 (Selected Years).

	1962	1965	1967	1968
England and Wales:				
Alcoholic Psychosis	2	–	4	1
Alcoholism	49	57	68	80
Cirrhosis (alcohol mentioned)	1,325	1,400	1,367	1,462
Total*	1,376	1,457	1,439	1,543
Scotland:				
Alcoholic Psychosis *or* Alcoholism	246	220	234	254
Cirrhosis (alcohol mentioned)	19	24	28	32
Total*	265	244	262	286

* Alcohol-related deaths account for less than .3% of all deaths in any year.

Source: Central Statistical Office. *Statistical Review for the Year 1969.*
H.M.S.O., London. 1970, and Scottish Home and Health Department.
Personal Communication. 1970.

In Scotland, there has been a smaller rise in deaths recorded from cirrhosis of the liver (alcohol-involved) and alcoholism or alcoholic psychosis (see Table 8—10).

Suicide

It is not uncommon for alcoholics to attempt or commit suicide. However, the exact rates among alcoholics are difficult to ascertain. Kessel (1965) surveyed a sample of 151 men and 314 women who were admitted to the Edinburgh Poison Centre during 1965 Thirty per cent of the men and 8% of the women were thought to be alcohol dependent. Of the 6 persons who successfully committed suicide within one year of discharge from the Poisons Centre five were alcoholics.

Kessel and Grossman (1961) followed up 131 consecutive alcoholic patients discharged from the Maudsley Hospital and 87 patients discharged from the St. Pancras Observation Ward. 8% of the first group and 7% of the second committed suicide during the period of follow-up.

REFERENCES

BOWMAN K.M. and JELLINEK E.M., 1942. Alcoholic mental disorders. *In* Jellinek E.M. (Ed.).
Alcohol Addiction and Chronic Alcoholism. Yale University Press, New Haven.
BRANDON D., 1971. *The Homeless in London.* Christian Action, London.
CHRISTIAN ECONOMIC AND SOCIAL RESEARCH FOUNDATION, 1970. *Drink Offences: Chief Constables' Reports. England and Wales. 1969.* C.E.S.R.F., London.
DAVIES D.L., 1962. Normal drinking in recovered alcohol patients. *Quart.J.Stud.Alc.* 23, 94.
DIXON M.F., 1960. *The Association Between Alcoholism and Gastrectomy.*
Unpublished Dissertation, University of London.
EDWARDS G., 1967. Classification of pathological drinking. In Dawson A.M. (Ed.).
Third Symposium of Advanced Medicine. Pitman Medical Publishing, London.
EDWARDS G., CHANDLER J., and HENSMAN C., 1971a. Correlates of normal drinking in a London suburb. *Quart.J.Stud.Alc.* In press.
EDWARDS G., CHANDLER J., HENSMAN C. and PETO J., 1971b. Correlates of trouble with drinking: An analysis of report by male drinkers in a London suburb. Unpublished report.
EDWARDS G., HAWKER A., WILLIAMSON V. and HENSMAN C., 1966a. London's Skid Row. *Lancet.* i, 249.
EDWARDS G., HENSMAN C., HAWKER A. and WILLIAMSON V., 1966b. Who goes to Alcoholics Anonymous? *Lancet.* ii, 1407.
EDWARDS G., HENSMAN C. and PETO J., 1970. Drinking problems among recidivist prisoners. Unpublished report.
EDWARDS G., KELLOGG-FISHER M., HAWKER A. and HENSMAN C., 1967. Clients of alcoholism information centres. *Brit.Med.J.* 4, 346.
EDWARDS G., WILLIAMSON V., HAWKER A., HENSMAN C. and POSTOYAN S., 1968. Census of a reception centre. *Brit.J.Psychiat.* 114, 1031.
GATH D., 1969. The male drunk in court. In *The Drunkenness Offence.* Ed. Gath D., Cook T. and Hensman C. Pergamon, Oxford.
GATH D., HENSMAN C., HAWKER A., KELLY M. and EDWARDS G., 1968. The drunk in court: A survey of drunkenness offenders from two London courts. *Brit.Med.J.* 4, 808.
GIBBENS T.C.N., 1963. *Psychiatric Studies of Borstal Lads.* Oxford University Press, London.
GIBBENS T.C.N. and SILBERMAN M., 1970. Alcoholism among prisoners. *Psychological Medicine.* 1, 73.
GLATT M.M., 1965. Crime, alcohol and alcoholism. *Howard Journal.* 11, 274.
GLATT M.M. and HILLS D.R., 1968. Alcohol abuse and alcoholism in the young. *Brit.J.Addict.* 63, 183.
GLATT M.M. and WHITELEY J.S., 1965. Problems of alcoholics at different social levels. *Mschr.Psychiat.Neurol.* 132, 1.
HASSALL C., 1968. A controlled study of the characteristics of young male alcoholics. *Brit.J.Addict.* 63, 193.
HASSALL C., 1969. Development of alcohol addiction in young men. *Brit.J.Prev.Soc.Med.* 23, 40.
HAWKER A., EDWARDS G. and HENSMAN C., 1967. Problem drinkers on the payroll. *Medical Officer.* 118, 313.
HENSMAN C., 1969. Problems of drunkenness amongst male recidivists. *In* Cook T., Gath D. and Hensman C. (Ed.) *The Drunkenness Offender.* Pergamon, Oxford.
HENSMAN C., CHANDLER J., EDWARDS G., HAWKER A. and WILLIAMSON V., 1968. Identifying abnormal drinkers: prevalence estimates by general practitioners and clergyman. *Medical Officer.* 120, 215.
HOME OFFICE, 1970a. *Offences of Drunkenness, 1969.* H.M.S.O., London.
HOME OFFICE, 1970b. *Offences Relating to Motor Vehicles.* H.M.S.O., London.
HOPWOOD J.S. and MILNER K.O., 1940. Some observations on the relation of alcohol to criminal activity. *Brit.J.Inebr.* 38, 51.
HORN J.L. and WANBERG K.W., 1969. Symptom patterns related to excessive use of alcohol. *Quart.J.Stud.Alc.* 30, 35.
HURLEY W. and MONAHAN T.M., 1969. Arson: the criminal and the crime. *Brit.J.Criminol.* 9, 1.
JELLINEK E.M., 1960. *The Disease Concept of Alcoholism.* Hillhouse Press, New Haven.
KENDELL, R.G., 1965. Normal drinking by former alcohol addicts. *Quart.J.Stud.Alc.* 26, 247.
KESSEL N., 1965. Self poisoning. *Brit.Med.J.* ii, 1629.
KESSEL N. and GROSSMAN G., 1961. Suicide in alcoholics. *Brit.Med.J.* 2, 1671.
KESSEL N. and WALTON H., 1965. *Alcoholism.* Penguin, London.
LODGE-PATCH I.C., 1970. Homeless man: a London survey. *Royal Soc.Med.* 63, 437.

LODGE-PATCH I.C., 1971. Homeless men in London: demographic findings in a lodging house sample. *Brit.J.Psychiat.* 118, 313.

McCLINTOCK F.H., and AVISON N.H., 1968. *Crime in England and Wales.* Heinemann, London.

McCLINTOCK F.H., AVISON N.H., SAVILL N.C. and WORTHINGTON V.C., 1963. *Crimes of Violence: an Enquiry by the Institute of Criminology into Crimes of Violence Against the Person in London.* MacMillan, London.

McGEORGE J., 1963. Alcohol and crime. *Med.Sci.Law.* 3, 27.

MELLOR C.S., 1969. *Drinking Behaviour and its Correlates in Alcohol Addicts.* Unpublished disseration, University of Manchester.

MORRIS T.P. and BLUM-COOPER L., 1969. *Criminal Homicide in England and Wales, 1957–68.* Interim report of Legal Research Unit, Department of Sociology, Bedford College, London.

MORRISON S.L., 1964. Alcoholism in Scotland. *Health Bulletin of Scottish Home and Health Department.* 22, 1.

MOSS M.C. and DAVIES, E. BERESFORD, 1968. *A Survey of Alcoholism Men in an English County.* Geigy, London.

NATIONAL ASSISTANCE BOARD, 1966. *Homeless Single Persons.* H.M.S.O., London.

NORRIS F.E., 1941. The delinquent's attitude towards alcohol. *Brit.J.Inebr.* 38, 112.

ODGERS F.J. and McCLINTOCK F.H., 1957. In Radzcinowicz, L. (Ed.). *Sexual Offences– A Report.* MacMillan, London.

OFFICE OF HEALTH ECONOMICS, 1970. *Alcohol Abuse.* O.H.E., London.

ORFORD J. and POSTOYAN S., 1970. Drinking behaviour and its determinants amongst university students in London. Paper presented at Third International Conference on Alcoholism and Addictions, Cardiff, Wales.

PARR D., 1954. Offences of drunkenness in the London area. *Brit.J.Criminol.* II, 272.

PARR D., 1957. Alcoholism in general practice. *Brit.J.Addict.* 54, 25.

PRIEST R.G., 1970. Homeless men: A U.S.A.–U.K. comparison. *Proc.Roy.Soc.Med.* 63, 441.

PRINCE J., 1969. Drinking habits of women in Holloway Prison and those dealt with at a London court. *In* Cook T., Gath D. and Hensman C. (Ed.) *The Drunkenness Offence.* Pergamon, Oxford.

PRYS-WILLIAMS G., 1965. *Chronic Alcoholics.* Rowntree Social Science Trust, London.

RATHOD R., 1967. An enquiry into a general practitioners' opinions about alcoholism. *Brit.J.Addict.* 62, 103.

REGISTRAR GENERAL, 1957. *Occupational Mortality. Decennial Supplement of England and Wales.* H.M.S.O., London.

ROBINSON C.B., PATTEN J.W. and KERR W.S., 1965. A psychiatric assessment of criminal offenders. *Med.Sci.Law.* 5, 140.

ROSS C.F.J., WARDER J. and MACRAE D., 1970. Alcoholism and its treatment in Scotland: A critical review. Unpublished report.

SCOTT P.D., 1968. Offenders, drunkenness and murder. *Brit.J.Addict.* 63, 221.

SPARKS R.F., 1971. The enforcement of fines. *Brit.J.Criminol.* In press.

WALTON H.J., 1968. Personality as a determinant of the form of alcoholism. *Brit.J.Psychiat.* 114, 761.

WEST D.J., 1967. *The Young Offender.* Penguin, London.

WHITE

WILLET T.C., 1964. *The Criminal on the Road.* Tavistock, London.

WILLIAMS L., 1960. *Tomorrow Will Be Sober.* Cassell, London.

WILSON G.B., 1940. *Alcohol and the Nation.* Nicholson and Watson, London.

WOODSIDE M., 1961. Women drinkers admitted to Holloway Prison during February, 1960: a pilot survey. *Brit.J.Criminol.* 1, 221.

WORLD HEALTH ORGANISATION, 1951. *Technical Report Series,* 42. W.H.O., Geneva.

WORLD HEALTH ORGANISATION, 1952. *Technical Report Series,* 48. W.H.O., Geneva.

WORLD HEALTH ORGANISATION, 1967. *Technical Report Series,* 363. W.H.O., Geneva.

CHAPTER 9
NON–MEDICAL USE OF CANNABIS

THE BACKGROUND OF CANNABIS USE IN GREAT BRITAIN

The moment at which a United Kingdom history of cannabis use should start is imprecise, but that it was used in Victorian Britain is in no doubt (Reynolds, 1890). However, the use of cannabis was not widespread before the end of the Second World War and there has been a gradual growth since that time. In the late 1940's there was some cannabis found on ships from Africa and Indian ports in small consignments for coloured seamen and entertainers in London docks and clubs. In the early 1950's police raids on jazz clubs provided evidence that cannabis smoking was being practised by the indigenous British population. In the 1960's white persons began to constitute the majority of cannabis offenders and this continues to be the case. (Advisory Committee on Drug Dependence, 1968, 'The Wootton Committee').

It is difficult to isolate, at this point in time a typical group of cannabis users, but one author, Kenneth Leech (1970), has traced three basic influences which have made contributions to the present developments. The first was the 'beatnik tradition' with its configuration of drop-out philosophy and genuine idealism. This was an influence largely due to American accounts of the drug and a number of authors and poets contributed to the stereotype (Lipton, 1962; Kerouac, 1958). Cannabis was used by the more avant garde of beat poets and writers in the 1950's for pleasure and spiritual insight. The second traditional movement comes through the 'jazz scene' from the 1920's to the 1950's. In Britain cannabis was probably originally smoked in jazz clubs. The third tradition has been from the immigration to Britain by citizens from the Commonwealth—India, Pakistan, West Africa and the Caribbean—which led to early clusterings of cannabis use around the docks (this was noticed by Banton, 1955).

These influences did not largely touch the domestic teenage population until around 1964 and were of little influence in studies of delinquent sub-culture before then (Downes, 1966). Schur (1963) found no evidence for a cannabis sub-culture. However, the situation at present in Britain has changed to the extent that cannabis use appears to have spread to a large number of people in all classes and to have crossed all social barriers.

This trend from cannabis use by the Commonwealth community to use by the indigenous population is shown in relative numbers of coloured and white cannabis offenders in the early 1960's.

Table 9—1.   Cannabis Offenders, 1963—1967.

Cannabis Offenders	1963	1964	1965	1966	1967
White	296	284	400	767	1,737
Coloured	367	260	226	352	656

Source: Advisory Committee on Drug Dependence (The Wootton Committee), 1968. HMSO, London.

THE EXTENT OF MISUSE AND CHARACTERISTICS OF THE USING POPULATION

Because of the nature of cannabis use, it is clearly impossible to form an exact opinion about the extent of such use in the United Kingdom. Unlike non-drug offences which become known to the police because a record of the offence itself exists, there is no record of any kind other than one of convictions. In as much as it is impossible to find reliable evidence of absolute figures for any one year, the changes between years are equally difficult to gauge. The illegal nature of cannabis use also means that users are reluctant to declare their use publically.

If we use as indicators the number of persons charged with various offences connected with cannabis use (see Table 9—2) and allow for changes in policing practices, there can be little doubt that there has been very substantial growth. There were estimates of the number of cannabis users made to the Wootton Committee (Advisory Committee on Drug Dependence, 1968), but these ranged from 30,000 to 300,000. The total numbers of cannabis convictions from 1963 to 1969 are set out below.

Table 9—2.   Total Cannabis Convictions, 1963—1969.

	1963	1964	1965	1966	1967	1968	1969
Total cannabis convictions	663	544	626	1119	2393	3071	4683

Source: Advisory Committee on Drug Dependence, 1968. HMSO, London. and Press Notice. Home Office. 18th September, 1970.

It is increasingly apparent to researchers in the field, and their evidence remains as informal as that cited by the Wootton Committee, that the growth of cannabis use over the last 20 years has accelerated in the last six. It is not uncommon to encounter large social groupings which have either constituted themselves around the use of cannabis, or which regard it as a normally used intoxicant. Some major cities in the United Kingdom have developed areas in which the cultural configurations surrounding cannabis use, expressed in literature and music lyrics, are particularly apparent.

The drug enjoys most popularity as an intoxicating agent among the young, and it appears to be used socially among small groups co-present during use rather than by solitary persons. It constitutes the centre of a particular type of small group activity. Whilst it seems to have been the case that the drug was confined, for the most part, to a middle-class milieu, the most recent indications are that its use has spread among young working class people.

The Wootton Report (Advisory Committee on Drug Dependence, 1968) found evidence of two main groups of users, one group well-adjusted to on-going social structures, and the other more hostile to these structures. In the first case the group was characterised by being law-abiding in matters other than cannabis use, by use of the drug for introspective purposes or as an aid to social relaxation and by their inclination to cease use at marriage when it was felt that the legal consequences of conviction for a cannabis offence were too onerous. The second group, who have been characterised as 'drop-outs', were believed to be showing some difficulties in social adjustment. They were actively discontented, rebellious and thought to be lacking in stability. The Report did not specifically discount the possibility that they also used cannabis for social relaxation and introspection. No attempt was made to estimate the sizes of these groups, but the Committee believed that in all probability, the latter was far smaller than the former.

ADVERSE REACTIONS TO CANNABIS USE

Several models have been developed as aids to considering cannabis effects. Leonard (1969) suggests that the person, his underlying personality, the environment, the conditions under which the drug is taken and the variety of cannabis taken are the key variables in the effect. The precise nature of these variables is in some doubt, there being few clear records of the personality structures of habitual users, the significance of circumstances, whether habitual or not, against which the psychological, social and physical consequences can be evaluated.

In general, reports have emphasised that there is no physical dependence on cannabis, and that no withdrawal symptoms or tolerance occurs.

'Cannabis is not a drug of addiction. It is an intoxicant'.
(Report of the Inter-Departmental Committee on Drug Addiction, 1961).

'Cannabis does not produce a real addiction. It does not give rise to biological dependence and withdrawal symptoms, neither does it establish a strong craving as in tobacco smoking or indulgence in alcohol'.
(Wolstenholme and Knight, 1964).

Users report stopping use without physical symptoms and without any strong craving to resume. Indeed, the Advisory Committee on Drug Dependence (1968) and Edwards (1968) consider that probably most smokers of the drug can control the effects they get and do not become incapacitated. Some research reports evidence of dependence (McMorris, 1967; Paton, 1968; Leonard, 1969), however, such reports usually refer to some kind of psychological dependence.

Reports of a specific cannabis psychosis have been rare in Great Britain. However, Tylden (1968) warned that widespread cannabis use would lead to an increasing number of 'cannabis psychotics'. However, Lewis states:

'Cannabis-psychoses have been frequently described and the accounts include practically every known variety of mental disorder ...'

'The term cannabis psychosis begs the question of the existence of such a syndrome ...'
There is no unequivocal evidence that cannabis can be the major or sufficient cause of any form of psychosis'.
(Advisory Committee on Drug Dependence, 1968).

Baker and Lucas (1969) investigated 82 cases of admissions to hospital in 1966 where cannabis was mentioned as a causal factor. Their analysis of 79 detailed case records was as follows:

Toxic confusional states leading to admission	8
Other physical or psychiatric symptoms leading to admission	9
Cannabis addiction irrelevant to admission	13
Cannabis addiction as a 'way of life' leading to social deterioration and eventual admission	20
Insufficient evidence or inadequate records records for a decision to be made	29
	79

SOCIAL CONSEQUENCES

There are an increasing number of convictions for cannabis use and these constitute one of the most obvious social consequences. There is conflicting evidence on the social effects of consumption of cannabis (Edwards, 1968; Glatt, 1969; Leonard, 1969).

The detailed analysis of cannabis cases dealt with by the courts in 1967 showed the following:

'Over two-third of all cannabis offenders (and nearly all found guilty of possessing more than 1 Kg.) did not have a record of non-drug offences. Nine out of ten of all cannabis offences were for possessing less than 30 grams (just over one ounce). About a quarter of all cannabis offenders were sent to prison (or borstal, detention centre, or approved school); only about 13% were made subject to a probation order; and about 17% of first offenders were sent to prison. There was notably greater emphasis on fines and imprisonment for possession of cannabis than of other dangerous drugs, but less use of probation and conditional discharge for possession of cannabis than for possession either of other dangerous drugs or of amphetamines and other 1964 Act drugs. Average fines for possession offences in 1967 were £36 in the case of cannabis: £39 in the case of other dangerous drugs: and £28. 10s. 0d. in the case of 1964 Act drugs.' (Advisory Committee on Drug Dependence, 1968).

The following table shows an analysis of the outcome of cannabis prosecutions in 1967 for those persons having up to 30 grams of cannabis, these represent 89% of all prosecutions. The total prosecution figure for up to 30 grams is 2,419 and the figure for upwards of 30 grams is 312.

RECOMMENDATIONS OF WOOTTON COMMITTEE
(ADVISORY COMMITTEE ON DRUG DEPENDENCE, 1968)

Some of the Committee's recommendations can be summarised as follows:

(a)   The association of cannabis with heroin was felt to be inappropriate and based on little evidence.

Table 9–3.   Analysis of Cannabis Prosecutions and Disposals Related to Age Groups and Weights of the Drug. (Up to 30 grams of Cannabis). 1967

AGE GROUPS

	Sex	15–20			21–25			26–35			Over 35			No age			Total		
		Fine £50+	Imprison-ment	Other	Fine £50+	Imprison-ment	Other	Fine £50+	Imprison-ment	Other	Fine £50+	Imprison-ment	Other	Fine £50+	Imprison-ment	Other	Fine £50+	Imprison-ment	Other
No previous convictions	M	112	24	501	116	90	278	89	66	135	42	44	79	10	5	43	369	229	1,036
	F	11	1	91	11	4	61	3	2	20	3	1	5	–	–	10	28	8	187
Previous offender (Drug offences only)	M	1	1	13	2	7	8	1	7	8	2	2	4	–	–	–	6	17	33
	F	–	–	2	1	2	3	–	–	–	–	–	1	–	–	–	1	2	6
Previous offender (Non-drug offences only)	M	21	10	110	20	18	62	15	27	27	7	11	16	3	1	1	66	67	216
	F	–	–	7	3	–	2	2	3	5	–	–	–	–	–	–	5	3	14
Previous offender (Drug and Non-drug)	M	3	2	28	5	12	23	3	15	7	1	15	6	–	–	–	12	44	64
	F	–	–	–	1	1	–	–	1	2	–	1	–	–	–	–	1	3	2
Total:	M	137	37	652	143	127	371	108	115	177	52	72	105	13	6	44	453	357	1,349
	F	11	1	100	16	7	66	5	6	27	3	2	6	–	–	10	35	16	209
Total for all weights of cannabis above 30 grams	M	5	1	33	7	31	21	13	55	17	16	43	13	1	3	2	42	133	86
	F	–	–	13	–	3	9	4	4	10	–	3	4	–	1	–	4	11	36

Source: Advisory Committee on Drug Dependence, 1968. HMSO, London.

(b)   Possession of small amounts of cannabis should not normally be regarded as a serious crime liable to punishment by imprisonment and, therefore, penalties for unlawful possession, sale or supply should be drastically lightened.

(c)   It recommended that the existing law, which inhibits research which requires the smoking of cannabis sativa by human experimental subjects, should be amended immediately to allow qualified workers to conduct such research.

(d)   There should be a review of the powers of the police to arrest and search persons in relation to suspected cannabis offences.

(e)   That legislation should be amended in the very near future along the lines recommended by the Advisory Committee. An attempt, it was believed, should be made to legislate differentially between those found in possession of small amounts of cannabis intended for their own use, and those found in possession with a view to dealing in the substance. Penalties for the latter offence would be considerably higher than for the former.

REFERENCES

ADVISORY COMMITTEE ON DRUG DEPENDENCE (The Wootton Committee), 1968. *Cannabis.* HMSO, London.

BAKER A.A. and LUCAS E.G., 1969. Some hospital admission associated with cannabis. *Lancet.* i, 148.

BANTON M.P., 1955. *The Coloured Quarter.* Tavistock, London.

DOWNES D., 1966. *The Delinquent Solution.* Routledge and Keegan Paul, London.

EDWARDS G., 1968. The problem of cannabis dependence. *The Practitioner.* 200, 226.

GLATT M.M., 1969. Is it all right to smoke pot? *Brit.J.Addict.* 64, 109.

HOME OFFICE, 1970. Press notice. 18th September, 1970.

INTERDEPARTMENTAL COMMITTEE ON DRUG ADDICTION, 1961. *Drug Addiction.* HMSO, London.

KEROUAC, J., 1958. *On the Road.* Andre Deutsch, London.

LEECH, K., 1970. *Pastoral Care and the Drug Scene.* S.P.C.K., London.

LEONARD B.E., 1969. Cannabis: a short review of its effects and possible dangers of its use. *Brit.J.Addict.* 64, 121.

LIPTON, L., 1962. *The Holy Barbarians.* New English Library, London.

McMORRIS S.C., 1967. What price euphoria? The case against marijuana. *Brit.J.Addict.* 62, 203.

PATON W.D.M., 1968. Drug dependence: Socio-pharmacological assessment. *Adv. of Science.* 12, 9.

REYNOLDS J.R., 1890. On the therapeutic uses and toxic effects of cannabis indica. *Lancet.* i, 637.

SCHUR E.M., 1963. *Narcotic Addiction in Britain and America.* Tavistock, London.

TYLDEN E., 1968. Cannabis taking in England. *Newcastle Med.J.* 30, 6.

WOLSTENHOLME G.E.W. and KNIGHT J., 1965. *Hashish: its Chemistry and Pharmacology.* Churchill, London.

CHAPTER 10

NON-MEDICAL USE OF L S D AND HALLUCINOGENIC DRUGS

HISTORIC OVERVIEW

As is the case with many drugs which are used in contemporary society, the hallucinogenic drugs have been used in antiquity. Records of hallucinogen drugs can be traced back through world-wide primitive literature (Leech, 1970).

In 1918, Mescaline had been synthesised, and in about 1938 the synthetic hallucinogenic agent Lysergic Acid Diethylamide (LSD) was discovered in Switzerland by Professor A. Hofmann whilst engaged in a course of study on ergot derivatives. Hofmann accidentally intoxicated himself with LSD and described many of the effects which are now commonly associated with the so-called 'mind expanding' drugs. Hofmann said of his experience:

'In the afternoon of 16th April, 1943, when I was working on this problem, I was seized by a peculiar sensation of vertigo and restlessness. Objects, as well as the shape of my associates in the laboratory, appeared to undergo optical changes. I was unable to concentrate on my work. In a dream-like state I left for home, where an irresistible urge to lie down overcame me. I drew the curtains and immediately fell into a peculiar state similar to drunkenness, characterized by an exaggerated imagination. With my eyes closed, fantastic pictures of extra-ordinary plasticity and intensive colour seemed to surge towards me. After two hours this stage gradually wore off.' (Laboratory notes of Dr. Hofmann quoted in Advisory Committee on Drug Dependence, 1970).

In contemporary society, a range of discussions and anxious enquiry has surrounded the use of hallucinogenic drugs. Huxley (1954, 1956) wrote extensively on his experiences with mescaline and has had considerable influence in articulating the perceptual and spiritual possibilities of hallucinogens. Similarly, lysergic acid diethylamide has had its active supporters. Many people who have engaged in experimentation with LSD have asserted that the drug has produced intense mystico-religious responses and has altered the deepest spiritual content of their lives (Leech, 1970).

By 1966, the medical press drew attention to the increasing use of hallucinogens, the potency of the drugs and their possible dangers (British Medical Journal, 1966). In the popular press, great alarm has been expressed about possible dangers of hallucinogenic drugs have been used in antiquity. Records of hallucinogenic drugs

EXTENT OF MISUSE AND CHARACTERISTICS OF THE USING POPULATION

There has been considerable reported use of LSD and other hallucinogens in the United Kingdom and there seems little doubt that there has been more extensive use in London and some provincial centres in the past few years. The years of largest growth appear to have been 1966–67. However, hard data on prevalence is entirely unavailable.

The illicit nature of LSD use and the minute amount of the drug (150 micrograms) needed for a 'trip', make it extremely difficult to estimate the extent of use. In 1968, there were seizures of LSD including some 175,000 potential 'trip' doses, and this would indicate a great deal more might be available for consumption. The frequent references to psychedelic experiences in the 'Underground' press and the widely known safeguards advised to avoid 'bad trips' suggest a growing number of users. The Advisory Committee on Drug Dependence (1970) noted the emphasis put by witnesses, who had used LSD, on the need for proper preparations and a 'guide' to help work through the drug experience.

Skill in dealing with 'bad trips' exists among the community of regular users.

The majority of present day LSD users seem to be young people under 25 years of age and come from all social backgrounds. While the earlier use of LSD was associated with intellectual pursuits, it is now part of the general drug taking scene.

Whilst the extensive use of LSD surrounds the 'hippie' cultural syndrome, a separate group of users can be discerned among those involved in the multiple-drug-use group. There is no evidence to suggest that there is a connection in this group between their use of hallucinogens and heroin that can be stated as causal, but there is a nexus of multiple-drug-use in some groups. However, it has been asserted that 'bad trips' may be a mechanism which discourages some drug users from any further experimentation with any drug whatever (Advisory Committee on Drug Dependence, 1970).

ADVERSE CONSEQUENCES

LSD and the hallucinogens do not produce physical dependence, but there may be a desire to continue taking the drug at regular intervals. A very small amount of LSD, one-millionth of a gram or even less per kilogram body weight, may affect autonomic, sensory and emotional functioning (Advisory Committee on Drug Dependence, 1970). A curious tolerance may develop rapidly so that a dose taken one or two days later may have little effect, but a dose five or six days later will have the full effect.

The most commonly stated risks attendant upon LSD use are the precipitation of lasting psychotic disturbance and possible chromosomal alteration. The overall incidence of lasting disturbance is difficult to estimate and Sir Aubrey Lewis has stated the present state of knowledge as follows:

'It is, at present, quite impossible to tell how frequently these dangerous reactions occur. In more than thirty papers, psychiatrists have communicated details of untoward reactions; some of them have seen only one such affected patient, others have seen three or four. But it cannot be assumed that most of the patients who have untoward reactions are seen by psychiatrists or by doctors, or that the doctors who do see them would report them in articles in the journals. Moreover, the number of persons who take LSD is quite unknown, and, consequently, the frequency of adverse reactions cannot be measured.' (Department of Health and Social Security, 1970).

The table 10–1 gives the persons admitted to National Health Hospitals, 1966–1968, who were known to use LSD. This table is only a crude indication of adverse reaction because it is not stated that LSD use itself was the reason for the admission and, on the other hand, other cases may have presented themselves, but the exact diagnosis was missed. There is also a marked reluctance to attend a hospital because of the illicit nature of LSD use, and many cases may have been attended by non-professionals.

Table 10—1.   Persons Admitted to N.H.S. Psychiatric Hospitals or Psychiatric Departments in 1966, 1967 and 1968, who were shown to have used LSD alone or with other drugs.

	1966			1967			1968		
	Male	Female	Total	Male	Female	Total	Male	Female	Total
Age under 18	1	1	2	3	2	5	5	1	6
18—24	8	1	9	24	–	24	19	1	20
25—29	1	–	1	5	2	7	4	–	4
30 and over	3	–	3	3	–	3	1	1	2
All ages using heroin and/or cocaine	7	1	8	11	3	14	11	8	19
Total:	20	3	23	46	7	53	40	11	51

Source: Advisory Committee on Drug Dependence. *The Amphetamines and Lysergic Acid Diethylamide—LSD.* H.M.S.O., London. 1970.

The evidence for possible chromosomal damage has received wide publicity in Britain and the Advisory Committee on Drug Dependence (1970) has summarised the evidence. They conclude that the 'verdict must be an open one', but that far more research must be done to resolve the issue.

There is much argument about social consequences of LSD use and its association with the 'hippie' sub-culture. Leech (1970) has given some of the sub-cultural configurations associated with LSD in Britain.

The table 10—2 sets out a detailed analysis of proceedings for unlawful possession of LSD in 1968. The social implications of legal action seem to apply to very few persons.

Table 10—2.   Analysis of Proceedings for Unlawful Possession of LSD 1968

	Unlawful possession of LSD
Number of charges brought	90
Charges withdrawn or dismissed	20
Hospital or Guardianship Order	—
Number of convictions	70
Absolute discharge	—
Recognizance	—
Conditional discharge	2
Hospital Order (S.60 Mental Health Act 1959)	1
Probation Order	7
Fit Person Order	—
Fine	24
Attendance Order	—
Suspended sentence	2
Remand Home	—
Detention Centre	—
Approved School	—
Police Cells	—
Imprisonment with fine	10
Borstal	—
Otherwise dealt with	24
Fines: minimum imposed	£10
maximum imposed	£75
total imposed	£780
Imprisonment:	
shortest sentence	6 months
longest sentence	2 years

Source: Adapted from Advisory Committee on Drug Dependence.
The Amphetamines and Lysergic Acid Diethylamide—LSD.
HMSO, London. 1970.

REFERENCES

ADVISORY COMMITTEE ON DRUG DEPENDENCE, 1970. *The Amphetamines and Lysergic Acid Diethylamide (LSD)*. H.M.S.O., London.
BRITISH MEDICAL JOURNAL, 1966. Effects of L.S.D. *Brit.Med.J.* 1, 1495.
DEPARTMENT OF HEALTH AND SOCIAL SECURITY, 1970. *Amphetamines, Barbiturates, LSD and Cannabis, Their Use and Misuse.* Reports on Public Health and Medical Subjects, No. 124. H.M.S.O., London.
HUXLEY A., 1954. *The Doors of Perception.* Chatto and Windus, London.
HUXLEY A., 1956. *Heaven and Hell.* Chatto and Windus, London.
LEECH, K., 1970. *Pastoral Care and the Drug Scene.* S.P.C.K., London.

CHAPTER 11

THE NON-MEDICAL USE OF AMPHETAMINE

HISTORICAL OVERVIEW OF AMPHETAMINE ABUSE

The origin of amphetamine abuse in Great Britain is not clearly documented. As early as 1937 a report appeared in The Pharmaceutical Journal on the possibility of Benzedrine abuse, and Guttman and Sargent (1937) mentioned a patient who was buying excessive quantities of amphetamine from a chemist shop. In June 1939, Benzedrine was placed in Part I of the Poisons List and in Schedule 1 of Schedule 7 of the Poisons Rules. This required the drug to be labelled as dangerous and recommended that it be taken only under medical supervision and only available under the supervision of a registered pharmacist. By 1954 the demand for amphetamine from the general public had grown and the Pharmaceutical Society recommended that the drug be restricted to availability only by a doctor's prescription. In 1956, when the amphetamines were placed under more restrictive control in Section 4 of the Poisons Rule, it was well-known that amphetamine pills and amphetamine inhalors were being abused by the public. These inhalors, which were used as decongestants, contained up to 325 mg. of amphetamine base, as compared to the normal dose in tablet form being 5 to 10 mg. The misuse of amphetamine inhalors was met by the voluntary co-operation of manufacturers following a request of the Pharmaceutical Society. The manufacturers responded either by withdrawing the product from the market or by altering the formulation.

THE EXTENT OF MISUSE AND THE CHARACTERISTICS OF SELECTED POPULATIONS

A series of medical studies of amphetamine psychosis (Connell, 1958; Beamish and Kiloh, 1960), amphetamine poisoning (Greenwood and Peachey, 1957) and amphetamine abuse in general practice surveys (Kiloh and Brandon, 1962; Brandon and Smith, 1962; Wilson and Beacon, 1964) indicated the extent and nature of amphetamine misuse from medical sources. Kiloh and Brandon (1962) in a survey of medical general practices in Newcastle-upon-Tyne (population 250,000) found 1% of the population (2,500 persons) to be receiving amphetamine-type drugs on a prescription and estimated that 20% of those receiving amphetamine were psychologically dependent on them. The majority were middle-aged women who had originally been prescribed amphetamines as treatment for depression or obesity.

Brandon and Smith (1962) showed that of patients receiving regular prescriptions for amphetamines or related drugs in general practice, 21% were thought by their doctors to be habituated. Wilson and Beacon (1964) in a study of 58 patients attending 11 medical practices, found that 58% were conditioned to Drinamyl in that they said they could not live without it.

Findings by McConnell (1963), Durrant (1965) and Johnson and Milner (1966) also portrayed amphetamine abuse as primarily the problem of the age group over 30. The table below sets out selected characteristics of patients in a number of the surveys above.

Table 11—1.   Characteristics of Patients in Five Studies on Amphetamine Psychosis or Dependence.

Locality	Numbers		Mean Age		Daily Max. Dose Mg./dose	Reference
	Male	Female	Male	Female		
London	27	15	33	32	975	Connell (1958)
Newcastle	6	2	33	26	300	Beamish and Kiloh (1960)
Belfast	11	20	Range 20—56		–	McConnell (1963)
Sussex	6	8	43	38	180	Durrant (1965)
Lancs.	4	10	26	47	200	Johnson and Milner (1966)

Source: Adapted from British Medical Association—Report of Working Party on Amphetamine Preparations, 1968,

The abuse potential of amphetamines is further evidenced by the number of persons admitted to National Health Service psychiatric hospitals or psychiatric departments, who were shown to have used amphetamines alone or with other drugs (except narcotics, LSD and cannabis). In 1968, 28% of persons admitted to hospital who were shown to be using amphetamines were women aged 30 and over.

Table 11—2.   Persons admitted to NHS psychiatric hospitals or psychiatric departments in 1966, 1967 and 1968 who were shown to have used amphetamines alone or with other drugs (except narcotics, LSD and cannabis).

Age	1966			1967			1968		
	Male	Female	Total	Male	Female	Total	Male	Female	Total
Under 18	22	7	29	18	16	34	23	24	47
18—24	86	47	133	115	28	143	131	73	204
25—29	33	31	64	33	34	67	30	31	61
30 and over	105	163	268	96	156	252	47	139	186
Total all ages:	246	248	494	262	234	496	231	267	498

Source: Advisory Committee on Drug Dependence, 1970. The Amphetamines and Lysergic Acid Diethylamide (LSD). HMSO, London.

The precise extent of the use and misuse of amphetamine drugs in the general population is impossible to ascertain. Laurie (1967) has applied the findings from Newcastle (Kiloh and Brandon, 1962) to the urban population of Great Britain and estimated that 23,000 persons may be dependent on prescribed amphetamines. However, Bewley (1966) has suggested that 80,000 persons may be slightly dependent on prescribed amphetamines, and that an additional 80,000 persons may be using amphetamines illicitly.

Only a comprehensive survey of medical general practices or a more detailed study of individuals' prescription forms could give an accurate estimate of the abuse of prescribed amphetamine. While the total number of prescriptions for amphetamine drugs has been falling since 1966, this does not take into account the size of each prescription or that dependent patients may be the most likely to continue receiving prescriptions. It is probable that dependence on amphetamines is exceeded only by dependence on cigarettes, alcohol and barbiturates in Great Britain (Bewley, 1966).

After changes in patterns of amphetamine misuse were reported by Connell (1958), an increasing number of articles appeared on the misuse of amphetamines taken in tablet form and obtained illegally by younger people (Linken, 1963; Connell, 1964, 1965a, b; Sharpley, 1964). Reports of forged prescriptions and stolen tablets were frequent by 1962 in the Pharmaceutical Journal. There was evidence that tablets were being sold illicitly and passed among friends and acquaintances. These were obtained from unused supplies originally obtained legitimately on a doctor's prescription by alteration or forgery of prescriptions and thefts from retailers, wholesalers and manufacturers. There was widespread use of these drugs in jazz clubs, coffee bars, and similar places where they were mostly consumed in sprees on weekends. They could be bought quite inexpensively in the early 1960's. However, there is no possible way to estimate the full extent of amphetamine abuse or non-therapeutic use among young people, as the majority using amphetamines illicitly neither appear before the courts, nor develop symptoms requiring medical consultation. The sources of illicit supply make it impossible to estimate the total amount of the drug that might be abused.

Scott and Wilcox (1965) in a study of two London remand homes found 18% of the boys had taken amphetamine very recently. They distinguished two categories of the young male amphetamine takers. First, the 'malignant' category who tended to increase their dosage, take a variety of forms of amphetamine in a reckless manner and take them mid-week as well as at weekends. Their school or work records fell off sharply. They invariably had grossly unfavourable home backgrounds. Essentially, their personality was characterised by lack of confidence in making personal relationships, together with an over-dependence on their parents. On the other hand, the 'benign' category confined their amphetamine use to weekends and did not increase their dose. They did not suffer from such unfavourable home backgrounds or such severe personality disorders. Their delinquency was parallel with their drug taking rather than caused by it.

Crockett and Marks (1969) in a survey of amphetamine taking among a sample of 972 youths in a remand centre population found an overall incidence of 6.9%. Personality assessment showed that the amphetamine takers tended to be more self-critical, more conflicting in feelings and attitudes, more honest in their responses and generally more neurotic.

In a study of 290 boys between 14 and 16 years old who were admitted to a detention centre in 1967, 8% admitted to taking amphetamines, although less than 1% were actually admitted on drug charges (Backhouse and James, 1969). This study examined the relationship of drug use, smoking and alcohol use and is discussed in more detail in Chapter 14.

In the summer of 1968 the practice of young people injecting ampoules of liquid methylamphetamine intravenously reached epidemic proportions in London. Until this time amphetamines were almost exclusively swallowed rather than injected, and only young opiate addicts used injections as a common way of self-administering drugs. As a result of spreading abuse of methylamphetamine, young people with amphetamine psychosis were encountered by medical and social work agencies (James, 1968; Glatt, 1968). The illicit market seemed to have been supplied indirectly from medical sources, with most of the methylamphetamine prescribed by a very few doctors working in private practice. Hawks et al (1969) surveyed 74 regular users of methylamphetamine injections. Those interviewed were predominantly British, single and under 25 years of age and a striking proportion had a history of parental separation, absence or bereavement. Twenty-three per cent had been sentenced to detention centre, borstal or approved school, and 20% had been sentenced to prison. In this sample, 30% were regularly misusing other non-amphetamine type drugs. This epidemic was curtailed in October 1968, when the manufacturers, by arrangement with the Ministry of Health and the British Medical Association, withdrew methylamphetamine from retail pharmacists. However, the practice of injecting amphetamines has continued to some extent, although it is necessary to pulverise amphetamine pills to make them suitable for injection.

CONSEQUENCES OF AMPHETAMINE ABUSE

One of the possible consequences of amphetamine abuse is amphetamine psychosis, described by Connell (1958). The amphetamine psychosis is now considered a paranoid state. The clinical picture also includes ideas of reference, paranoid delusion, auditory and visual hallucinations in a setting of clear consciousness. There is a general picture of restlessness, irritability, anti-social acts and obsessive compulsive behaviour. A generalized type of over-stimulation is most apparent. There is controversy over whether the amphetamines produce physical dependence (Oswald and Thracore, 1963), thought it is clear that they produce tolerance and psychological dependence. If amphetamines are taken by injection there is the added hazard of complications from careless injection practice—these complications are described in Chapter 13 on opiate abuse.

SOCIAL CONSEQUENCES

The most obvious social consequence of illicit amphetamine use is that of arrest under the Drugs (Prevention of Misuse) Act, 1964. The total number of convictions under that Act has increased from 958 in 1965 to 3,214 in 1968, and the great majority of these offences relate to amphetamine. Conviction figures are difficult to interpret and they may rise because of greater interest and activity on the part of the police or for other reasons, as well as a real increase in the use of a particular drug. The table 11—3 sets out an analysis of proceedings brought under the Drugs (Prevention of Misuse) Act.

RECOMMENDATIONS FROM THE REPORT BY THE
ADVISORY COMMITTEE ON DRUG DEPENDENCE

The following recommendations were made by the Committee with respect to the amphetamines.

The Government should consider introducing legislation to control the trafficking of drugs in certain public premises such as coffee bars, discotheques, clubs and dance halls. Some local town Acts and the Dangerous Drugs Act, Section 5, already make reference to possible punishment of the owners of premises where illicit drugs are consumed.

The Committee recommended that the powers of the General Medical Council be extended so that it is able to discipline doctors for reckless over-prescribing. This discipline system should recognise all the legal rights and safeguards appropriate to such a procedure. To make this possible it was recommended that the Home Office and Health Departments devise a method for early identification from prescriptions of doctors who might warrant investigation.

Table 11—3.   Analysis of Proceedings by Category of Offence Relating to
Amphetamines, 1968.

	Unlawful Possession	Unlawful import	Larceny	Offences under other Statutes	Total
Number of charges brought	2,231	5	561	323	3,120
Charges withdrawn or dismissed	212	–	12	10	234
Hospital or Guardianship order	–	–	–	1	1
Number of convictions	2,019	5	549	312	2,885
Absolute discharge	27	–	3	4	34
Recognisances	1	–	–	–	1
Conditional discharge	260	–	22	36	318
Hospital Order (S.60 Mental Health Act (1959))	10	–	–	3	13
Probation Order	377	–	68	66	511
Fit Person Order	–	–	–	–	–
Fine	658	3	124	61	846
Attendance Centre	–	–	3	–	3
Suspended Sentence	115	–	17	22	154
Remand Home	–	–	–	–	–
Detention Centre	77	–	43	3	123
Approved School	14	–	3	–	17
Police Cells	3	–	–	–	3
Imprisonment without fine	160	–	63	32	255
Borstal	75	–	31	2	108
Otherwise dealt with	242	2	172	83	499
Fines: minimum imposed	£1	£50	£1	£2	–
maximum imposed	£350	£50	£100	£100	–
total imposed	£15,673	£150	£3,731	£1,397	£20,951
Imprisonment:					
shortest sentence	1 month	–	2 weeks	1 month	–
longest sentence	2 years	–	3 years	3 years	–

The number of different persons proceeded against was 2603. These figures do not agree with
the total shown above as a number of persons were charged with more than one offence.

Source: Advisory Committee on Drug Dependence, 1970. HMSO, London.

This would have to include private as well as National Health Service prescriptions.
The former are currently subject to no scrutiny at all and the latter are scrutinised
basically for bulk pricing.

The establishment of out-patient treatment clinics and day centres should be
encouraged in areas where drug use is prevalent, and counselling should be
available to both young persons and parents. The report points to the need for
more extensive research on the social and personal factors involved in drug use.

In general, the Committee also recommends 'penalties should reflect the relative
harmfulness of the different forms of drug misuse. The occasional oral use of
a pep-pill ought to be regarded as a much less serious matter than the injection
of amphetamines, which is as dangerous as any form of drug misuse'.
(Advisory Committee on Drug Dependence, 1970).

REFERENCES

ADVISORY COMMITTEE ON DRUG DEPENDENCE, 1970. *The Amphetamines and Lysergic Acid Diethylamide (LSD).* HMSO.

BACKHOUSE, C.I. and JAMES, I.P., 1969. The relationship and prevalence of smoking, drinking and drug taking in (delinquent) adolescent boys. *Brit.J.Addict.* 64, 75.

BEAMISH, P. and KILOH, L.G., 1960. Psychosis due to amphetamine consumption. *J.Ment.Sci.* 106, 337.

BEWLEY, T.H., 1966. Recent changes in the pattern of drug abuse in the United Kingdom. *Bulletin of Narcotics.* 18(4), 1.

BRANDON, S. and SMITH, D., 1962. Amphetamines in general practice. *J. Col. Gen. Pract.* 5, 603.

BRITISH MEDICAL ASSOCIATION, 1968. *Report of the Working Party on Amphetamine Preparations.* British Medical Association, London.

CONNELL, P.H., 1958. *Amphetamine Psychosis.* Maudsley Monograph No.5. Oxford University Press, London.

CONNELL, P.H., 1964. Amphetamine misuse. *Brit. J. Addict.* 60, 9.

CONNELL, P.H., 1965 (a). The assessment and treatment of adolescent drug takers with special reference to amphetamine. *Proc. Leeds Symposium on Behavioural Disorders.* May and Baker.

CONNELL, P.H., 1965 (b). Adolescent drug taking. *Proc. Roy. Soc. Med.* 50, 409.

CROCKETT, R. and MARKS, V., 1969. Amphetamine taking among young offenders. *Brit. J. Psychiat.* 115, 1203.

DRUGS (PREVENTION OF MISUSE) ACT, 1964. HMSO.

DURRANT, B.W., 1964. Amphetamine addiction. *Practitioner.* 194, 649.

GLATT, M.M., 1968. Letter to the Editor. *The Lancet.* ii, 215.

GREENWOOD, R. and PEACHEY, R.S., 1957. Acute amphetamine poisoning: an account of three cases. *Brit. Med. J.* 1, 742.

GUTTMANN, E. and SARGANT, W., 1937. Observations on benzedrine. *Brit. Med. J.* 1, 1013.

HAWKS, D., MITCHESON, M., OGBORNE, A. and EDWARDS, G., 1969. Abuse of methylamphetamine. *Brit. Med. J.* 2, 715.

JAMES, I.P., 1968. Letter to the Editor. *The Lancet.* i, 916.

JOHNSON, J. and MILNER, G., 1966. Amphetamine intoxication and dependence in admissions to a psychiatric unit. *Brit. J. Psychiat.* 112, 617.

KILOH, L.G. and BRANDON, S., 1962. Habituation and addiction to amphetamines. *Brit. Med. J.* 2, 40.

LAURIE, Peter, 1967. *Drugs: Medical, Psychological and Social Facts.* Penguin, London.

LINKEN, A., 1963. *Sunday Times.* 27th January, 1963.

McCONNELL, W.B., 1963. Amphetamine substances in mental illness in Northern Ireland. *Brit. J. Psychiat.* 109, 218.

OSWALD, I. and THACORE, V.R., 1963. Amphetamine and phenmetrazine addiction— Physiological abnormalities in the abstinence syndrome. *Brit. Med. J.* 2, 427.

PHARMACEUTICAL JOURNAL, 1937. 20th June, 1937.

PHARMACY AND POISONS ACT, 1933. HMSO.

SCOTT, P.D. and WILLCOX, D.R.C., 1965. Delinquency and the amphetamines. *Brit. J. Psychiat.* 111, 865.

SHARPLEY, Anne, 1964. *Evening Standard.* 3—6th February, 1964.

WILSON, C.W.M. and BEACON, S., 1964. An investigation in the habituating properties of an amphetamine-barbiturate mixture. *Brit. J. Addict.* 60, 81.

CHAPTER 12
NON-MEDICAL USE OF HYPNOTICS
AND TRANQUILLISERS

HISTORIC OVERVIEW

Barbiturates were introduced into clinical practice in 1903 (Department of Health and Social Security, 1970). They were first discussed in Great Britain at a meeting of the British Medical Association in 1905 (Glatt, 1962) and were proclaimed an excellent drug. The drug became widely used for insomnia, disturbances due to anxiety, worry, tension, depression and other conditions requiring sedative action. Glatt (1962) traces the history of 'the battle of the barbiturates' from 1905 to 1960 along with changes in the consumption of barbiturates in medical practice and all data available on barbiturate poisoning and habituation up to 1960. The danger of habituation was pointed out by Wilcox in 1913 and has subsequently been confirmed. The evidence of Glatt shows that dependence on barbiturates is not uncommon and it has been calculated that barbiturates account for the most widespread dependence to any drug in Great Britain save perhaps cigarettes. (Bewley, 1966).

The data on prescription of barbiturate and non-barbiturate hypnotics is shown in Chapter 6 and the increasing use of hypnotic drugs has given rise to concern about self poisoning and dependence (British Medical Journal, 1968).

THE EXTENT OF MISUSE AND CHARACTERISTICS OF
SELECTED POPULATIONS

Two studies of barbiturate prescribing in general practice allow some estimates of the extent of dependence on barbiturates by patients who are receiving legitimate prescriptions. Adams et al (1966) investigated a London general practice of 10,000 patients during an eight week period. Four per cent of the patients received prescriptions for barbiturates and 58% of those had been taking barbiturates for more than one year. There were three and a half times as many female as male patients taking the barbiturates and the majority of patients were aged 40 and older.

Johnson and Clift (1968) studied an industrial general practice in the north of England. Ninety-seven patients (1.3% of the practice) were receiving repeat prescriptions for hypnotics (74 barbiturate type, 23 non-barbiturate type). While only two were described as severely dependent, only four patients were able to discontinue their hypnotic drug, which suggests that the remaining 91 should be called mildly dependent or perhaps 'reliant'. They had been taking hypnotics for a mean of 5.6 years. In this study as well, the patients were predominantly female and in the older age groups (mean 62.7 years) with an excess of widows. Both studies would indicate that more than one million adults may consume hypnotics but extrapolation from these samples, which may not be representative of the general population, would be dangerous. Bewley (1966) estimated that 100,000 persons might be dependent on barbiturates and 500,000 were using them regularly without dependence.

Glatt (1962) cites numerous case studies and reports on small groups of patients in the older age groups abusing barbiturate-like drugs. There is also increasing evidence of hypnotic drug abuse among younger aged persons. Informal reports from social workers, hospitals, police and drug users themselves suggest that there has been an increase in the abuse of hypnotic drugs. There is an impression that sedatives are partly replacing amphetamines as a drug of abuse, particularly in the south of England. One such south of England town has reported a change in the drug of choice from Mandrax brand of methaqualone in 1968, to barbiturates in 1969 based on cases known to the police and of younger persons admitted to casualty wards of local hospitals.

In the course of investigations on younger drug users, several studies have indicated the increasing use of hypnotic drugs. Bewley (1965) reported that five of 33 heroin addicts seen in 1963 and 1964 were taking barbiturate-like drugs. Bewley and Ben-Arie (1968) studied 100 consecutive heroin dependent patients and subsequent morbidity from October 1964 to December 1966. They found that 40 of the 100 had used barbiturates. Camps (1968) investigating the cause of death in cases of drug dependency found that in the analysis of post mortem specimens, 31% had traces of barbiturates. James (1969) in a study of 50 heroin addicts admitted to Brixton Prison during the summer of 1967 showed that 66% admitted to regular or occasional concurrent use of barbiturates with opiates. Hawks et al (1969) when studying methylamphetamine abuse found that 53% of the methylamphetamine users had used sedatives and tranquillisers. Stimson and Ogborne (1970) in their study of a random sample of patients prescribed heroin at London treatment centres found that 103 of 108 subjects reported the use of sedatives at some time, and that 75% had used them in the month prior to interview.

A study by the Addiction Research Unit (Mitcheson et al, 1970) specifically concentrated on sedative abuse by heroin addicts. Sixty-two of 65 persons interviewed had taken barbiturates, 52 of these had injected the drug. Of the 40 who had received sedative drugs on prescription, 29 had received prescriptions under the National Health Service and 18 had obtained private prescriptions. In that sample, three-quarters of the subjects had taken barbiturates daily at one time and just over half had taken Mandrax daily at one time previous to interview. Concern with the abuse of hypnotics such as Mandrax has also been voiced by de Alarcon (1969), among others.

The increasing prevalence of sedative abuse among the younger age groups reflects the general trend to poly-drug abuse in Great Britain. The restriction of heroin and cocaine to specific treatment centres (see Chapter 13) seems in part to have caused young drug abusers to try a variety of other drugs for pleasure. As with amphetamines (see Chapter 11), there is an increasing tendency for hypnotic drugs to be injected rather than taken orally.

The Advisory Committee on Drug Dependence is presently considering barbiturates and sedatives and their report is expected within the next year.

CONSEQUENCES OF THE ABUSE OF BARBITURATES AND HYPNOTICS

The principle dangers arising from the abuse of barbiturates are dependence and self-poisoning. Barbiturates are physically addictive and tolerance does occur over time. The addictive properties of the barbiturates are less severe than morphine-type drugs, and the non-barbiturate type of hypnotics carry less risk.

The characteristics of dependence to hypnotics and sedatives have been reported by Glatt (1962) and Oswald (1970), among others.

Aside from dependence problems, barbiturate and barbiturate-like drugs are often involved in self-poisoning. The total number of barbiturate deaths in 1967 (2048) is a twofold increase from the 1960 figures, a fivefold increase from 1950 figures and 25 times the number of deaths from barbitures in 1940. This annual figure would indicate that almost 40 people are dying each week from accidental or deliberate overdose from barbiturates. There has been little change in the overall suicide rate since 1940, but there has been this sharp rise in barbiturates as a means of suicide. The barbiturate mortality rates among hospital admissions has been calculated by Locket (1957) as up to 7 or 8% (Glatt, 1962). Below is the age breakdown of deaths from barbituric acid or derivatives in 1967.

Table 12−1.   Deaths by Barbituric Acid and Derivatives, 1967.

Ages at death	Male	Female	Ages at death	Male	Female
All ages	802	1,246	40−	91	135
0−	−	−	45−	91	132
1−	−	−	50−	86	126
5−	−	−	55−	98	138
10−	−	−	60−	96	144
15−	14	18	65−	76	127
20−	33	40	70−	42	110
25−	38	35	75−	29	68
30−	40	60	80−	9	37
35−	53	62	85 and over	5	14

Source: Registrar General, 1967. HMSO, London.

Matthew et al (1969) have reported on the organisation of a poisoning treatment centre in Edinburgh. Between 1963 and 1968 the number of admission to the centre has doubled. In 1968 there were 1067 cases admitted with the following drugs involved:

Barbiturates	26%
Aspirin preparations	14%
Minor tranquillisers	12%
Mandrax preparations	10%
Other drugs	38%

(Matthew et al, 1969).

REFERENCES

ADAMS B.G. and HORDER E.J., HORDER J.P., MODELL M., STEEN C.A., WIGG J.W., 1966.
Patients receiving barbiturates in an urban general practice. J.Coll.Gen.Practit. 12, 24.

BEWLEY T.H., 1965. Heroin and cocaine addiction. *Lancet.* i, 808.

BEWLEY T.H., 1966. Recent changes in the pattern of drug abuse in the United Kingdom.
Bull.Narcot. 18(4), 1.

BEWLEY T.H. and BEN-ARIE O., 1968. Study of 100 consecutive in-patients. *Brit.Med.J.*
1, 727.

BRITISH MEDICAL JOURNAL, 1968. Current Practice–Today's Drugs. *Brit.Med.J.* 2, 409.

CAMPS F.E., 1968. Investigation of the cause of death in cases of drug dependency. In *Lectures
Presented at the International Conference on Drug Dependence.* OPTAT, Quebec.

de ALARCON R., 1969. Letter in *Brit. Med. J.* 1, 319.

DEPARTMENT OF HEALTH AND SOCIAL SECURITY, 1970. *Amphetamines, Barbiturates,
LSD and Cannabis, Their Use and Misuse.* Reports on Public Health and Medical Subjects,
No. 124. HMSO, London.

GLATT M.M., 1962. The abuse of barbiturates in the United Kingdom. *Bull.Narcot.* 14(2), 19.

HAWKS, D., MITCHESON M., OGBORNE A. and EDWARDS G., 1969. Abuse of methylamphetamine. *Brit.Med.J.* 2, 715.

JAMES I.P., 1969. Delinquency and heroin addiction in Britain. *Brit.J.Crim.* 9, 108.

JOHNSON J. and CLIFT A.D., 1968. Dependence on hypnotic drugs in general practice.
Brit.Med.J. 4, 613.

LOCKET S., 1957. The abuse of barbiturates. *Brit.J.Addict.* 53, 105.

MATTHEW H., PROUDFOOT A.T., BROWN S.S. and AITKEN R.C.B., 1969. Acute poisoning:
organisation and workload of a treatment centre. *Brit.Med.J.* 3, 489.

MITCHESON M., DAVIDSON J., HAWKS D., HITCHINS L. and MALONE S., 1970.
Sedative abuse by heroin addicts. *Lancet.* i, 606.

OSWALD I., 1970. Dependence upon hypnotic and sedative drugs. *Brit.J.Hosp.Med.* 4, 168.

REGISTRAR GENERAL, 1968. *Statistical Review of England and Wales for the Year 1967.*
HMSO, London.

STIMSON G.V. and OGBORNE A., 1970. Survey of addicts prescribed heroin at London
clinics. *Lancet.* i, 1163.

CHAPTER 13

THE NON-MEDICAL USE OF OPIATES

AN OVERVIEW OF OPIATE USE IN GREAT BRITAIN

Opiate drugs were abused in Great Britain as early as 1600 and accounts of addiction to opium and laudanum were widely publicised in the 19th century (Laurence, 1966). Morphine was derived from opium in the 1830's and heroin, synthesised in 1874 at St. Mary's Hospital, London, was introduced into clinical practice in 1898 as a cure for morphine addiction (Laurence, 1966). Since that time more than one hundred opiate preparations have been produced. The first Dangerous Drugs Act, restricting the use of opiate substances and cocaine, was introduced in 1920.

The pattern of opiate abuse in this century was relatively stable up to 1950. Opium was only rarely abused in Britain and then mostly by persons of Chinese origin (Spear, 1969).

'By the end of the Second World War the Dangerous Drugs Acts had been in operation for nearly 25 years and during this time there had been no evidence of widespread abuse of Dangerous Drugs in this country, nor any reason to suppose that the statistics relating to offences involving Dangerous Drugs (see Table 13–1) and the number of addicts coming to the notice of the Home Office (see Table 13–2), did not provide a fairly accurate picture of the extent and nature of drug abuse in the United Kingdom.' (Spear, 1969).

The number of known addicts varied between 300 and 700. Most of the persons who came to notice were addicted to opiates in the course of medical treatment (therapeutic addicts). They tended to be middle aged and female with the drug involved usually morphine (see Table 13–3). An appreciable proportion of the known addicts were members of the medical profession or from associated occupations, such as chemists or nurses (professional addicts).

In the mid-1950's there was an increase of persons known to be addicts in the United Kingdom and a marked change in the characteristics of those addicts (Bewley, 1965). The new opiate users tended to be younger and include a higher percentage of males with heroin as the drug of choice, rather than morphine (see Tables 13–2, 13–3, 13–4). There were indications that other drugs were being abused as well by these same young people. The new users were motivated to start taking heroin for its own intrinsic pleasure rather than in the course of a medical treatment (non-therapeutic addicts). Opiate abuse of a non-therapeutic origin previously confined to London began to spread to the provinces (Hawks, 1970).

Spear (1969) has examined the 'first clues' surrounding the change in the general pattern of drug abuse in Great Britain. The change seems traceable to a young man trafficking drugs in London who had broken into a hospital dispensary and stolen a large quantity of morphine, cocaine and heroin in 1951. By 1964, 63 addicts 'who could not be linked directly with (this young man), but who were known to be close associates of some of his original "customers" ', had come to the notice of the Home Office. It appears there was little or no heroin circulating in the West End of London until this man appeared with the stolen supplies, and this 'coincided with a scarcity of cannabis . . . with the result that many persons who had been smoking cannabis began to use heroin and cocaine as substitutes'. (Spear, 1969). The impact of this change in opiate use was not felt until the early 1960's, when large numbers of non-therapeutic heroin addicts came to notice (see Table 13–2, 13–3, 13–4).

In 1968 specialised treatment centres for drug addicts were opened. Since that time there has been an increase in the use of methadone with a corresponding decrease in heroin use. The use of sedatives has become widespread among addicts and there is a trend for many drugs to be abused concurrently by addicts (de Alarcon, 1970; Hawks et al, 1969; Bewley, 1970).

GOVERNMENT COMMITTEES ON DRUG ADDICTION IN THE UNITED KINGDOM

Since the enactment of the Dangerous Drugs Acts in 1920, there have been three major Committee reports on drugs addiction—the Departmental Committee on Morphine and Heroin Addiction (the Rolleston Committee) 1926, the Report of the Interdepartmental Committee on Drug Addiction, 1961 and the Second Report of the Interdepartmental Committee on Drug Addiction 1965 (The Brain Committees).

The Rolleston Committee considered the circumstances, if any, in which morphine and heroin should be supplied to addicts by the medical profession and to consider any precautions that might be necessary with such a policy. Their recommendations formed the basis of the British approach to addiction until the first fundamental changes in the Dangerous Drugs Acts were made in 1967 (see Chapter 4). Essentially, the Committee found that opiate addiction was a rare condition and should be considered as an illness rather than 'a mere form of vicious indulgence'. The medical profession should be free to administer heroin or morphine to:

'(a)   those who are undergoing treatment for cure of the addiction by the gradual withdrawal method';

'(b)   persons for whom, after every effort has been made for the cure of the addiction, the drug cannot be withdrawn, either because:'

'(i)   Complete withdrawal produces serious symptoms which cannot be satisfactorily treated under the ordinary conditions of private practice; or'

'(ii)   the patient, while capable of leading a useful and fairly normal life so long as he takes a certain non-progressive quantity, usually small, of the drug of addiction ceases to be able to do so when the regular allowance is withdrawn.' (Departmental Committee on Morphine and Heroin Addiction, 1926).

The right of practitioners to prescribe opiates for addicts who lead 'a useful and fairly normal life' has been the mainstay of British policy.

In 1961 the Interdepartmental Committee on Drug Addiction (the first Brain Committee) reported on their consideration of the Rolleston Committee recommendations in the light of more recent developments. It was the first official review of the 1926 findings in 35 years. The Committee found that the problem of opiate abuse was 'still very small' and despite the use of new synthetic opiates there was 'no cause to fear that any real increase (in opiate use) is at present occurring'. Further, the illicit use of opiates was said to be 'almost negligible'. The Committee recommended that addiction should be regarded as a medical condition requiring treatment and not a form of criminal behaviour, that there were no grounds for compulsory treatment of addiction, that a system of registration of addicts would not be desirable, and that statutory control in addition to existing legislation was unnecessary (Interdepartmental Committee on Drug Addiction, 1961).

By 1965, when the Second Report of the Interdepartmental Committee on Drug Addiction (the second Brain Committee) was published, the situation had altered considerably. There had been an alarming increase in the total number of addicts to Dangerous Drugs, especially by persons in the younger age group taking heroin for non-therapeutic reasons (see Tables 13–2, 13–3, 13–4). The Committee felt that the supply for these new addicts was not imported or adulterated heroin, but rather 'that the major source of supply has been the activity of a very few doctors who have prescribed excessively for addicts.' This over-prescription allowed excess heroin to become available in the illicit market.

The Committee recommended three basic changes which were later incorporated in the Dangerous Drugs Act 1967 and subsequent regulations.

(i)   A system for the notification of addicts should be established whereby it would be the statutory duty of a medical practitioner to notify to a central authority any addict he might deal with professionally.

(ii)   Specialised treatment centres should be established, especially in London, for the treatment of addiction.

(iii) Statutory controls should be introduced to confine to doctors on the staff of the proposed treatment centres, the prescribing of *heroin* and *cocaine* to drug addicts. (Interdepartmental Committee on Drug Addiction, 1965).

The recommendation, that general practitioners no longer had the right to supply heroin and cocaine to addicts, led to a fundamental change of approach 41 years after the Rolleston Committee.

PREVALENCE OF OPIATE ABUSE IN THE UNITED KINGDOM

Data relating to the prevalence of opiate abuse in Britain has been compiled by the Home Office. Offences committed under the Dangerous Drugs Acts have been recorded since their enactment in 1920 (see Table 13–1).

The number of addicts who came to the notice of the Home Office between 1935 and 1968 is set out in (Table 13–2). Prior to the introduction of the Dangerous Drugs (Notification of Addicts) Regulations, which came into force on 22nd February, 1968 (see Chapter 4), there was no statutory notification of opiate users. Previously, the figures were compiled from information received through the routine inspection of pharmacists' records and the voluntary information supplied by doctors, police, prison sources and hospitals.

Table 13—1.   Drug Offences* for Opium and Manufactured Drugs** 1921—1969.

Year	Opium	Manufactured drugs	Year	Opium	Manufactured drugs
1921	184	67	1945	206	20
1922	94	110	1946	65	27
1923	167	128	1947	76	65
1924	48	50	1948	78	48
1925	35	33	1949	52	56
1926	50	45	1950	41	42
1927	27	33	1951	64	47
1928	41	21	1952	62	48
1929	39	31	1953	47	44
1930	16	48	1954	28	47
1931	26	40	1955	17	37
1932	37	43	1956	12	37
1933	17	32	1957	9	30
1934	39	33	1958	8	41
1935	13	33	1959	18	26
1936	17	35	1960	15	28
1937	9	27	1961	15	61
1938	6	35	1962	16	71
1939	13	36	1963	20	63
1940	14	37	1964	14	101
1941	201	25	1965	13	128
1942	199	27	1966	36	242
1943	147	40	1967	58	573
1944	256	32	1968	73	1099
			1969	53	1359

* From 1921—1953 inclusive figures relate to prosecutions.
From 1954 figures relate to convictions.
** Manufactured drugs are essentially manufactured opiates (e.g. heroin, pethidine, etc.) and cocaine.

Source: Spear, H.B. The growth of heroin addiction in the United Kingdom. *Brit.J.Addict.* 64, 245. 1969.

Table 13–2. Number of Known Addicts, Sex, Origin and Drugs Used. 1935–1968.

Year	No. of known addicts	Sex		Origin*			Drugs used**					Profession-al Addicts
		M	F	T	N/T	UK	Morphine	Heroin	Cocaine	Pethidine	Methadone	
1935	700 approx.				This information was not collected prior to 1958 (except for heroin addicts).		Exact numbers not available, but the proportion of addicts using morphine has varied from approx. 90% in 1935 to 60–67% in 1950–54.	Exact numbers not available, but the proportion of addicts using heroin has varied from 5% in 1935 to 19% in 1952.	Exact numbers not available, but less than 10% of the addicts used cocaine.	From 1948 to 1954 the proportion of addicts using pethidine varied between 12–19%.	Exact numbers not available except in 1949 and 1951, when there were 2 and 3 respectively.	120 approx.
1936	616	313	300									147
1937	620	300	320									140
1938	519	246	273									143
1939	534	269	265									131
1940	503	251	254									90
1941	503	252	251									91
1942	524	275	249									98
1943	541	280	261									94
1944	559	185	274									93
1945	367	144	223									80
1946	369	144	225									79
1947	383	164	219									87
1948	395	198	197									119
1949	326	164	162									100
1950	306	158	148									95
1951	301	153	148									77
1952	297	153	144									75
1953	290	149	141									71
1954	317	148	169					57				72
1955	335	159	176				179	54	6	64	21	86***
1956	333	163	170				176	53	6	64	20	99
1957	359	174	185				178	66	16	92	31	88
1958	442	197	245	349	68	25	205	62	25	117	47	74
1959	454	196	258	344	98	12	204	68	30	116	60	68
1960	437	195	242	309	122	6	177	94	52	98	68	63
1961	470	223	247	293	159	18	168	132	84	105	59	61
1962	532	262	270	312	212	8	157	175	112	112	54	57
1963	635	339	296	355	270	10	172	237	171	128	59	56
1964	753	409	344	368	372	13	171	342	211	128	62	58
1965	927	558	369	344	580	3	160	521	311	102	72	45
1966	1349	886	463	351	982	16	157	899	441	123	156	54
1967	1729	1262	467	313	1385	31	158	1299	462	112	243	56
1968	2782	2161	621	306	2420	56	198	2240	564	120	486	43

*The origin of addiction; T = therapeutic, N/T = non-therapeutic, UK = unknown.
**Alone or in combination with other drugs.
***Nurses included in 'professional' for first time; hitherto they had been included in 'other.'

Source: Spear, H.B. The growth of heroin addiction in the United Kingdom. *British Journal of Addiction.* 64, 245. 1969.

The annual figures would not include addicts who were able to obtain their supplies entirely from illicit sources but, on the other hand, it is impossible to know if all persons notified would be considered addicted by a medical practitioner. Only since 1968 was a medical opinion necessary for a person to be notified as an addict. The Home Office has also instituted a new method of reporting the 1969 figures for known addicts which will be discussed below.

The origin of heroin addicts and the age structure of addicts are set out below.

Table 13—3.   Number and Origin of all Heroin Addicts and of New Heroin Addicts 1945—1968.

Year	Total no. of heroin addicts	Thera- peutic	Non- thera- peutic	Unknown	No. of new heroin addicts in year	Thera- peutic	Non- thera- peutic	Unknown
1945					1	1	–	–
1946					1	–	1	–
1947					3	–	3	–
1948					4	1	3	–
1949			Not available		3	1	2	–
1950					3	1	1	1
1951					1	–	1	–
1952					8	3	5	–
1953					4	–	4	–
1954	57	20	37	–	16	2	14	–
1955	54	18	36	–	10	1	9	–
1956	53	17	36	–	10	1	9	–
1957	66	21	45	–	7	2	5	–
1958	62	19	43	–	11	3	8	–
1959	68	21	47	–	11	2	9	–
1960	94	22	72	–	24	1	23	–
1961	132	20	112	–	56	2	54	–
1962	175	18	157	–	72	–	72	–
1963	237	15	222	–	90	–	90	–
1964	342	13	329	–	162	2	160	–
1965	521	12	509	–	259	1	258	–
1966	899	13	885	1	522	3	518	1
1967	1299	9	1290	–	745	–	745	–
1968	2240	8	2232	–	1306	2	1304	–

Source: H.B. Spear. The Growth of Heroin Addiction in the United Kingdom. *Brit.J.Addict.* 64, 245. 1969.

The statistics of drug addiction in the United Kingdom for 1969 were recorded in new form.

'Refinement in the procedures for recording particulars of drug addicts notified to the Home Office has enabled the end of year "population" to be stated for the first time. In previous years the statistics (as explained at the time of publication and in Parliamentary statements) were based on the total number of addicts who actively came to notice from *beginning to end* of a calendar year. Cumulative figures of that kind necessarily included addicts who by reason of imprisonment, cure, disappearance or death have ceased by the year's end to use drugs, but they were not separately accounted for.'

Table 13—4.   Ages of Addicts known to the Home Office. 1959—1968.

Age	1959	1960	1961	1962	1963	1964	1965	1966	1967	1968
Under 20										
All drugs	–	1	2	3	17	40	145	329	395	764
(heroin)	–	(1)	(2)	(3)	(17)	(40)	(134)	(317)	(381)	(709)
20–34										
All drugs	50	62	94	132	184	257	347	558	906	1530
(heroin)	(35)	(52)	(87)	(126)	(162)	(219)	(319)	(479)	(827)	(1390)
35–49										
All drugs	92	91	95	107	128	138	134	162	142	146
(heroin)	(7)	(14)	(19)	(24)	(38)	(61)	(52)	(83)	(66)	(78)
50 and over										
All drugs	278	267	272	274	298	311	291	286	279	260
(heroin)	(26)	(27)	(24)	(22)	(20)	(22)	(16)	(20)	(24)	(20)
Age unknown	34	16	7	16	8	7	10	14	7	82

*Precise details of age groupings were not included in Annual Reports until 1959.

Source: Spear, H.B. The growth of heroin addiction in the United Kingdom. *British Journal of Addiction.* 64, 245. 1969.

'For purposes of comparison, the "balance sheet" for 1968 and 1969 may be expressed as follows'—

1968
'During this year 2,782 addicts actively came to notice—(10 notifications were later found to be invalid)—but by the end of the year 61 of them had died and there was no evidence that 965 were then receiving drugs at all'.

1969
'The new method of analysis shows that altogether 2,881 addicts actively came to notice during the year. The year-end total was determined as follows'—

ADDICTS known to be receiving drugs at 1.1.69:		1,746
Less number not known to be receiving drugs at 31.12.69:		752
		994
NEW addicts notified during 1969:	1,135	
Less number not known to be receiving drugs at 31.12.69:	663	472
		1,466 '

(Home Office. *Press Notice.* 18th September, 1970)

The figures above indicate that 58% of the new addicts notified in 1969 did not appear as addicts receiving narcotic drugs at the end of the year and that 44% of the addicts receiving narcotic drugs on 1st January, 1969 do not appear as known addicts on 31st December, 1969.

Data based on statutory notification under the Dangerous Drugs (Supply to Addicts) Regulations, 1968 and examination of prescription records indicates that the drugs received by the 1,466 known addicts on 31st December, 1969 were as follows:

'1011 addicts receiving methadone
       (of whom 295 were also receiving heroin);

  204 addicts receiving heroin
       (either alone or in combination with drugs other than methadone);

  251 addicts receiving drugs other than methadone or heroin
       (for the main part, morphine or pethidine), whose addiction is mostly of
       therapeutic origin.'

(Home Office. *Press Notice.* 18th September, 1970).

THE PREVALENCE AND SPREAD OF HEROIN USE IN SELECTED COMMUNITIES

In addition to the Home Office statistics on drug addiction in the United Kingdom, there have been several studies of heroin use in smaller geographic areas. A series of investigations in Crawley New Town were undertaken to discover if there was an undetected pool of heroin users in the community and to establish methods for early detection of such cases (Rathod, de Alarcon and Thomson, 1967; de Alarcon and Rathod, 1968; de Alarcon, Rathod and Thomson, 1969). Crawley had a population of 62,130 in 1966 with 41% of the population under 20 years of age. Information about young heroin users in the town was gathered from the Probation Service, police and heroin users who were already known. In addition, surveys of hepatitis in the community and of admissions to the local casualty department for overdoses of stimulants or hypnotics were initiated. These screening methods yielded 98 names which were then classified into 50 confirmed heroin users, 5 probable heroin users, 37 suspected heroin users and 6 non-users. Only 8 of the confirmed cases had been first detected by the normal channel of general practitioner referral to a hospital. The most productive sources for discovering young heroin users were the known addicts and the jaundice survey (de Alarcon and Rathod, 1968). On the basis of these figures, a one year prevalence rate for 1967 in the age group 15–20 was 8.5 per 1,000 of the population. If only cases known to the Home Office had been used in calculating an addiction rate the comparable figure would have been 1.4 per 1,000.

De Alarcon (1969) has reported detailed data on the spread of heroin use in Crawley New Town. He summarises his findings as follows:

'(i)   1962–1965; a small number of Crawley youngsters are initiated in other towns;
(ii)   first half of 1966; a nucleus of established heroin users, initiated by the former, develops in Crawley;
(iii)   second semester 1966–first semester 1967; heroin abuse spreads explosively in the town.'
(De Alarcon, 1969).

A comparable study was reported by Kosviner et al (1968) in an unidentified provincial town. The town was described as compact and long-established, with a population of under 100,000. It had an unusually high proportion of middle-class people and had a university and technical college. The aim of the survey was to find any person in the town who had been using heroin, in any dosage, at the time of the study or in the previous three months. Heroin users were traced through other users already known to the investigators. In addition, official records and medical sources were consulted to alert the investigators to people who might possibly be using heroin. Thir†y-seven heroin users were found, including 17 daily users, 13 irregular users (less than daily) and seven persons who were institutionalised at the time of the study, but were known to have taken heroin in the previous three months. All the medical and official agencies that had been consulted under estimated the extent of heroin use in the town. Subsequent follow-up studies (Zacune et al, 1969; Hitchins et al, 1971) have extended the work to 63 known opiate users in the town.

Only a small number of the known users were receiving heroin on prescription at this time of the study, and the rest generally obtained their supplies by different users going to London each week to buy heroin from registered addicts there. There was no evidence of anyone 'pushing' heroin, but rather there seemed to be a co-operative system for getting supplies (Kosviner et al, 1968). The use of heroin seemed to spread through existing friendship groups, but this pattern has been altered by the establishment of a treatment clinic in the town (Zacune et al, 1969).

CHARACTERISTICS OF SELECTED POPULATIONS

Nationality

The great majority of heroin addicts in the United Kingdom are of British nationality. Bewley (1965) reported in a review of all new cases of heroin addiction known between 1955–1964 that 77% (348) were British, 20% (88) Canadian, American, Australian or New Zealander and only 3% (14) were of other nationalities. The Canadians form the largest non-British group of heroin addicts. Ninety-one Canadian heroin addicts have come to Great Britain since 1959 (Spear, 1971) and their social functioning in Canada and Great Britain has been reported by Zacune (1971).

A study of 519 persons known to the Home Office as addicts in 1965 showed that 83% were of British nationality (Hancock and Hawks, 1970). In a representative sample of addicts being prescribed heroin at London treatment clinics, 79% came from England, Wales or Scotland, 12% from Northern or Southern Ireland and 9% from outside the British Isle, including three Americans and four Canadians (Stimson and Ogborne, 1970a). Studies of largely non-notified opiate users have confirmed that heroin use is largely a problem of the white, indigenous British population (de Alarcon and Rathod, 1968; Zacune et al, 1969; Murphy, 1969).

Age

The number of known addicts in the younger age groups has been increasing since 1960 (see Table 13–4). While there were no addicts under the age of 20 in 1959, by 1968 they constituted 27% of the total of known addicts. Stimson and Ogborne (1970a) found 69% of their London clinics sample to be aged 25 and under.

Sex

In 1958 the ratio of male to female addicts known to the Home Office was 1:1.2. By 1968 the ratio was 3.6 male to 1 female, reflecting the consistent trend in the 1960's of males to become increasingly predominant in the use of heroin.

Socio-Economic Status

There have been very few systematic studies into the socio-economic status of addicts and most investigators have reported the addict's own best or present employment, though given the youthfulness of the addict population these provide unreliable indices (Hawks, 1970). Early studies (Hewetson and Ollendorf, 1964; Glatt et al, 1967) indicated that all social classes were represented among the addicts. De Alarcon and Rathod (1968) found no indication that their addicts had a different social background from many of the families in the Crawley area.

Consideration of the addicts' fathers' socio-economic status in the study of a provincial town (Kosviner et al, 1968) and in a representative sample of heroin addicts in treatment clinics (Stimson and Ogborne, 1970b) indicated that the professional workers, employers and managers were over-represented in comparison with control populations. The table below gives the socio-economic groups of addicts based on their own present or last occupation and their father's occupation.

Table 13—5.   Socio-Economic Group of Addicts Prescribed Heroin at London Treatment Centres and of Addicts' Father

Addict's Classification	Socio-economic Groups *	Subject's occupation no.	%	Population statistics **	Father's occupation no.	%	Population statistics *** %
Professional workers	3, 4	2	1.6	5.6	10	7.8	4.5
Employers and managers	1, 2, 13	10	7.8	12.0	23	18.0	10.6
Foremen, skilled manual workers & own account workers (other than professional)	8, 9, 12, 14	12	9.4	35.0	36	28.1	39.4
Non-manual workers	5, 6	43	33.6	23.5	20	15.6	17.1
Personal service workers, semi-skilled manual workers and agricultural workers	7, 10, 15	33	25.8	14.5	10	7.8	18.0
Unskilled manual workers	11	23	18.0	8.0	15	11.7	8.3
Members of armed forces and persons with inadequately described occupations	16, 17	1	0.8	1.3	3	2.4	3.0
Not known	–	4	3.1	–	11	8.6	–
Total:	–	128	–	–	128	–	–

*Registrar General Classification of Occupation, 1966.
**Economically active males, Greater London Area, Sample Census, 1966.
***Economically active males, Great Britain, Sample Census, 1966.

Source: Stimson, G.V. and Ogborne A. A survey of a representative sample of addicts prescribed heroin at London clinics. *Bulletin of Narcotics.* 22(4), 13. 1970.

Education

When educated has been investigated, addicts do not seem to lack in educational opportunity compared with the rest of the population. Stimson and Ogborne (1970b) reported 24% of their sample attended grammar or public school and Kosviner et al (1968) reported that 57% of their sample attended grammar, public or direct grant schools. James (1969) found in a prison sample of heroin users that 28% had obtained places in grammar schools, compared with 6% of a prison control group matched for age.

While there is some evidence for poor school performance and a tendency for addicts to 'drop-out' of school (Kosviner et al, 1968; James, 1969), Murphy (1969) reported no difference between his sample of drug takers and a control group. Bewley and Ben Arie (1968) did not find any difference in school achievements between their sample of hospital in-patient addicts and the general population.

EMPLOYMENT, SOURCES OF INCOME AND RESIDENCE

Heroin addicts have a fairly high rate of unemployment. In the London clinic sample 40% were employed full-time (Stimson and Ogborne, 1970a) and in other studies between 25% and 38% of the addicts were in full-time employment (Kosviner et al, 1968; Hitchins et al, 1971; Murphy, 1969).

Roughly half of any sample of heroin users would be living with their parents, and to some extent supported by them (Hawks, 1970). However, more residential instability may be found in prison populations and D'Orban (1970) found 53% of the female prisoners in his sample said they were sleeping rough or had no fixed address.

The ways in which a representative sample of London clinic patients support themselves are set out below.

Table 13—6.   Types of Support in last month reported by London Addicts at London Treatment Centres.

	No.	%
Own income only	29	26
Own income plus social security only	*17	15
Social security only	8	7
Own income plus social security plus hustling** and/or illicit	12	11
Social security plus hustling and/or illicit	26	23
Hustling only	7	6
Hustling and illicit only	12	11

*Own income and social security were not necessarily concurrent for these people but both sources were used during the month before interview.

**'Hustling' means borrowing, selling, money from friends, begging, pawning and gambling.

Source: Stimson G.V. and Ogborne A. A survey of a representative sample of addicts prescribed heroin at London clinics. *Bull.Narcot.* 22 (4), 13. 1970.

Criminality

Approximately half the known addicts in Great Britain committed criminal offences before receiving opiates on prescription (Hawks, 1970) and several studies have shown that a proportion of notified addicts continue to commit offences, often of a minor nature, which are not obviously related to obtaining or being in possession of drugs (James, 1969; Willis, 1969; Kosviner et al, 1968; Zacune et al, 1969; Stimson and Ogborne, 1970b; Mitcheson et al, 1970).

James (1969) in a study of 50 addicts in prison found that 44% had appeared before a juvenile court, and 76% had been convicted by a court before addiction. In the provincial town studies (Kosviner et al, 1968; Zacune et al, 1969), the original sample had only petty non-drug offences which were all committed before trying heroin, but in subsequent samples the newer users had more serious delinquency records. The users with more convictions before and after their drug use were on the whole more working class and had spent less time in formal education than the original users. In the London clinic sample (Stimson and Ogborne, 1970b) 79% admitted to a conviction of some sort and 51% had convictions for a non-drug offence before their first use of heroin.

Drug Use

Heroin addicts are known to use a wide range of drugs concurrently with opiates. Hicks (1969) found that 63% of the addicts referred to a London treatment centre took heroin in combination with another drug. The increasing abuse of sedatives by heroin addicts has been documented (Bewley and Ben Arie 1968; Camps, 1969; James, 1967; Mitcheson et al, 1970). In addition, the use of amphetamines, cannabis and cocaine concurrently with heroin have been noted (Bewley, 1966; Kosviner et al, 1968; Zacune et al, 1969; Murphy, 1969).

The table below illustrates the use of other drugs by the representative sample of heroin users at London treatment centres.

Table 13—7.   Drug Use by Heroin Addicts at London Treatment Centres (N=111).

Drug	In last month: Prescribed		In last month: Used		Ever used	
	No.	%	No.	%	No.	%
Methadone	91	82	95	86	107	97
Other opiates (e.g. morphine, opium, pethidine)	0	0	25	22		
Amphetamine, amphetamine/barbiturate mixtures, and other stimulants	14	13	49	44	109	98
Sedatives and hypnotics	51	46	83	75	103	95*
Tranquillisers	5	4	19	17	90	81
Cocaine	14	13	32	29	104	94
Cannabis	0	0	68	61	111	100
Psychedelics	0	0	13	12	72	65

*N = 108.

Source: Stimson G.V. and Ogborne A. A survey of a representative sample of addicts prescribed heroin at London clinics. Bull.Narcot. 24(3), 13. 1970.

Morbidity and Mortality

Bewley and Ben-Arie (1968) studied 100 male heroin addicts discharged from a London hospital between October 1964 and the end of December, 1966. Of these patients, 39% reported suffering septic complications at some time, 29% reported hepatitis, 21% reported psychosis due to drug use, 17% had suffered overdoses and 12% had other drug related conditions. Most patients admitted were noted to be under-weight and the chances of hepatitis with jaundice were very high in groups of addicts who had shared one another's needles. When following this group for just over two years, the patients were found to have had a further 155 admissions to hospital. By the end of the follow-up 12% were not known to be taking heroin by the Home Office, and these might include some abstinent cases, however, 53% were still using opiates, 21% were in institutions (prisons or hospitals), 12% were dead and 5% out of the country.

Marks and Chapple (1967) found that 80% of liver function tests given to an unselected group of heroin and cocaine users treated at a psychiatric unit showed some abnormality. Bewley, Ben-Arie and Marks (1968) examining 284 in-patients with liver function tests, found that 60% had some degree of liver damage (mild 28.9%, moderate 13.7% severe 17.6%). Where jaundice occurs it is most often attributable to sharing someone else's needle. Stimson and Ogborne (1970) found that only 11% of their sample could be said to use sterile injection practices.

The mortality rate among British heroin users is extremely high. Bewley, Ben-Arie and James (1968) reviewing all addicts first reported to the Home Office between 1947 and 1966 (1272 cases) found 89 deaths among the non-therapeutic addicts and 16 among the therapeutic. They estimated the death rate to be 28 times in excess of the comparable age group in the general population. The mean age of death among non-therapeutic addicts between 1955–1964 was 30.3 years, while in 1965–1968 it had dropped to 24.8 years. James (1967) looked at the period 1955–1964 and found the mortality rate twenty times as high as expected in the general population for male non-therapeutic addicts and a rate five times higher than the general population for females. Gardner (1970a) has investigated the circumstances of 112 deaths of opiate users in the years 1965–1968. Non-suicidal overdose was the major cause of death in these cases with an increasing number of deaths involving methadone (Gardner, 1970a, b).

Bewley, Ben-Arie and James (1968) report suicide and violent death in 22% of the cases; suicidal overdose, accidental overdose, sudden death and septic conditions in 61% and natural causes 17%. These so-called natural causes, however, were almost invariably linked with drug addiction, for example death from the inhalation of vomit during barbiturate withdrawal. Camps (1968) giving data from a preliminary report about investigations into the cause of death in cases of drug dependence in Greater London reports 54% of these deaths due to drug poisoning or overdose, 19% to septicaemia, abscesses, inhalation of vomit, malnutrition or bronchial pneumonia following drug intoxication, and 26% to other causes.

Bewley, Ben-Arie and James (1968) suggest that this extremely high mortality, over twice that of heroin addicts in New York, possibly reflects the high doses taken by United Kingdom addicts and their use of other drugs in combination. James (1967) concludes from similar evidence that the practice of maintaining narcotic addicts on legally supplied drugs substantially increases the mortality risk and that it is not a satisfactory substitute for abstinence programmes.

REFERENCES

BEWLEY T.H., 1965. Heroin addiction in the United Kingdom (1954–1964). *Brit.Med.J.* 2, 1284.
BEWLEY T.H., 1968. Recent changes in the incidence in all types of drug dependence in Great Britain. *Proc.Royal Soc. Med.* 62, 175.
BEWLEY T.H., 1970. An introduction to drug addiction. *Brit.J.Hosp.Med.* 4(2), 150.
BEWLEY T.H. and BEN-ARIE O., 1968. Study of 100 consecutive in-patients. *Brit.Med.J.* 1, 727.
BEWLEY T.H., BEN-ARIE O. and JAMES I.P., 1968. Survey of heroin addicts known to the Home Office. *Brit.Med.J.* 1, 725.
BEWLEY T.H., BEN-ARIE O. and MARKS V., 1968. Relation of hepatitis to self-injection technique. *Brit.Med.J.* 1, 730.
CAMPS F.E., 1968. Investigation of the cause of death in cases of drug dependency. In *Lectures Presented at the International Conference on Drug Dependence.* OPTAT, Quebec.
de ALARCON R., 1969. The spread of heroin abuse in a community. *Bull.Narcot.* 21, 17.
de ALARCON R., 1970. The extent of the drugs problem. In B. McAlhone (Ed.) *WHERE on Drugs: a Parents' Handbook.* Advisory Centre for Education, Cambridge.
de ALARCON R. and RATHOD N., 1968. Prevalence and early detection of heroin abuse. *Brit.Med.J.* 2, 549.
de ALARCON R., RATHOD N.H. and THOMSON I., 1969. Observations on heroin abuse by young people in Crawley New Town. In H. Steinberg (Ed.). *The Scientific Basis of Drug Dependence.* Churchill, London.
d'ORBAN P.T., 1970. Heroin dependency and delinquency in women: a study of heroin addicts in Holloway Prison. *Brit.J.Addict.* 65, 67.
DEPARTMENTAL COMMITTEE ON MORPHINE AND HEROIN ADDICTION (THE ROLLESTON COMMITTEE), 1926. *Report.* H.M.S.O., London.
GARDNER R., 1970a. Deaths in United Kingdom of opoid users 1965–69. *Lancet.* ii, 650.
GARDNER R., 1970b. Methadone use and death by overdosage. *Brit.J.Addict.* 65, 113.
GLATT M.M., PITTMAN D., GILLESPIE D. and HILLS D., 1967. *The Drug Scene in Great Britain: Journey into Loneliness.* Edward Arnold, London.
HANCOCK J. and HAWKS D., 1970. A retrospective study of heroin addicts known to the Home Office in 1965: interim analysis. Unpublished report.
HAWKS D.V., 1970. The epidemiology of drug dependence in the United Kingdom. Bull. Narcot. 22(3), 15.
HAWKS D.V., MITCHESON M., OGBORNE A. and EDWARDS G., 1969. Abuse of methylamphetamine. *Brit.Med.J.* 2, 715.
HICKS R.C., 1969. The management of heroin addiction at a general hospital drug addiction treatment centre. *Brit.J.Addict.* 64, 235.
HITCHINS L., MITCHESON M., ZACUNE J. and HAWKS D., 1971. A two year follow-up of a cohort of opiate users in a provincial town. In press.
HOME OFFICE, 1970. *Press Notice.* Home Office, 18th September, 1970.
INTERDEPARTMENTAL COMMITTEE ON DRUG ADDICTION (THE BRAIN COMMITTEE), 1961. *Drug Addiction.* H.M.S.O., London.
INTERDEPARTMENTAL COMMITTEE ON DRUG ADDICTION (THE BRAIN COMMITTEE), 1965. *Drug Addiction.* H.M.S.O., London.
JAMES I.P., 1967. Suicide and mortality amongst heroin addicts. *Brit.J.Addict.* 62, 391.
JAMES I.P., 1969. Delinquency and heroin addiction in Britain. *Brit.J.Crim.* 9, 108.
KOSVINER A., MITCHESON M., OGBORNE A., MYERS K., STIMSON G., ZACUNE J. and EDWARDS G., 1968. Heroin use in a provincial town. *Lancet.* i, 1189.
LAURENCE D.R., 1966. *Clinical Pharmacology.* Churchill, London.
MARKS V. and CHAPPLE P.A.L., 1967. Hepatic dysfunction in heroin and cocaine users. *Brit.J.Addict.* 62, 189.
MITCHESON M., DAVIDSON J., HAWKS D., HITCHINS L. and MALONE S., 1970. Sedative abuse by heroin addicts. *Lancet.* i, 606.
MURPHY F.W., 1969. Drug abuse in a London suburb. Unpublished report.
RATHOD N., de ALARCON R. and THOMSON I., 1967. Signs of heroin usage selected by drug users and their parents. *Lancet.* ii, 1411.
SPEAR H.B., 1969. The growth of heroin addiction in the United Kingdom. *Brit.J.Addict.* 64, 245.
SPEAR H.B., 1971. The influence of Canadian addicts on heroin addiction in the United Kingdom. In press.
STIMSON G.V. and OGBORNE A., 1970a. Survey of addicts prescribed heroin at London clinics. *Lancet.* i, 1163.

STIMSON G. and OGBORNE A., 1970b. A survey of a representative sample of addicts prescribed heroin at London clinics. *Bull. Narcot.* 22(4), 13.

WILLIS J., 1969. The natural history of drug dependence: some comparative observations on United Kingdom and United States subjects. In H. Steinberg (Ed.). *The Scientific Basis of Drug Dependence.* Churchill, London.

ZACUNE J., 1971. A comparison of Canadian narcotic addicts in Great Britain and Canada. In press.

ZACUNE J., MITCHESON M. and MALONE S., 1969. Heroin use in a provincial town—one year later. *Int.J.Addict.* 4, 557.

CHAPTER 14
POLY-DRUG USE AND ESCALATION

POLY-DRUG USE

The view that drug dependence could be adequately described by reference only to the abuse of discrete psycho-active substances, such as morphine or amphetamine, is no longer tenable. Young drug users in Great Britain are now most commonly multiple drug takers who are likely to experiment with a wide range of psycho-active substances. The patterns of drug experimentation and substitution do not have any logic dictated by the pharmacological effects of drugs. The same person may readily use hallucinogens, stimulant and hypnotic drugs in the same week. This would seem to be determined partly by the desire to enjoy varieties of drug experiences, and partly to be related to what drugs are readily available on the illicit market. When a drug user cannot obtain his drug of choice or enough of that drug, he may supplement his use by what comes to hand. Leech and Jordan (1967) called attention to young drug users in central London who would consume any available pills at the weekends. Various 'fashions' in drug use have occurred, leading to widespread abuse of such drugs as methylamphetamine, barbiturates and methadone (see Chapters 11, 12 and 13 respectively).

The concurrent use of sedatives by heroin addicts has been reported by James (1969) and Mitcheson et al (1970). In the latter work, 95% of addicts had used barbiturates, and in addition:

> 'alcohol, cannabis, heroin and methadone injections had been taken by all patients at least once; amphetamine or amphetamine/barbiturate tablets and methylamphetamine injections by all but one'. (Mitcheson et al, 1970).

The table 14—1 shows the frequency of drug use in that sample.

In the second year follow-up study of a cohort of 63 opiate users in an English provincial town, Hitchins et al (1971) report that in the year 1969, 79% of the sample took heroin, 65% methadone injections, 49% oral methadone, 56% amphetamines, 71% barbiturates and sedatives, and 68% cannabis.

The findings of Stimson and Ogborne (1970) on a representative sample of addicts being prescribed heroin at London treatment centres, are reported in Chapter 13 (see Table 13—7). Hawks et al (1969) in a study of methylamphetamine users analysed the maximum and current intensity of other drug use. The table 14—2 is a summary of their more detailed findings.

Table 14—1.   Drug Use in a Sample of Heroin Addicts.

Drug	Ever used No.	Ever used %	% ever used daily	% ever used weekly	% used in last month	% used daily in last month
Alcohol	65	100	52	34	35	3
Amphetamines and amphetamine/ barbiturate	64	99	57	29	32	19
Cannabis	65	100	77	8	49	12
Cocaine*	50	77	59	8	25	9
Hallucinogens	48	74	8	27	9	0
Heroin	65	100	100	0	91	66
Methylamphetamine injections	64	99	95	3	2	0
Methadone injections	65	100	N.K.	N.K.	83	65
Barbiturates*	62	95	75	12	72	37

* Information lacking in 1 case. Columns 3 and 4 are mutually exclusive.
N.K. — Not known.
All percentages in the body of the table are calculated in the terms of the total sample, N = 65.

Source: Mitcheson M., Davidson J., Hawks D., Hitchins L. and Malone S., 1970.
Sedative abuse by heroin addicts. *Lancet*. i, 601.

Table 14—2.   Drug Use in a Sample of Methylamphetamine Users

	Cannabis %	Amphetamine barbiturate mixtures %	Heroin %	Amphetamine tablets %	Methadone %	Sedatives and tranquillisers %	Hallucinogens %	Cocaine %	Other opiates %
Use of drugs in the past*	93	89	86	70	61	51	53	53	46
Current use of drugs**	56	44	50	22	40	28	21	9	8

*This includes isolated, intermittent and regular use.
**This includes occasional and regular use.

Source: Adapted from Hawks D., Mitcheson M., Ogborne A. and Edwards G., 1969.
Abuse of Methylamphetamine. *Brit.Med.J.* 2, 715.

In addition to the studies above, many more general works have commented on the changing fashions in drug use and the poly-drug use phenomenon (Leech, 1970; Willis, 1969; Newmark, 1968). The spread of poly-drug abuse has several implications. It makes it difficult to explain drug-taking in accordance with the pharmacological action of drugs. Drugs do not seem to be used by individuals just to make them more calm or more alert and invigorated. The influences of availability and fashion need to be taken into account and further study of the 'economics' of drug use is necessary. Poly-drug use also implies that treatment or prevention directed at specific drugs or limited groups of drugs will not necessarily be effective. Any basic alteration in an individual's behaviour or in the social context of drug use will have to come about from an attack on the whole of the underlying complexities of drug use.

CONCURRENT USE OF ALCOHOL AND OTHER DRUGS

It has been reported that drug abusers tend to dislike alcohol, but there is a small amount of data to suggest that a young person who is becoming drug involved might also have been a heavy drinker. Hawks et al (1969) reported that among methylamphetamine users 24% have a history of previous drinking problems. In a survey of cannabis use, Webb et al (1970) found that those who had used cannabis more intensively had also more often got drunk. Backhouse and James (1969) found a relationship between early smoking, alcohol use and drug taking. For some individuals it seems possible that alcohol may just be another drug to be used in the poly-drug use syndrome.

In the older age group there is some documentation of a small proportion of alcoholics concurrently abusing other drugs or that the alcoholics may proceed to these drugs after stopping drinking. Glatt (1962) reported that of 41 women alcoholics admitted to a hospital in 1961, 17 (41.5%) were taking barbiturates concurrently with alcohol. In a second study between 1958 and 1960 more than one in three women alcoholics treated at a hospital had habitually taken drugs to excess. Forty per cent of 68 women alcoholic patients at another hospital and 25% of 200 male alcoholic patients had formed a habit in relation to drugs (Glatt, 1962).

The combined use of alcohol and other drugs is most likely if (i) an alcoholic patient is carelessly started by a doctor or hospital on barbiturates or similar drugs, (ii) if an alcoholic such as a doctor, nurse or chemist has ready access to other drugs, or (iii) in the case of young poly-drug users.

ESCALATION

There is continuing controversy about the hypothesis that the use of one drug, in particular cannabis, leads onto the use of more harmful drugs, such as the opiates. Studies which have examined the chronology of drug use have consistently shown that cannabis and amphetamines (or amphetamine/barbiturate mixtures) are the most frequent drugs taken first by drug addicts (Hawks et al, 1969; Mitcheson, et al, 1970; Kosviner et al, 1968; Chapple, 1968; Paton, 1968; George and Glatt, 1967; Leonard, 1969).

The evidence gathered from retrospective studies of heroin users can never be conclusive. On the assumption that cannabis smoking is still confined to a small, but growing, section of the population, the evidence that a high proportion of addicts have smoked cannabis would only suggest that a cannabis smoker is more likely to take heroin than a non-smoker. This does not constitute any proof of escalation in itself because it does not give any clue to the crucial question of the frequency of progression among cannabis smokers as a whole. It is clear that if there were a simple relation of cannabis smoking to heroin use, there would be many more heroin addicts in Great Britain and a large percentage would be coloured. The coloured population is proportionately under-represented among the addict population (Leech, 1970). Paton (1968) has used a statistical argument to show that a substantial proportion of cannabis users do progress to heroin, however, Edwards (1968) has expressed the view that a postulated cannabis-heroin escalation is logically quite untenable.

A direct link between cannabis and heroin seems unlikely, but other reasons for the suggested progression have been put forward. The Wootton Committee (Advisory Committee on Drug Dependence, 1968) and others have examined the view, that through association with the illicit drug scene, cannabis users will come into contact with dealers who supply opiate drugs. While it is possible that some social mixing takes place between cannabis and opiates, there is strong indication that 'supplies of cannabis in this country are not necessarily obtained in the same places as heroin' (Advisory Committee on Drug Dependence, 1968).

Chapple (1966) hypothesised a number of channels of escalation: a shortage of cannabis coupled with a plentitude of heroin could lead some persons to use the more dangerous drug; the use of large amounts of cannabis may reduce the feeling of being 'high' and encourage a change to a more potent drug; heroin being cheaper than cannabis in England might lead to greater use, and finally, that the use of cannabis 'loosened some moral sense' making escalation possible.

Leonard (1969) feels that 'dependence upon the euphoric effect' of cannabis brings about a disposition to seek the effects of more potent and dangerous substances. The Advisory Committee on Drug Dependence (1968) suggests that there are particular groups of persons who are 'emotionally deprived' with 'disturbed personalities' who may try a wide range of illegal drugs, including cannabis, before taking heroin. The Committee states, 'it is the personality of the user, rather than the properties of the drug, that is likely to cause progression to other drugs'.

Leech (1970) has summarised his views on the escalation questions as follows:

'The truth behind the escalation thesis is that cannabis users are more likely to become heroin addicts than non-cannabis users. In view of the apparent and increasing spread of cannabis and of the social and cultural traditions associated with its use, this is likely to become less and less significant an axiom as the years go on. Heroin addiction is more likely to be averted by attention to the underlying personal problems of the potential addict than by concern about cannabis or any other external features present within the scene'.

The question of escalation from non-opiate drugs in general to narcotics has been investigated in a high risk group.

Noble (1970) carried out a retrospective survey of 67 boys referred to a London Remand Home during the years 1965—1967, all of whom were known to have taken drugs. The boys were divided into a 'hard' and 'soft' group according to whether they had taken narcotic drugs or not. These groups were compared on background, personal and social variables. Subsequently, in June 1969, an examination of the Home Office files showed that 19% of boys in the soft group had progressed to hard drugs. These boys were more similar to the 'hard' drugs group than others in the original 'soft' group in that the ones who progressed showed a high degree of personality disturbance, poor work records and had families with a high incidence of psychiatric illness.

Backhouse and James (1969) report a study in which they investigated the relationship and prevalence of cigarette smoking, drinking and drug taking in delinquent adolescent boys. Of the 290 adolescent boys (14—16 years old) interviewed at a detention centre, 83% admitted smoking cigarettes, 63% drank alcohol and 12% admitted taking drugs. It was established that there was a positive relationship between drinking, smoking and drug taking among those interviewed. The study was replicated the following year, and the combined findings are presented below.

Table 14—3.   Relationship of Smoking to Drinking and Drug Taking.

	Non-smokers (N = 119)	Moderate smokers (N = 391)	Heavy smokers (N = 139)
Regular or excessive drinkers (1)	22 19%	90 24%	55 40%
Drug takers (2)	7 6%	36 9%	29 21%

(1) X^2 = 18.46 (d.f. = 2) p. $<$ .001
(2) X^2 = 18.19 (d.f. = 2) p. $<$ .001

Source: Backhouse C.I. and James I.P. (1970). Clinical note—Dependency habits in delinquent adolescents. *Brit.J.Addict.* 64, 417.

REFERENCES

ADVISORY COMMITTEE ON DRUG DEPENDENCE, 1968. *Cannabis.* HMSO, London.

BACKHOUSE C.I. and JAMES I.P., 1969. The relationship and prevlance of smoking, drinking and drug taking in delinquent adolescent boys. *Brit.J.Addict.* 64, 75.

BACKHOUSE C.I. and JAMES I.P., 1970. Clinical note—dependency habits in delinquent adolescents. *Brit. J. Addict.* 65, 417.

CHAPPLE P.A.L. and GRAY G., 1968. One year's work at a centre for the treatment of addicted patients. *Lancet.* i, 908.

EDWARDS, G., 1968. The problem of cannabis dependence. *The Practitioner.* 200, 226.

GEORGE H.R. and GLATT M.M., 1967. A brief survey of a drug dependency unit in a psychiatric hospital. *Brit.J.Addict.* 62, 147.

GLATT M.M., 1962. The abuse of barbiturates in the United Kingdom. *Bull.Narcot.* 14(2), 19.

HAWKS D., MITCHESON M., OGBORNE A. and EDWARDS G., 1969. Abuse of methylamphetamine. *Brit.Med.J.* 2, 715.

HITCHINS L., MITCHESON M., ZACUNE J. and HAWKS D., 1971. A two year follow-up of a cohort of opiate users from a provincial town. In press.

JAMES I.P., 1969. Delinquency and heroin addiction in Britain. *Brit.J.Crim.* 9, 108.

KOSVINER A., MITCHESON M., MEYERS K., OGBORNE A., STIMSON G., ZACUNE J. and EDWARDS G., 1968. Heroin use in a provincial town. *Lancet.* i, 1189.

LEECH, K. *Pastoral Care and the Drug Scene.* S.P.C.K., London.

LEECH K. and JORDAN B., 1967. *Drugs for young people; their use and misuse.* Religious Education Press, London.

LEONARD B.E., 1969. Cannabis: a short review of its effects and possible dangers of its use. *Brit.J.Addict.* 64, 121.

MITCHESON M., DAVIDSON J., HAWKS D., HITCHINS L. and MALONE S., 1970. Sedative abuse by heroin addicts. *Lancet.* i, 606.

NEWMARK, P., 1968. *Connexions: Out of Your Mind?* Penguin, London.

NOBLE P.J., 1970. Drug-taking in delinquent boys. *Brit.Med.J.* 1, 102.

PATON W.D.M., 1968. Drug dependence: socio-pharmacological assessment. *Adv. of Science.* 12, 9.

STIMSON G. and OGBORNE A., 1970. Survey of addicts prescribed heroin at London clinics. *Lancet.* i, 1163.

WEBB M., HAWKS D. and KOSVINER A., 1969. Cannabis use in a student population. Unpublished report.

WILLIS J., 1969. *Drug Dependence, a Study for Nurses and Social Workers.* Faber, London.

SECTION 4

TREATMENT AND REHABILITATION

The structure of treatment and rehabilitation services for alcoholism and drug dependence are reviewed in Chapter 15 and 16. These chapters also consider research on samples of alcoholics or drug dependent patients as well as research on the efficacy of various approaches to treatment and rehabilitation.

CHAPTER 15
ALCOHOL DEPENDENCE
TREATMENT AND REHABILITATION

Treatment and rehabilitation for alcohol dependence are provided by the Department of Health and Social Security and the Home Office in England and Wales, and similar departments in Scotland and Northern Ireland (The Home and Health Department and the Ministry of Health and Local Government). The services provided include the Government financed National Health Service, the Probation Service, Prison Medical and Welfare facilities, and Local Authority health and welfare organisations. Some private medical practitioners in general practice treat cases of alcohol dependence in private clinics or in hospitals where patients must pay for private treatment. In addition to the government services, there are a large number of specialist and non-specialist voluntary organisations.

Medical Services within the National Health Service

The structure of the National Health Service in England and Wales is a tripartite structure under the direction of the Department of Health and Social Security. The services provided by general medical practitioners, dentists, pharmacists and opticians are run by local Executive Councils. The hospital and specialist services, except for teaching hospitals where medical students are trained, are administered by Regional Hospital Boards. Local Authority health services, which concentrate on the prevention of illness and the provision of practical help within homes, are administered by local government authorities through the county Medical Officer of Health. The present structure has been the subject of two government proposals ('Green Papers') which recommend the unifying of all these health services under local area health authorities (Ministry of Health, 1968a, Department of Health and Social Security, 1970). The implications of the proposed changes in the structure of the health service are discussed in memoranda of the Royal Medico-Psychological Association (1969, 1970). The memoranda discuss the special difficulties of treating alcoholics within the present system because the distinction between medical and social care is often artificial in these cases.

The role of the National Health Service is central in the treatment of alcohol dependence and the medical consequences of alcoholism. Care is provided by general practitioners, general hospital casualty and in-patient facilities, and psychiatric hospital out-patient and specialist services.

General Practitioner Services

Everyone in Great Britain is entitled to the services of a general medical practitioner, paid by National Health Service funds, who does not only provide medical service himself, but should be the initial point of referral to any specialist treatment that an individual may require. Most general practitioners, however, have had little medical education concerning alcohol dependence (see Chapter 18) and the concept that alcoholism is a disease requiring medical attention has only recently been widely accepted in Britain. The general practitioner services are understaffed (Cartwright, 1967) and it is often difficult for a general practitioner to involve himself in the treatment of alcohol dependence which can be time-consuming, relatively unrewarding and stressful. A Joint Committee of the British Medical Association and the Magistrates Association (1961) urged that general practitioners become more involved in the treatment of alcohol dependence. However, Parr (1957), Rathod (1967), Moss and Davies (1968), and Hensman et al (1968) have found that general practitioners in Britain often remain unaware of many alcoholics in their practices. Edwards et al (1967) found that 74% of the clients at three alcoholism information centres reported they had attempted to 'fool' a doctor by giving false reasons for requiring a medical certificate during the previous year and 18% of a sample of Alcoholics Anonymous members believed their doctors to be unaware of their alcoholism (Edwards et al, 1966). While it is possible that more adequate hospital and community services for alcohol dependence might encourage general practitioners to treat alcoholics themselves, at the present time most practitioners refer alcoholic patients to the hospital services.

Specialised Treatment Units for Alcohol Dependence

In 1962, a Ministry of Health (now Department of Health and Social Security) memorandum recommended that 'treatment for alcoholism and alcohol psychosis should as far as possible be given in specialised units'. The memorandum recommended that each of the 20 Regional Hospital Boards should initially set up one unit in its region to be run by, or in association with psychiatrists, given 'the full support of ancillary staff'. It was recommended that the units should have between 8 and 16 beds and should be responsible for out-patient as well as in-patient care. The units should co-operate fully with the local health authorities, Alcoholics Anonymous and other interested agencies (Ministry of Health, 1962).

By 1970, there were, however, only 14 units in England and Wales covering ten regions (four units being in metropolitan London), with a total capacity of 298 beds. Although the proportion of alcoholics treated in specialised units is rising (Ministry of Health, 1968b), the number of places provided is still inadequate.

Psychiatric In-Patient Treatment for Alcohol Dependence—
Non-Specialised Units

Aside from the specialised treatment units for alcohol dependence, there are 154 mental illness hospitals in England and Wales and an additional 105 psychiatric units at general hospitals. Patients may be treated in these hospitals (or units) for alcoholism or alcohol psychosis with or without other related conditions. The number of admissions to mental hospitals in England and Wales for alcoholism as a primary or secondary diagnosis increased by more than three times between 1959 and 1969 (see Table 15–1).

These figures do not include out-patient treatment for alcoholism or admissions to general (as opposed to psychiatric) hospitals. It is possible that there is some element of under-reporting due to alcoholism being diagnosed as 'depression', 'personality disorder' or similar categories. Further, it is difficult to interpret the rise in the numbers admitted to hospital for alcohol dependence. While this may reflect a true increase in the incidence of alcoholism, it is more likely to be accounted for by the increase of National Health Service treatment facilities.

In Scotland, admissions for alcohol dependence to mental hospitals or to psychiatric units of general hospitals have increased nearly threefold between 1960 and 1968. However, alcoholics account for a much higher proportion of total

Table 15–1.   Admissions to Mental Illness Hospitals and Units of Patients having Primary or Secondary Diagnosis of Alcoholism or Alcoholic Psychosis in Selected Years from 1959–1969, England and Wales.

Year	Total Alcoholism Admissions (Primary diagnosis) (A)	Total Alcoholism Admissions (Secondary diagnosis) (B)	Total Alcoholism Admissions (D)	Increase over Previous Year (%) (D)	Total Number of Mental Illness Admissions (E)	A as Proportion of E (F)
1959	2044	315	2359	15.4%	105,742	1.93%
1964	5423	1160	6583	21.4%	158,861	3.41%
1966	6088	1268	7356	20.8%	163,980	3.71%
1967	6252	1409	7661	22.5%	168,438	3.71%
1968	6391	1425	7816	22.3%	179,021	3.57%
1969	6689	1376	8065	20.6%	182,260	3.67%

* The proportion of alcoholism admissions to total mental illness admissions.

Source: Department of Health and Social Security. *Personal Communication.* 1971.

admissions to mental hospitals or psychiatric units in Scotland than they do in England and Wales (see Table 15–2). The facilities available in Scotland for the treatment of alcohol dependence are discussed by the Scottish Home and Health Department and Scottish Health Services Council (1965).

Table 15–2.   Number of Admissions, Re-Admissions and Transfers to Scottish Mental Hospitals and Psychiatric Units for Alcoholism and Alcoholic Psychosis. 1960–1968.

Year	Total Alcoholic Admissions	Total Mental Illness Admissions	Alcoholic Admissions expressed as percentages of total admissions
1960	1091	12,892	8.5%
1961	1347	13,686	9.8%
1962	1617	14,724	11.0%
1963	2307	18,739	12.3%
1964	2698	19,903	13.6%
1965	2736	20,967	13.0%
1966	2761	20,290	13.6%
1967	2936	20,682	14.2%
1968	3095	21,874	14.1%

Source: Scottish Home and Health Department. *Personal Communication.* 1969.

Psychiatric Out-Patient Departments

Out-patient treatment for alcohol dependence is generally run in association with in-patient facilities. The alcoholic patient will most usually be seen in a general psychiatric out-patient clinic, although some psychiatrists may run special alcohol clinics. In many regions the waiting list for both general and specific forms of psychiatric treatment is long. The service offered to an alcoholic on an out-patient basis varies, but at best will entail a comprehensive physical, psychiatric, psychological and social work assessment, followed by induction into treatment. The methods used may include individual or group psycho-therapy, drug therapy including Antabuse (disulfiram) or Abstem (citrated calcium carbimide), behaviour therapy or social work directed towards the family. Research at a London teaching hospital (Edwards and Guthrie, 1967) indicated that carefully structured out-patient treatment can be as effective as in-patient care.

General Hospital Casualty and Emergency Departments

It is not uncommon for alcoholics to attend casualty departments in general hospitals as the result of injuries, traffic accidents, collapse or suicidal attempt. A survey conducted in the casualty department of one London teaching hospital (Watson, 1969) showed that approximately 1% of all attenders in 1967 had alcohol mentioned on their case records in connection with their admission. One-quarter of those with alcohol mentioned in the notes 'showed aggression or were generally unco-operative' and it was estimated that 'chronic alcoholism was a possible diagnosis in about one-third of these' (Watson, 1969). It is probable that alcoholics are not often referred to other agencies from most casualty departments although this could be an important opportunity for specialised referral.

Private Medical Practice

Private care for alcohol dependence by psychiatrists and general practitioners exists in parallel to the National Health Service, although its use is limited due to the high cost and perhaps to a reluctance of private physicians and nursing homes to deal with alcoholic patients. It is not known to what extent private insurance schemes will contribute to the expenses incurred by a private patient seeking treatment for alcoholism. The treatment of private patients has been reported by Williams (1960).

TREATMENT WITHIN THE PENAL AND PROBATION SERVICES

As the government department responsible for internal law enforcement, the Home Office, through its prison, police, probation and after-care departments, is responsible for the treatment of alcoholism in any way connected with persons committing crimes or offences. The Home Secretary was responsible for establishing the Working Party on Habitual Drunken Offenders which was appointed in 1967 'to consider the treatment, within the penal system, of offenders who habitually committed offences involving drunkenness, to assess the extent and nature of the need for such treatment, including the use and provision of hostels, and to make recommendations' (Working Party on Habitual Drunken Offenders, 1971).

Treatment Orders

When an individual commits an offence that is punishable by imprisonment, the courts can impose treatment orders under certain conditions specified in the Mental Health Act, 1959. The provisions under the Act are discussed in Chapter 16 with reference to drug dependence, and the same limitations and uses apply to the treatment of alcohol dependence. It is also possible for the courts to include in a probation order the requirement that a person shall submit for up to 12 months to treatment under the supervision of a duly qualified medical practitioner (Section 4 of the Criminal Justice Act, 1948).

The Probation Service

Daily throughout Great Britain the courts deal with drunkenness offenders. If a man has appeared before the same magistrate on several occasions over a short time on the charge of drunkenness, the magistrate may remand him in custody and ask for a probation officer's or a prison medical officer's report. Additionally, a probation order can be made for one to three years which places the offender under the supervision of the Probation Department. Probation officers have many alcoholics under their care and offer long term support and social help which they give to all offenders. While probation officers often have little formal training about alcoholism, the probation service is becoming more concerned about special problems created by the alcoholic and special facilities may eventually be developed. The probation service also staffs the prison welfare service within the penal system.

The Prison Service

It is now known that a high proportion of prisoners have drinking problems (see Chapter 8). In the past comparatively little was done to help the alcoholic prisoner who may well be serving a longer sentence than that which is usual for a drunkenness offender. However, the prison service is now more aware of the problem and within the limits of understaffing problems, more is being done to help alcoholic offenders. Special prison units, such as Grendon Underwood in Buckinghamshire, have been developed to deal with psychiatrically disturbed prisoners and no doubt more formalised help with alcoholics will be developed in the future. An experiment in which drunkenness offenders in London were sent to an open prison in the country is no longer in operation, but was fully reported at the time (Kelly, 1966).

In most prisons, treatment will depend on the interest of the prison medical officer. In addition, Alcoholics Anonymous runs approximately 40 prison groups at present, after first starting such a group at Wakefield Prison nine years ago. This work is co-ordinated throughout the country and up to £5-worth of literature a year may be sent to each prison at the expense of the Prison Department.

RECEPTION CENTRES

The Supplementary Benefits Commission of the Department of Health and Social Security is responsible for running 'reception centres' which provide nightly accommodation for vagrants and for those 'without a settled way of living' and 'no fixed abode'. These centres used to be the responsibility of local authorities and were later under the direction of the National Assistance Board until it amalgamated with the Ministry of Health in 1968 into the present Department. These reception centres evolved from the 'work houses' of 19th century Britain.

A full census of all reception centres in the country was carried out by the National Assistance Board (1966) and a census of a London reception centre had been completed in the previous year (Edwards et al, 1968). While both studies indicated that alcoholism was prevalent, more recent work in a London reception centre indicates that as many as 2,500 alcoholics may pass through the centre during the course of a year. Five hundred of these cases will be previously unknown (Tidmarsh, Personal Communication, 1971). Persons who use these reception centres are either self-referred, brought in by the police or referred by a variety of social agencies. They are primarily offered shelter on a casual basis, although an attempt at resettlement is increasingly being made in some centres.

EVALUATION OF TREATMENT PROGRAMMES

As in other countries, claims for the efficacy of specific treatments and regimes have not been adequately evaluated in the United Kingdom. Few investigations have attempted to include control groups, define carefully characteristics of the population which they were treating, or give a complete description of the type of treatment employed. The validity of data is often not thoroughly checked and reports of outcome are frequently limited to considerations of abstinence or not adequately specified. In all, several studies have been concerned with the assessment of treatment results but few have met the methodological requirements for proper evaluation (Edwards, 1967).

Davies, Shepherd and Myers (1956) followed up 50 alcohol dependent patients treated at the Maudsley Hospital in general psychiatric wards and later as out-patients. For the 39 men and 11 women in the sample, therapy was broad-based and included the establishment of a close doctor/patient relationship, the use of drugs, contact with Alcoholics Anonymous and vocational guidance. After discharge from hospital, vigorous attempts were made to keep in contact and to continue assistance. Group therapy was not employed at any time. Two years following treatment, 36% were found to be either totally abstinent or abstinent most of the time. A further 42%, despite light or fairly heavy drinking, had maintained social efficiency. Good prognosis was found to be associated with a good previous personality and previous social stability.

Glatt (1961) reported the results of the treatment of approximately 200 male alcoholics who were treated with a variety of methods. He found that one-third of the sample abstained totally, another third improved in their social functioning though they continued drinking, and one-third deteriorated.

One-hundred and eleven consecutive male in-patients at the Warlingham Park Alcoholism Unit were followed up for two years by Rathod et al (1966). With treatment mainly consisting of group psycho-therapy, over 50% of the patients were found to be abstinent at one year's follow-up. This abstinence was closely associated with improved work record and improved relationships at home. It was also found that of 14 patients who discharged themselves from hospital prematurely, five remained abstinent.

Edwards and Guthrie (1967) compared in-patient treatment in a general psychiatric ward with intensive out-patient care. In this study, 40 alcohol dependent men were randomised between the two forms of therapy. The in-patients stayed an average of 8–9 weeks with treatment being variable, but emphasis placed on a good doctor/patient relationship, the use of Abstem (citrated calcium carbimide), Alcoholics Anonymous attendance and social work help with family and employment problems. The out-patients were treated similarly and on average received 7–8 weeks 'intensive treatment'. Both groups were followed up for one year with monthly assessments of progress by independent raters. No significant difference between the two groups was found, indicating that out-patient care was as effective as in-patient for the entire group.

These English studies of treatment for alcohol dependence do not indicate any major differences in results between the two main types of in-patient care, that is, group therapy in a specialised unit or selective therapy in a general psychiatric hospital. There is no evidence that in-patient care is necessarily better than out-patient. The studies have emphasised that prognosis is determined to a great extent by the previous personality and social stability of the alcoholic and that this may be more relevant to prognosis than the particular treatment given. There is also very little work on the selection of patients for various different treatment programmes.

In Scotland, Smith and Sclare (1964) studied 100 alcoholic admissions to the psychiatric unit at one of Glasgow's general hospitals. Eighty-nine of the admissions were male and 11 female, the majority being between the ages of 35 and 49, with a drinking history lasting 5–15 years. The authors suggested that the absence of patients over the age of 50 could be explained by admissions to medical or surgical wards for these older alcoholics presenting physical symptoms of chronic alcoholism, or the absence of social pressure in these older age groups. Alternatively, spontaneous remission of alcoholism may occur or these alcoholics may be dying. Vallance (1965) following up alcoholics treated at another Glasgow hospital, reported a lack of ability in alcoholics to keep out-patient appointments following discharge and noted that out of 65 male patients only 25% were assessed as improved, while 30% suffered further deterioration.

The largest number of evaluative studies in Scotland have been carried out at the Royal Edinburgh Hospital's Alcoholism Unit, where out-patient facilities exist in addition to Unit beds. Walton et al (1966) in following up a cohort of alcoholic patients, differentiated features associated with favourable outcome assessed both in terms of drinking and of social adjustment. They found that only slightly better results were obtained with in-patients than with out-patients, but that better results were obtained with 'loss of control' drinkers than with 'inability to abstain' drinkers. Both higher social class and older age were associated with good prognosis. As with English studies (Davies et al, 1956; Edwards and Guthrie, 1967), abstinence at six months following treatment was highly correlated with abstinence at 12 months. The profile of a Scottish alcoholic receiving out-patient care with a good prognosis was an alcoholic with 'loss of control' drinking, mild rather than severe personality disorder, a long history of alcohol addiction, previous experience with Alcoholics Anonymous, good marital relations and evidence of abstinence before first attendance at hospital. Successful outcome following in-patient treatment was associated with a current marriage, absence of a history of drunkenness arrests and a late start to heavy drinking. Ritson and Hassall (1970) report a further series of patients treated at the same unit, with special reference to younger alcoholics.

McCance and McCance (1969) investigated alcoholic patients admitted to one or other of the two principal psychiatric hospitals in Aberdeen. They compared three groups of alcoholic patients—one receiving aversion therapy, one receiving group therapy and the third receiving routine ward treatment. While there was no ultimate difference in outcome between the three treatment groups, there were large differences between the two hospital populations. In this study, good prognosis was associated with no experience of delirium tremens, absence of a heavy drinking sub-culture, living with others, higher social class, marital stability, length of drinking and absence of police convictions. McCance and McCance concluded that the presence or absence of these factors affects the outcome more than the type of treatment received. It is possible that favourable results obtained at various hospitals may be caused by a bias of selection of patients, rather than effectiveness of treatment.

REHABILITATION

Local Authority Services

Local county borough and city authorities provide a wide variety of rehabilitation services, some of which they have a statutory duty to administer and others which they can provide if they so wish. These authorities enjoy considerable autonomy so that the adequacy and availability of services varies widely. The services provided for alcoholics by these authorities are carried out by local health and welfare departments which have been re-organised by the Personal Services Act, 1970, which will come into force during 1971. This Act will put into force the recommendations of the Seebohm Committee (Committee on Local Authority and Allied Personal Social Services, 1968) whereby all local authority welfare services will be amalgamated under one Director of Social Services. It is too early to assess the effects of the Act, but it is certain that Children's Officers (responsible for the welfare of children of school age in their own homes and in residential institutions), Housing Welfare Officers (responsible for those families having difficulty in paying rent), Welfare Officers for the physically handicapped and Mental Welfare Officers—all of whom come into contact with alcoholism—will be integrated into one service organised locally by area teams.

Hostel Accommodation for Alcoholics

A Ministry of Health (now Department of Health and Social Security) memorandum on the treatment of alcoholism was sent to all hospital authorities in England and Wales in May, 1968 affirming that 'alcoholism is a chronic, relapsing disease which destroys personal relationships and leads to social decline'. This memorandum, in addition to reiterating the need for special hospital units which had been recommended in an earlier memorandum (Ministry of Health, 1962), noted that it was essential for medical services to be linked with social services in the community and whenever possible 'for those (social services) to be attached with the family'. The final three paragraphs of this memorandum (Ministry of Health, 1968b) were devoted to the problem of after-care and stress was laid on the necessity for arrangements being made for alcoholics coming out of hospital. The need for many more hostels was cited which should be provided either by local authorities or voluntary bodies. Hostels, it was stressed, should take account of the 'different needs of alcoholics'. The lengths of stay that would be necessary would vary from a few weeks upwards to 'indefinite provision'. The management regime of these hostels should range from the 'conventionally authoritarian' to that of 'varying degrees of permissiveness' which would allow residents to accept some degree of responsibility along the lines of therapeutic communities which have been advocated by Maxwell Jones (1968).

The memorandum above was very much in line with an earlier report of the Working Party on the Place of Voluntary Service in After-Care (1965). This Committee was 'to consider what contribution voluntary effort could make to the after-care of discharged offenders and to advise on what particular project should be considered for assistance from public funds'. The Report concerned itself with residential provision for homeless discharged offenders. The Home Office After-Care Hostels Grant scheme, introduced in 1965, now provides a grant of £150 per annum for each hostel place reserved for offenders and up to £250 per place for hostels providing special facilities for particularly 'difficult' categories of offenders, such as those formerly addicted to drink and drugs. The National Association for Voluntary Hostels, an organisation supported by various government and local authority bodies, which serves as a placement agency throughout the country, estimated that they placed 226 alcoholics out of 4062 placements in 1969.

The Report of the Working Party on the Place of Voluntary Service in After-Care (1965) divided discharged offenders (those having left a penal establishment) into three categories: those of 'low dependency' who could be relied upon to find their own way; those of 'intermediate dependency' who require accommodation in a 'more tolerant and less frustrating surrounding with trained staff to maintain equilibrium'; and those of 'high dependency' or the chronically handicapped needing special care, including alcoholics. Following this, the Special After-Care Trust advocated setting up a number of experimental ventures and money was subsequently obtained from a charitable foundation which allowed five experimental hostels to be started on a two year basis. Specialised hostels for alcoholics were recommended, as alcoholics constituted 'perhaps the largest single category of men requiring specialised hostel facilities'. The first two year's progress at those experimental hostels has been described in Cook and Pollak (1970). It was also urged that additional accommodation be found at non-specialised hostels 'understanding the problem and willing to accept mild cases or those already partially treated elsewhere'. The Report also recommended that single group centres or 'family like hostels' linked with a psychiatric hospital providing a high degree of support and treatment be established, but this recommendation has not been executed to date. The National Association for the Care and Resettlement of Offenders estimates that there were approximately 25 hostels taking alcoholics in the London area, plus 35 elsewhere in England and Wales at the end of 1970.

The assessment of the treatment provided in hostels has been made by comparing the first year in a hostel with the previous years in terms of employment, drunkenness arrests and convictions (Cook, Morgan and Pollak, 1968). An up-to-date assessment of hostel accommodation, including those provided for alcoholics, is given in two recent reports (Hinton, 1970; Griffiths, 1970).

The Role of Voluntary Organisations in the
Treatment of Alcohol Dependence

Despite the ever increasing development of National Health Service and other statutory facilities for the treatment of alcohol dependence, voluntary organisations continue to play an important part both nationally and locally. The Committee on Habitual Drunken Offenders (1971) comments:

'The role played by the voluntary societies in providing facilities is crucial to any consideration of the present position of the drunken offender.'

Aside from hostels, voluntary organisations run crypts and shelters of all sizes (both for alcoholics and other homeless persons within the community) clubs, clinics, information centres, organisations providing food ('soup kitchens') and self-help groups, such as Alcoholics Anonymous.

The variety and number of these organisations throughout the country are too great to be described in detail. Crypt services, for instance, are more predominant in the London area and range from old style handouts of clothes and food, to certain crypts which provide accommodation for vagrant and/or alcoholic men. The most active crypt service outside London is probably that offered in Leeds, where benches are available for overnight sleeping and basic food and clean clothing are offered. Between 100 and 180 men seek shelter there each night with a large proportion of these being considered to be heavy drinkers and alcoholics.

Other voluntary organisations are those having residential and non-residential facilities in London and other cities which are filled by men and women who have been found sleeping rough by the organisation's voluntary workers. The workers in such communities often receive no pay.

Alcoholics Anonymous is the largest voluntary organisation specifically caring for alcoholics. As of December, 1970, a total of 274 Alcoholics Anonymous groups were reported meeting regularly in England, 13 in Wales, 93 in Scotland and 29 in the six counties of Northern Ireland. Alcoholics Anonymous groups meet in various centres, alcoholic treatment units, and prisons. The total active membership of Alcoholics Anonymous was estimated at approximately 3,000 'regular attenders' during 1970 (Committee on the Habitual Drunken Offender, 1971).

A sample of London AA groups was surveyed by Cooper and Maule (1962) and later by Edwards et al (1966). The organisation was shown to draw most of its strength in London from middle-aged and middle class persons dependent on alcohol. Alcoholics Anonymous undoubtedly provides a service for continuing follow-up and support of hospital treated patients, as well as getting patients to accept initial hospital treatment. The organisation has, in its own right, a high degree of therapeutic success.

Al-Anon family groups, a relatively new part of Alcoholics Anonymous' services, now have an extensive organisation and some 70 groups were active at the end of 1970. In addition, Alateen—for the teenage sons and daughters of alcoholics—is also becoming active.

Collaboration between Organisations Treating Alcohol Dependence

The need for close collaboration among all organisations treating alcohol dependence has been emphasised by the Committee on Habitual Drunken Offenders (1971), whose recommendations include advice that central government departments should 'consider what further steps can be taken to improve liaison' among such bodies. At present, close collaboration is taking place only in certain localities. Evans et al (1966) have demonstrated that effective collaboration can be achieved between hospitals, local authorities and voluntary services, and that this has resulted not only in more efficient treatment and after-care for the alcoholic and his family, but also proved useful for research and education of the public. The National Council on Alcoholism has suggested that its existing information centres might be used as co-ordinating bodies in local areas. Edwards et al (1967) found that these centres were used by a wide variety of alcoholics and that the centres could perform a useful function in 'reaching out' to alcohol dependent persons who otherwise might not know where to find help.

The need for elaboration and co-ordination of services is emphasised by the Ministry of Health memorandum (1968b) in that 'the absence of a reliable cure for alcoholism requires that treatment facilities should be organised so as to permit flexibility, experiment and research'.

REFERENCES

BRITISH MEDICAL ASSOCIATION AND MAGISTRATES ASSOCIATION, 1961.
   Alcoholism: A Memorandum Prepared by the Joint Committee, British Medical Association,
   London.
CARTWRIGHT A., 1967. *Patients and their Doctors.* Routledge and Keegan Paul, London.
COMMITTEE ON LOCAL AUTHORITY AND ALLIED PERSONAL SOCIAL SERVICE
   (THE SEEBOHM COMMITTEE), 1968. *Report of the Committee.* H.M.S.O., London.
COOK T., MORGAN H.G. and POLLAK B., 1968. The Rathcoole experiment: first year at a
   hostel for vagrant alcoholics. *Brit.Med.J.* 1, 240.
COOK T. and POLLAK B., 1970. *In Place of Skid Row: The Rathcoole Experiment—the First
   Two Years.* National Association for the Care and Resettlement of Offenders, London.
COOPER J. and MAULE H.G., 1962. Problems of drinking. *Brit.J.Addict.* 58, 45.
DAVIES D.L., SHEPARD M. and MYERS E., 1956. The two year prognosis of 50 alcohol
   addicts after treatment in hospital. *Quart.J.Stud.Alc.* 17, 485.
DEPARTMENT OF HEALTH AND SOCIAL SECURITY, 1970. *National Health Service: The
   Future Structure of the National Health Service.* H.M.S.O., London.
EDWARDS G., 1967. The meaning and treatment of alcohol dependence. *Hospital Medicine.*
   2, 272.
EDWARDS G. and GUTHRIE S., 1967. A controlled trial of in-patient and out-patient treatment
   of alcohol dependence. *Lancet.* i, 555.
EDWARDS G., HENSMAN C., HAWKER A. and WILLIAMSON V., 1966. Who goes to
   Alcoholics Anonymous? *Lancet.* ii, 1407.
EDWARDS G., KELLOG-FISHER M., HAWKER A. and HENSMAN C., 1967. Clients of
   alcoholism information centres. *Brit.Med.J.* 4, 346.
EDWARDS G., WILLIAMSON V., HAWKER A., HENSMAN C. and POSTOYAN S., 1968.
   Census of a reception centre. *Brit.J.Psychiat.* 114, 437.
EVANS M., FINE E.W. and PHILLIPS W.P., 1966. Community care for alcoholics and their
   families. *Brit.Med.J.* 1, 1531.
GLATT M.M., 1961. Treatment results in an English mental hospital alcoholic unit.
   Acta.Psych.Scand. 37, 143.
GRIFFITHS D.J., 1970. *Hostels in the 1970's.* National Association for the Care and
   Resettlement of Offenders, London.
HENSMAN C., CHANDLER J., EDWARDS G., HAWKER A. and WILLIAMSON V., 1968.
   Identifying abnormal drinkers: prevalence estimates by general practitioners and clergymen.
   Med.Officer. 120, 215.
HINTON N., 1970. *The Voluntary Concept in the Hostel System for Discharged Offenders.*
   National Association for the Care and Resettlement of Offenders, London.
JONES, M., 1968. *Social Psychiatry in Practice.* Penguin, London.
KELLY M., 1966. The medical investigation of short-term alcoholics in the open prison at
   Spring Hill. Unpublished report.
McCANCE C. and McCANCE P.F., 1969. Alcoholism in north-east Scotland: its treatment and
   outcome. *Brit.J.Psychiat.* 115, 519.
MINISTRY OF HEALTH, 1962. *Memorandum on Hospital Treatment of Alcoholism 43/62.*
   Ministry of Health, London.
MINISTRY OF HEALTH, 1968a. *Administrative Structure of the Medical and Related Services
   in England and Wales.* H.M.S.O., London.
MINISTRY OF HEALTH, 1968b. *Memorandum on the Treatment of Alcoholism 37/68.*
   Ministry of Health, London.
MOSS M. and DAVIES E.B., 1968. *A Survey of Alcoholism in an England County.* Geigy,
   London.
NATIONAL ASSISTANCE BOARD, 1966. *Homeless Single Persons.* H.M.S.O., London.
PARR D., 1957. Alcoholism in general practice. *Brit.J.Addict.* 54, 25.
RATHOD R., 1967. An enquiry into general practitioners' opinions about alcoholism.
   Brit.J.Addict. 62, 103.
RATHOD N.H., GREGORY E., BLOWS D. and THOMAS G.H., 1966. A two year follow-up
   study of alcoholic patients. *Brit.J.Psychiat.* 112, 683.
RITSON B. and HASSALL C., 1970. *The Management of Alcoholism.* Livingstone, London.
ROYAL MEDICO-PSYCHOLOGICAL ASSOCIATION, 1969. Memorandum on the Green
   Paper on the Administrative Structure of the Medical Services in England and Wales.
   Brit.J.Psychiat. 115, 601.
ROYAL MEDICO-PSYCHOLOGICAL ASSOCIATION, 1970. Memorandum on the Second
   Green Paper on the Future of the National Health Service. *Brit.J.Psychiat.* 117, 577.
SCOTTISH HOME AND HEALTH DEPARTMENT AND SCOTTISH HEALTH SERVICES
   COUNCIL, 1965. *Alcoholics: Report on Health Services for their Treatment and
   Rehabilitation.* H.M.S.O., Edinburgh.

SMITH M. and SCLARE A., 1964. Alcoholism in Glasgow. *Scot.Med.J.* 9, 514.
VALLANCE M., 1965. Alcoholism: a two year follow-up study of patients admitted to the psychiatric department of a general hospital. *Brit.J.Psychiat.* 3, 348.
WALTON H.J., RITSON E.B. and KENNEDY R.I., 1966. Response of alcoholics to clinic treatment. *Brit.Med.J.* 2, 1171.
WATSON J.P., 1969. Alcohol in the casualty department. *Brit.J.Addict.* 64, 547.
WILLIAMS L., 1960. *Tomorrow Will Be Sober.* Cassell, London.
WORKING PARTY ON THE PLACE OF VOLUNTARY SERVICE IN AFTER-CARE, 1965. *Residential Provision for Homeless Discharged Offenders.* H.M.S.O., London.
WORKING PARTY ON THE PLACE OF VOLUNTARY SERVICE IN AFTER-CARE, 1967. *Second Report.* H.M.S.O., London.
WORKING PARTY ON HABITUAL DRUNKEN OFFENDERS, 1971. *Habitual Drunken Offenders.* H.M.S.O., London.

CHAPTER 16
DRUG DEPENDENCE
TREATMENT AND REHABILITATION

Drug dependence in the United Kingdom is treated both by local psychiatric and medical services and by specialised treatment centres for opiate dependence. Treatment of middle-aged and elderly people who have become dependent on psychoactive drugs, such as barbiturates (see Chapter 12) or amphetamines (see Chapter 11), is usually managed by the patient's general medical practitioner who may request advice from local hospital psychiatric services. Normally the dependence arises from the immoderate use of these drugs which are legitimately prescribed. If in-patient treatment is required this is provided by the general psychiatric or medical services, and after-care would be the joint responsibility of the general practitioner with the advice of a psychiatrist and the local mental welfare services which are discussed in relation to alcohol dependence (see Chapter 15).

Young people consuming a variety of psychoactive substances (see Chapters 9, 10, 11, 12, 13, 14) may come to the notice of the medical services either by requesting a general practitioner to prescribe drugs or as the result of criminal prosecution when the person was referred for medical treatment by the court, or a doctor was requested to make a report (Bewley, 1970). In general, there are very few special provisions for the assessment and treatment of young persons dependent upon sedatives, hallucinogenic or stimulant drugs and the general medical and welfare services are used (see Chapter 15).

Special treatment facilities are provided in England, Wales and Scotland for the treatment of opiate (especially heroin and cocaine) addiction. These treatment centres were established following the recommendations of the Interdepartmental Committee on Drug Addiction, 1965 (see Chapter 13). Legislation concerning the establishment of treatment centres, the restriction of heroin and cocaine prescribing to licensed doctors, and the compulsory notification of addicts is discussed in Chapter 4 (Dangerous Drugs Act, 1967; Dangerous Drugs (Supply to Addicts) Regulations, 1968; Dangerous Drugs (Notification of Addicts) Regulations, 1968).

The licensing of practitioners to supply heroin and cocaine effectively restricted the care of people dependent on these drugs to specialist hospital centres. Following the enactment of the Dangerous Drugs (Supply to Addicts) Regulations on 16th April, 1968, it was stated that 545 medical practitioners had been issued licenses to prescribe heroin and cocaine. 529 of these doctors were on the staff of 219 National Health Service hospitals, seven were in the prison service and nine practitioners were in three non-National Health Service hospitals (British Medical Journal, 1968). At the end of 1970 there were 14 special treatment facilities for addicts in greater London which were separately staffed within the National Health Service hospitals, and 13 units outside London which could be called 'treatment centres' along the lines of the London out-patient models

(Personal communication, Department of Health and Social Security). In addition, some facilities exist where doctors are licensed to prescribe heroin and cocaine to addicts without these hospitals having specialised addiction units. Since February, 1968, 42 hospitals outside London have reported cases of addiction in accordance with the Dangerous Drugs (Notification of Addicts) Regulations, 1968 (Personal communication, Department of Health and Social Security).

A memorandum was circulated throughout the National Health Service in 1967 anticipating the setting up of the special treatment centres for addicts which still describes the basic aims of the clinics.

'Within the measures to contain the spread of addiction to heroin, the role of the hospital service is of special importance. It is necessary for hospital treatment centres to provide not only for those patients who are willing to agree to treatment by withdrawal, but for those who are not for the time being willing to accept withdrawal, who nevertheless require drugs and in consequence need medical supervision.'

'In-patient facilities are required for patients who will accept withdrawl treatment. These will usually be provided in mental illness hospitals, but may be provided in psychiatric departments of general hospitals. Where there are sufficient patients, there are advantages in treating them in small groups, probably not exceeding 12: this assists in the development of specialised treatment by medical and nursing staff, brings into play the mutual support which is helpful to patients and staff, makes it easier to prevent drugs from being brought in to addicts, and provides more favourable conditions for research. The constitution of groups of addicts is a matter for clinical discretion and it may be considered desirable to treat in separate groups patients addicted to heroin and those addicted to other drugs or to alcohol, or to separate the younger heroin addicts from the elder ones. Accommodation which permits sub-divisions of this kind will therefore be required.'

'*Rehabilitation.* Withdrawal is only the first step in treatment and longer term rehabilitation will often be required. The main difficulty lies in maintaining the interest and co-operation of the patient after completing the withdrawal stage, and some modification of the usual occupational and recreational activities and arrangements for after-care may be necessary in order to meet the needs of those heroin addicts who are young, active and intelligent.'

'*Out-Patient Services.* Some addicts will not accept withdrawal treatment, at any rate to start with, and complete refusal of supplies will not cure their addiction— it will merely throw them on the black market and encourage the development of an organised illicit traffic on a scale hitherto unknown in this country. The aim is to contain the spread of heroin addiction by continuing to supply this drug in minimum quantities where this is necessary in the opinion of the doctor, and where possible to persuade addicts to accept withdrawal treatment. For these purposes the medical supervision of addicts is necessary; this will include attention to those physical illnesses to which addicts are prone and the maintenance of a therapeutic relationship which may at any time render withdrawal treatment acceptable to the patient. Out-patient services are required and will generally entail the provision of separate sessions for addicts, either in existing out-patient departments or in separate premises.'

'The organisation of services will depend on the method of supplying drugs that is adopted by clinicians. It is, however, desirable in any area that there should be a fairly uniform approach; otherwise the organisation of services and the share of the load will be obstructed because addicts will gravitate to those clinics where they think drugs are easiest to get. While administration of drugs by the medical staff of the treatment centre is not excluded, supply by the hospital or by retail prescription is likely to be more generally practicable. Guidance on measures necessary to prevent misuse of prescriptions by patients will be forwarded separately.'

'To guard against duplication of supply, a system of identifying addicts will be needed, which can be linked with the central records which are to be established.' (Ministry of Health and Home Office, 1967)

The recommendations contained in the memorandum form the basis of the present British approach to the treatment of heroin addiction. Edwards (1969) has identified six central hypotheses underlying the British system of opiate treatment.

1. 'The clinic doctor will not start a new patient on heroin unless he is absolutely sure that the patient is addicted and truly needs the drug.'

2. 'The doctor in the new centre will prescribe conservatively and this will much lessen the risk of his patient having surplus heroin to sell.'

3. 'By the controlled medical prescribing of heroin the likelihood of a well-organised criminal black market is diminished—why buy expensive illegal heroin when legal heroin is free? The Mafia, it is believed, will see any attempt by them to move on to the British scene as likely to be under-cut and unprofitable.'

4. 'Addicts are taken on by the clinics not for the continuing hand-out of drugs but for treatment: the patient may not initially be motivated to accept withdrawal but, through contact with clinic staff, motivation will gradually be built, dosage gradually decreased, and the offer of admission for withdrawal finally accepted.'

5. 'Since successful treatment ultimately depends on the patient's own motivation, there is no place for the use of compulsory admission procedures.'

6. 'There are believed to be some patients who cannot—or cannot for the time being—function without the drug, but who on a regular maintenance dose can live a normal and useful life as "stabilised addicts"; such patients will be maintained on heroin rather than have their drug withdrawn.' (Edwards, 1969).

All of these hypotheses point to difficulties with the treatment of addicts in Great Britain. In some cases the underlying assumptions are unsound while in others the practical problems are pervasive although not insuperable.

The assessment of a new patient attending a treatment centre is notoriously difficult. The doctor may take a case history from the individual, examine his arms for needle marks, give a urine test for the presence of an opiate and use intuitive judgement as to the genuine needs of the patients. None of these methods can adequately ensure that a doctor may not accidentally prescribe an opiate for a person who is not really addicted (Edwards, 1968; Chapple and Gray, 1968; Gardner and Connell, 1970).

Gardner and Connell (1970) asked the Home Office if each new clinic case was already known, and contacted the general practitioner, clinic or supply chemist where patients had previously received drugs on prescription. They further evaluated the medical, drug and psychiatric histories of the individuals and took specimens of urine for analysis. Marks et al (1969) used a combination of methods for assessing new patients including urine testing and a nalorphine test when it was urgent to know whether a patient was addicted or not.

Edwards (1969) suggests that the only safe method for assessment of new cases is the in-patient observation of withdrawal symptoms. However, this method is time consuming and costly when hospitals are already crowded. The new patient demanding an opiate prescription presents several difficulties:

i)   'An over-stretched clinic may accidentally turn a non-addict into an addict.'

ii)   'If refused heroin, a non-addict may simply go on to another and perhaps more dangerous drug.'

iii) 'The patient whose needs are not gratified may bully, exploit, manipulate, and indeed terrorise his family.'

iv)   'Failure of communication between clinics may result in the adolescent who has been refused at one centre being given heroin at another.'

(Edwards, 1969).

After deciding to prescribe for an addict, the practitioner must be able to provide just the right amount of heroin—not too little so that the patient suffers from withdrawal symptoms and seeks supplementary supply from illicit sources, or not so much that the patient has surplus narcotics to sell to others. Unfortunately, no biochemical tests can indicate the dose an opiate user is on. Nonetheless, Marks et al (1969) have found urine analysis valuable both for detecting improper drug use and for monitoring the efficacy of treatment.

The policy of prescribing for addicts can function only if it eliminates a criminally organised black market. The supplies of over-prescribed National Health Service heroin have undoubtedly decreased, but there still is some excess on the market despite the conservative prescribing of clinic doctors. Illegally imported heroin has been reported on a few occasions, but it has posed little problem to date. Nonetheless, that source may be dangerous in the future.

However, another potential source of opiates is created by the fact that present regulations apply only to heroin and cocaine. Addicts can receive supplies of methadone, morphine or other opiates from general practitioners who may not have specialist skills in dealing with addiction.

The clinic's function of providing drugs while trying to build motivation to come off heroin is extremely difficult. The dilemma can be illustrated by the two different approaches below:

(i)   'The clinic staff could go all out to offer reality help to the addict, aiding him with accommodation and financial problems, and generally showing kindness and evident concern, so that a transference is built up, communication is established and maintained, and the patient gradually won round to accepting the staff's view that he should come off drugs. However, the result of such a human policy may sadly be the reverse of that intended: the drug taker is protected from all adverse social consequences of his addiction, and all motivation for withdrawal is sapped.'

(ii) 'The alternative policy would be to limit the clinic's activity to prescribing heroin, to hold out the offer of withdrawal, and to refuse to do anything to protect the addict from the social consequences of his behaviour, hoping that his suffering will drive him to accept help. Such an approach to the care of a sick person would to many doctors seem distasteful, and its consequence might be to destroy any hope of a good and therapeutically useful relationship being maintained. (Edwards, 1969).

Compulsory treatment for drug addicts was recommended by the second Brain Committee (Interdepartmental Committee on Drug Addiction, 1965; see Chapter 13), but this recommendation has not been accepted to date. The issue of compulsion has been discussed for many years (Glatt, 1967; Lendon, 1967), but compulsory treatment for addicts can be effected only under the general provisions of the Mental Health Act, 1959 (see below).

The concept of the 'stable addict' was applied to the therapeutic addicts which were prominent up to 1960, and it may not be applicable to the younger, more unstable, addicts now attending treatment centres. The efficacy of the various treatment regimes must be monitored to ensure that the programmes are both helping to cure individual addicts and prevent the spread of addiction.

Finally, adequate staffing of treatment centres, continual willingness to try new modes of treatment, and the provision of adequate long term rehabilitation are necessary pre-requisites to a successful system.

Connell (1969) has outlined the basic challenges of the British approach to heroin addiction. These include (i) the need for treatment centres to work together and create a relatively uniform approach, (ii) the development of reliable qualitative and quantitative tests for the detection of drugs, (iii) data on the cause and spread of drug taking, and (iv) the production of hard data on the efficacy of treatment. The greatest handicap in assessing treatment results has been the failure to provide adequate controls in methodology and the use of treatment methods from other countries, such as America, may not necessarily be applicable in Great Britain (Connell, 1970a; Connell, 1970b).

COMPULSORY TREATMENT

The Mental Health Act, 1959, provides for Emergency and Observation Orders (Section *29* and *25*).

Under an observation order, patients may be detained up to 28 days in hospital, and in an emergency the first three days on the recommendation of a doctor and mental welfare officer or a relative of the patient. An application for admission for observation may be made on the grounds:

a) 'that he is suffering from mental disorder of a nature or degree which warrants the detention of a patient under observation . . . and'

b) 'that he ought to be detained in the interests of his own health or safety or with the view to the protection of other persons.'

It must be stressed that being physically ill or addicted is *not* usually interpreted as being sufficient reason for detention under the Mental Health Act. However, emergency or observation orders might be appropriate in the case of someone suffering an acute amphetamine psychosis, or an acute depressive reaction.

A three day detention order is possible under Section *136*, if a constable finds a person in 'a place to which the public have access if the person appears to be suffering from mental disorder and to be in immediate need of care and control'. This might be used in the case of an acute LSD psychosis.

The Mental Health Act, 1959, also provides for *Treatment Orders* in Section *26*.

Patients may be detained up to one year in the first instance. Apart from persons under the age of 21, a person may be detained for treatment provided:

a) 'that he is suffering from mental illness or severe subnormality and that the disorder is of a nature or degree which warrants the detention of the patient in a hospital for medical treatment . . . and'

b) 'that it is necessary in the interests of the patient's health or safety, or for the protection of other persons, that the patient should be so detained.'

It would probably not be possible to detain a person over 21 years of age under this section unless there was evidence of mental illness concurrent with addiction.

If a person is under 21 years of age he can be detained under Section *26* with a diagnosis of 'psychopathic disorder'. A psychopathic disorder is defined as:

'a persistent disorder or disability of the mind (whether or not including subnormality of intelligence) which results in abnormally aggressive or seriously irresponsible conduct on the part of the patient, and requires, or is susceptible to, medical treatment.'

Here again, there would probably have to be evidence of persistent abnormal behaviour aside from drug addiction to allow such an order to be made.

Certain treatment orders can be made provided the person has appeared before a court for an offence that is punishable by imprisonment. Under Section *60* (Hospital Order) of the Mental Health Act, 1959, a court may authorise the admission of and detention in a hospital of a person who has been convicted before a Court of Assize or Quarter Sessions of an offence, other than an offence the sentence for which is fixed by law; or is convicted by a magistrates court of an offence punishable on summary conviction with imprisonment, provided:

a) 'the offender is suffering from mental illness, psychopathic disorder, subnormality or severe subnormality, and'

b) 'the mental disorder is of a nature or degree which warrants the detention of the patient in a hospital for medical treatment, and'

c) 'the court is of the opinion that the most suitable method of disposing of the case is by means of an order under this section.'

In these cases the Court must be satisfied that arrangements have been made for admission to a hospital and that the hospital concerned is willing to accept the patient. All provisions for hospital orders by the Courts can only be effected if the person is convicted. (Mental Health Act, 1959; British Medical Journal, 1967).

TREATMENT RESEARCH

The early research on the treatment of drug dependence in the United Kingdom was reported by general practitioners who treated addicts. For the most part these reports dealt with the characteristics of their patients and methods used to treat addiction. Most later research has outlined the progress of the specialised treatment centres, but to date there have not been any control trials reported.

Frankau and Stanwell (1961) reported on a series of 51 patients treated in their general practices between August, 1958 and March, 1960. Three groups of addicts were described: a group of therapeutic addicts, a small group of stable addicts 'from the higher social and economic levels' and 36 patients who showed the now familiar characteristics of non-therapeutic addicts who took heroin and a variety of drugs for pleasure. The treatment of the three groups is specified and a substantial number were reported off drugs. However, the short time interval and uncertainty of the follow-up methods casts some doubt on the results.

Clark (1962) has reported the follow-up of 65 patients admitted to Crighton Royal Hospital between 1949 and 1960, all of whom were drawn from the medical or nursing professions. Fifty-six per cent of the patients were addicted to drugs controlled by the Dangerous Drugs Acts and 44% to other drugs. Clark found that 28% of the patients had overcome their addiction, though only 14% of those addicted to opiates or cocaine remained drug free. The largest group were those who had resorted to drugs for varying periods of time since being discharged. Glatt (1968) has reported the outcome of treatment in respect of doctors and nurses dependent upon alcohol or drugs admitted to two different hospitals in the 1960's.

A year's intensive work with one hundred heroin and cocaine addicts is described by Hewetson and Ollendorf (1964). They describe the clinical state of the addicts and the extra time needed by a general practitioner to deal with the demands of the addicts. By 1967 this general practice had contacted 213 addicts (Hewetson, 1967). In 144 cases the treatment was temporary or the patients had lost contact. Of the remaining 69 cases, four had been off narcotics more than three years, 32 had been off 1–3 years and 20 for a year or less. In addition, 29 of the 144 patients who had not been in continuous treatment were off narcotics according to Home Office information (Hewetson, 1967).

The treatment of addicts in general practice is discussed by Merry (1967) and Ollendorf (1968). The latter considers the factors of personality, self-destruction, sex negation, psychoticism, pharmacology and group pressure to be most important. Chapple (1967) considered that treatment in a community setting was essential and that the British approach to the treatment of addiction should be experimental with different approaches for different types of addicts. The importance of research in establishing the efficacy of treatment has been stressed by Connell (1967).

Beckett (1968) and Myers (1968) have used group techniques for motivating addicts towards seeking a permanent cure. The view of addiction as a problem of community mental health has been put forward by Owens (1967). Owens recommends a policy of containing addiction by the identification and registration of addicts in a defined geographical area. Chemists, police, doctors and other community bodies should deal with the problem in an integrated approach.

Table 16—1.   Clinical Groups in a London Treatment Centre

Group	Home Office	Source of drug	Chemist	No. of patients	Mean age (yr.)	Age range (yr.)	Mean duration opioid misuse (yr.)	Mean daily opioid (mg.)
I	Known	G.P. (years)	Known	19	41.12	28—63 *	17.3	610
II	Known	G.P. (weeks or months)	Known	11	23.8	16—39 **	5.4	200
III	Known	Other treatment centre	Known	15	25.0	16—49	4.4	75
IV	Known	Illegal	Not Known	16	21.8	17—26	3.2	95
V	Not Known	Illegal	Not Known	46	23.7	14—79 ***	1.7	60

*Four patients misusing pethidine (one), methadone (one on ampoules), morphine (one).
**One USA addict aged 39, only in UK for a few months; one Canadian aged 31, withdrawn in hospital and restarted on methadone ampoules by GP; and one English addict aged 26 with history of opiate misuse for 8 years only recently obtaining drugs from his GP.
***Included Indian opium addict aged 79.

Source: Gardner R. and Connell P., (1970). One year's experience in a drug dependence clinic. *Lancet.* ii, 455.

A year's work at the National Addiction and Research Centre in London is reported by Chapple and Gray (1968). During 1967, the authors treated 225 patients addicted to heroin alone or in combination with other drugs. Patients were allocated to either a general supportive programme with heroin on prescription or to a methadone maintenance programme. One hundred and twenty-two patients were still under treatment with 33 off drugs altogether.

Behaviour therapy has been attempted with addicts. Rathod and Thomson (1968) have published a preliminary report of aversion treatment. The technique used involved injecting 30 mg. Scoline so that paralysis was produced at approximately the same time as the patient injected himself. The patient was then subjected to forceful accounts on the dangers of using heroin. Ten patients underwent treatment having a total of 49 sessions. None ever used the heroin left with them after each treatment session. Eight of the patients continued to be drug free while in hospital for an average period of 13 weeks. One patient was discharged immediately after the fifth treatment session and remained drug free in the community for a period of 23 weeks. One patient relapsed eight weeks after the fifth treatment session and was treated again, after which he remained drug free for 17 weeks. This conditioning procedure is part of a total therapeutic regime including other forms of therapy and support.

Kraft (1969) has described the successful treatment of a case of barbiturate addiction by the method of systematic desensitisation. A similar technique was less successful with narcotic addition (Hawks, 1970).

James et al (1969) comment on the methods of treatment for addicts in prison. In Brixton Prison alone 237 narcotic addicts were treated in 1968.

Opiate users identified in a community survey (Kosviner et al, 1968) were followed up by Zacune, Mitcheson and Malone (1969). Six of the original sample of 37 heroin users were not using heroin one year later, while 16 were daily users and 12 used irregularly. Of the six persons who were off heroin, four had been daily users in the original survey. New cases of opiate use in the year and general trends were also reported.

The organisation, starting and operation of a treatment centre which opened prior to the Dangerous Drugs (Supply to Addicts) Regulations, 1968 is reported by Hicks (1969). Clinical and social data on the first 57 patients are given along with a description of the treatment programme for gradual withdrawal of heroin.

Gardner and Connell (1970) report on the first year's experience in a treatment centre from March, 1968 to February, 1969. They differentiate five distinctive clinical groups (see Table 16—1). The initial management of patients is described and they report that 27% of patients had negative urine tests for opiate at first attendance. The general policy of dealing with assessment, relapse and hospital admission are discussed and the establishment of adequate clinical facilities recommended for all clinics.

REHABILITATION FACILITIES FOR DRUG ADDICTS

The need for the establishment of rehabilitation facilities for drug addicts has been recognised for some time by the Department of Health and the Home Office. In November, 1967 and again in April, 1969 the Department of Health issued circulars (Department of Health and Social Security, 1967, 1969) stressing the need for special after-care hostels as well as other rehabilitation measures They defined rehabilitation in the context as 'the re-education of the individual to live without drugs' and suggested that it should start 'as soon as a doctor accepts an addict as his patient'. It noted that the type of rehabilitation required would vary depending on the needs of the individual, but that it might involve a prolonged period in hospital followed by job placement. The importance of adequate social support throughout was stressed. Psychiatric support on an out-patient basis should also be available. If the patient should not be satisfactorily discharged to his parents home, lodgings should be sought with a reliable, understanding family. It was recognised that a number of ex-patients would require accommodation in special hostels. The establishment of such hostels is the responsibility of the Local Authorities who, it was said, 'may discharge their functions either by providing hostels themselves or supporting hostels run by voluntary bodies'.

In their special report on rehabilitation, the Advisory Committee on Drug Dependence (1968) spoke strongly for the need for such hostels and recommended that four hostels should be set up in 'metropolitan areas' of London, one of these being for women. It was suggested that the hostels should cater for up to 12 ex-patients, and perhaps be best sited in the outer suburbs, but in view of the lack of experience in England to date the Committee stressed that its recommendations were tentative and that they 'should not like their views to hinder any particular project'. A small number of residential centres catering for ex-addicts were in operation at this time, both in and outside of London, but the number of places available was considered inadequate to cope with London's growing problem.

The London Boroughs Association agreed in principle to the establishment and support of such hostels in London, but whilst they were prepared to share the financial burden of supporting these hostels, no one borough came forward with plans for establishing one at that stage. The London Boroughs Association therefore decided to support two hostels (one in and one outside the metropolis) proposed by voluntary bodies as pilot schemes with representatives of the London Boroughs Association on the management committees of these hostels.

It is difficult to assess as yet whether the facilities currently available are adequate. The general feeling is that a variety of approaches must be utilised in order to meet the many different needs of patients and because no one yet knows what is the best approach for which person. The question of residential accommodation for the using addict has been raised by the Advisory Committee who said that 'there is a need for hostels for the homeless addict attending an out-patient clinic. In the first instance plans should be made to obtain one for each sex, each taking up to 12 persons, in the metropolitan region'. Although there are hostels who will accept using addicts, so far as we know, there are none as yet which deal specifically with the care of the using addict. In addition to residential facilities, there are a small number of day centres for addicts. The intention of these in the main is to motivate using addicts towards an alternative drug-free way of life. Methods employed include drug substitution and group therapy.

CO-ORDINATION OF SERVICES

There have been a few attempts by voluntary agencies to gain an overview and attempt to co-ordinate and assess the gaps in services currently available for addicts, but to date there has been no marked success in this field. It is hoped that in the future such co-ordination and assessment will take place at a central level. The task is considerable and complex as it involves co-operation between voluntary and statutory agencies and between various Government departments, each with their special responsibilities. There is no central person or department responsible for co-ordination of rehabilitation in the drug field.

RESEARCH ON EFFECTIVENESS

There has not yet been any systematic assessment of the functioning of a rehabilitation programme, but it is possible that such research will shortly be started into the workings of two rehabilitation programmes, one in London and one in Portsmouth. Both these projects are based on principles of rehabilitation as employed by such programmes as Synanon, Day Top village and Phoenix House in the United States. Such programmes—intensive therapeutic communities based on the self-help principle and largely staffed by ex-addicts—have had a considerable degree of success in America and despite legal and cultural differences between England and America (Edwards, 1967), these techniques may be able to adapt successfully to the situation in England.

REFERENCES

ADVISORY COMMITTEE ON DRUG DEPENDENCE, 1968. *The Rehabilitation of Drug Addicts.* H.M.S.O., London.

BECKETT D., 1968. The Salter Unit, an experimental in-patient treatment centre for narcotic drug addiction. *Brit.J.Addict.* 63, 51.

BEWLEY T.H., 1970. An introduction to drug dependence. *Brit.J.Hosp.Med.* 4(2), 150.

BRITISH MEDICAL JOURNAL, 1967. Compulsory detention of narcotic addicts. *Brit.Med.J.* 2, 517.

BRITISH MEDICAL JOURNAL, 1968. Parliamentary Report. *Brit.Med.J.* 2, 311.

CHAPPLE P.A.L., 1967. Treatment in the community. *Brit.Med.J.* 2, 500.

CHAPPLE P.A.L. and GRAY G., 1968. One year's work at a centre for the treatment of addicted patients. *Lancet.* i, 908.

CLARK J.A., 1962. The prognosis in drug addiction. *J.Ment.Sci.* 108, 411.

CONNELL P.H., 1967. Importance of research. *Brit.Med.J.* 2, 499.

CONNELL P.H., 1969. Drug dependence in Great Britain: a challenge to the practice of medicine. In H. Steinberg (Ed.). *The Scientific Basis of Drug Dependence.* Churchill, London.

CONNELL P.H., 1970(a). Clinical aspects of drug addiction. *J.Royal Coll. Phycns.* 4, 254.

CONNELL P.H., 1970(b). Treatment of narcotic and non-narcotic drug dependence: the need for research. In R.V. Phillipson (Ed.). *Modern Trends in Drug Dependence and Alcoholism.* Butterworths, London.

DANGEROUS DRUGS ACT, 1967. H.M.S.O., London.

DANGEROUS DRUGS (NOTIFICATION OF ADDICTS) REGULATIONS, 1968. H.M.S.O., London.

DANGEROUS DRUGS (SUPPLY TO ADDICTS) REGULATIONS, 1968. H.M.S.O., London.

DEPARTMENT OF HEALTH AND SOCIAL SECURITY, 1967. *Local Authority Circulars 21/67.* H.M.S.O., London.

DEPARTMENT OF HEALTH AND SOCIAL SECURITY, 1969. *Local Authority Circular 7/67.* H.M.S.O., London.

EDWARDS, G., 1967. Relevance of American experience of narcotic addiction to the British scene. *Brit.Med.J.* 3, 425.

EDWARDS, G., 1969. The British approach to the treatment of heroin addiction. *Lancet.* i, 768.

FRANKAU I. and STANWELL,P., 1961. The treatment of drug addiction. *Lancet.* ii, 1377.

GARDNER R. and CONNELL, P.H., 1970. One year's experience in a drug dependence clinic. *Lancet.* ii, 455.

GLATT M.M., 1967. Correspondence in *Brit.Med.J.* 2, 309.

GLATT M.M., 1968. Correspondence in *Brit.Med.J.* 1, 380.

HAWKS D., 1970. The epidemiology of drug dependence in the United Kingdom. *Bulletin of Narcotics.* 22(3), 15.

HEWETSON J., 1967. Correspondence in *Brit.Med.J.* 1, 425.

HEWETSON J. and OLLENDORF R., 1964. Preliminary survey of 100 heroin and cocaine addicts. *Brit.J.Addict.* 59, 109.

HICKS R.C., 1969. The management of heroin addiction at a general hospital drug addiction treatment centre. *Brit.J.Addict.* 64, 235.

INTERDEPARTMENTAL COMMITTEE ON DRUG ADDICTION, 1965. *Drug Addiction.* H.M.S.O., London.

JAMES I., GRANT R., MAGUIRE T. and WARNANTS L., 1970. Correspondence in *Lancet.* i, 37.

KOSVINER A., MITCHESON M., MYERS K., OGBORNE A., STIMSON G.V., ZACUNE J. and EDWARDS G., 1968. Heroin use in a provincial town. *Lancet.* i, 1189.

KRAFT T., 1969. Successful treatment of a case of chronic barbiturate addiction. *Brit.J.Addict.* 64, 115.

LENDON N.C., 1967. Correspondence in *Brit.Med.J.* 2, 444.

MARKS V., FRY D., CHAPPELL P. and GRAY G., 1969. Application of urine analysis to diagnosis and treatment of heroin addiction. *Brit.Med.J.* 2, 153.

MENTAL HEALTH ACT, 1959. H.M.S.O., London.

MERRY J., 1967. Out-patient treatment of heroin addiction. *Lancet.* i, 205.

MINISTRY OF HEALTH AND HOME OFFICE, 1967. *Memorandum.* H.M.(67)16.

MYERS K., 1968. Heroin dependence–a community experiment in therapeutics. *Lancet.* i, 574.

OLLENDORF R., 1968. Assessment of the function of the general practitioner. *Proc.Royal Soc.Med.* 61, 181.

OWENS J., 1967. Integrated approach. *Brit.Med.J.* 2, 501.
RATHOD R. and THOMSON I.G., 1968. Aversion therapy for heroin dependence. *Lancet.* ii, 382.
ZACUNE J. MITCHESON M. and MALONE S., 1969. Heroin use in a provincial town—one year later. *Int.J.Addict.* 4, 557.

SECTION 5
EDUCATION, ADVERTISING, PREVENTION AND RESEARCH

The dissemination of information about alcohol and drug dependence is discussed in Chapter 17.

Chapter 18 deals with specialised education and training for the professions which are most likely to come into contact with alcohol or drug problems.

The role of advertising in the promotion of alcohol and drugs is reviewed in Chapter 19. The findings on alcohol promotion relate to how alcohol is displayed in the press, television, and other media to the general population. Drug advertising concerns the mass promotion of household medicines and techniques used by the pharmaceutical manufacturers to promote their products to medical practitioners.

Approaches to the prevention of alcohol and drug dependence and the role of research are examined in Chapters 20 and 21.

CHAPTER 17
EDUCATION OF THE PUBLIC ON ALCOHOL AND DRUG DEPENDENCE

The general population of Great Britain is exposed to a large variety of sources of education in relation to alcohol and drug dependence. This chapter examines the role of the school in providing information about alcohol and other drugs. The availability of general books and specialised information available to the public is considered, along with various organisations and bodies who include among their activities providing educational material on alcohol and/or drug dependence. Information contained in the newspapers, television and radio is discussed in Chapter 19 which is concerned with the response of the mass media.

EDUCATION IN SCHOOLS ABOUT THE USE OF ALCOHOL AND OTHER DRUGS

Government departments can make recommendations with regard to the contents of school and public education, but have no power to compel local authorities or individual schools to teach any particular subject (except religious instruction). The Department of Education and Science encourages health education on drugs, alcohol and tobacco, devoting a chapter to these subjects in *A Handbook of Health Education* (Department of Education and Science, 1968). This book, quoting a letter from the Principal Medical Officer of the Department of Education and Science to Principal School Medical Officers (dated 25th July, 1967), said:

'As regards the identification of children taking drugs, it is well-known that a diagnosis of drug dependence is extremely difficult and that in the early stages of the condition there are no specific signs or symptoms whereby it may be recognised with certainty. Whilst it may manifestly affect a child's behaviour in a variety of ways, such behaviour may equally be due to other causes than the taking of drugs. Insofar as the incentive to experiment with drugs is primarily social in origin, though it may ultimately lead to a situation calling for medical, including psychiatric help, the detection of drug dependence lies in the early recognition of a measure of mal-adjustment that warrants investigation. For this reason it is especially important that those who are in daily contact with young people, and particularly teachers, should be alert to behaviour clearly uncharacteristic of the child, or to a developing pattern of behaviour likely to interfere with his educational progress and social development. Furthermore it is essential that they should be fully appraised of the need to seek medical advice regarding children showing such behaviour. This advice should be available from school doctors, to whom head-teachers (acting also for class teachers) should turn in the first place'.

The Handbook gives information on the misuse of alcohol and various drugs and then recommends:

'Teachers will also wish to give pupils the kind of help which might prevent drug taking. While objective, scientific information about the dangers of drug taking may protect pupils, the subject should not be handled in such a way as to lend unnecessary glamour or to encourage its concealment. Thus, drug taking should be discussed in its proper context as an aspect of health education, the proper use of medicaments and the solving of social problems....'

'Health education should attempt to inform young people about the risks of misuse of both tobacco and alcohol and, even more important, should try to impart attitudes which allow young people to make independent decisions and free them from the necessity of always following the social group. ...'

'Teaching about alcohol should, as with drugs, be put into its proper context, in order to avoid the "limelight" treatment as in the delivery of special lectures on the dangers of alcohol and its improper use.' (Department of Education and Science, 1968).

The Department of Health and Social Security has, since 1968, channelled its educational work on alcohol and drug use through the Health Education Council. The Council is an independent organisation financed to the extent of 88% by the Government, but also receiving a certain amount of support from local authorities and private donations. It has a bibliography and list of films and filmstrips about alcohol and drugs which can be forwarded to schools on request. The Health Education Council concentrates mainly on educating the educators by supplying factual information to teachers and groups of teachers.

A survey of the policies and practices on drug education in schools by local education authorities was undertaken by the Advisory Centre for Education (McAlhone, 1970). All principal and divisional school medical officers listed in the current Education Committee's Year Book (272 in all) were asked in a postal survey what was being done about drug education in their areas. Full replies were received from 116 medical officers giving a response rate of just over 42%. The services provided by the local authorities were divided into six categories:

1) 'Providing written and/or visual materials.
2) Holding or planning to hold day conferences for pupils.
3) Holding or planning to hold conferences for teachers.
4) Arranging lectures, talks or discussion for pupils, sometimes by health educators.
5) Arranging lectures, talks or discussion for teachers.
6) Including teaching on drugs in the health education syllabuses in schools'. (McAlhone, 1970).

Fifty-four of the authorities provided three or more of the services listed above, which included education for both teachers and pupils. Fifty-one local authorities provided one or two services with all but three authorities providing educational material for pupils. Eleven of the authorities (9%) replied that they provided no services for drug education in that area. (McAlhone, 1970).

It is difficult to draw any broad conclusions from this survey since 58% of the authorities did not reply and it is impossible to know whether they are doing anything or not. Nonetheless, it is clear that while some authorities have carefully thought out policies on drug education, many others have not.

In general, the methods used for imparting information on alcohol and drugs vary considerably, and depend to a large extent on the policy of the local education authority and the attitudes of the particular headmaster or headmistress in a school. Drug or alcohol education is in some places, introduced as a part of a general course in personal relationships, biology, or social education. In other schools specialised methods and techniques are employed, such as filmstrips, tape-recordings, films or lecturers brought in from outside the school. There is no general agreement about the efficacy of the various methods employed in promoting attitude change.

The Advisory Committee on Drug Dependence (1970) commented that in relation to drugs: 'The preventive role that the schools can play is crucial, if only because the school is the one universal meeting ground for all boys and girls between the ages of 5 and 15....'. The local education authorities have made some effort to distribute booklets, tape recordings, films and other material about drugs and alcohol. Aside from the list of material supplied from the Health Education Council, there is also a more limited list circulated by the Teachers' Advisory Council on Alcohol and Drug Education. A number of small, inexpensive booklets are available to schools. The two most widely used are pamphlets by Wood (Undated) who is now with the Health Education Council, and booklets by Schofield et al (undated and Wright (undated). For more detailed study by the older age groups in schools, there is a booklet by the Office of Health Economics (1967) concerned with drugs, and two books intended for fifth and sixth form students (Leech and Jordan, 1967; Newmark, 1968). Booklets used in schools concerning alcoholism include Kemp (undated) and Eliot (undated) as well as a pamphlet by the Office of Health Economics (1970) on alcohol abuse.

In the survey by the Advisory Centre for Education (McAlhone, 1970) the film, filmstrip and audio-tape materials available were more heavily criticised by teachers and medical officers than the pamphlets and books. Many of the available films were made in America and show a different cultural setting for alcohol or drugs misuse, and otherwise most of the films were felt to be either horrific or too tedious. There is no doubt about the need for better audio-visual educational material about alcohol and drug dependence.

BOOKS GENERALLY AVAILABLE ON ALCOHOL AND DRUG DEPENDENCE

There are a large number of readily available publications on drug dependence. Among the books intended for research workers or for the education of professionals are the books by Steinberg (1969), Wilson (1968), Willis (1969) and Lingeman (1970). Books aimed at a more general audience describing the drug scene in Great Britain include Glatt et al (1967), Laurie (1967), Silberman (1967) and the pamphlet put out by the Office of Health Economics (1967). General books describing drugs in relation to the law or specialised social problems associated with drug abuse include Jones (1968), Dawtry (1968), Coon and Harris (1970), Deedes (1970), Mitchell (1969), Birdwood (1969) and the National Council for Civil Liberties (1969). The use of drugs among a sample of school children is described by Weiner (1970).

Books that are generally available about alcohol dependence include Kessel and Walton (1965), Williams (1967), Glatt (1970) and Ritson and Hassall (1969). Two pamphlets on alcoholism are available by Prys Williams (1965a, 1965b) and a pamphlet on the abuse of alcohol by the Office of Health Economics (1970). A survey on alcoholism in a defined geographic area is reported by Moss and Davies

(1967) and a general history of public houses in England is published by Monckton (1969).

NATIONAL AND LOCAL ORGANISATIONS CONCERNED WITH EDUCATION OF THE PUBLIC ON THE PROBLEMS OF ALCOHOL AND OTHER DRUGS

While it is beyond the scope of this book to provide a directory to all national and local organisations concerning themselves with alcohol and/or drug dependence, it is important to indicate the scope of activities undertaken by non-Governmental organisations. The organisations cited are selected to indicate various areas of concern, but this listing is in no way comprehensive.

Organisations Concerned with Alcoholism

The National Council on Alcoholism was founded in 1963 to educate the general public about alcoholism and to act as a referral agency to help the alcoholic, his friends and employers. The Council publishes material relating to alcohol dependence and has local councils and information centres throughout Great Britain. Information centres operate in Glasgow, Edinburgh, Liverpool, Coventry, Exeter, Southampton and Bristol. Regional councils, such as the Merseyside Council in Liverpool, pursue independent activities in line with the policy of the national body.

Autonomous regional councils on alcoholism include the Camberwell Council on Alcoholism which operates in south east London, and has organised an international symposium on the drunkenness offence (Cook et al, 1969), and is associated with the Summer School on Alcoholism (see Chapter 18). The Tower Hamlets Council on Alcoholism in east London is manned by voluntary workers and is applying for affiliation to the National Council.

Three other local councils are concerned with both alcoholism and addiction to other drugs in Gloucester, Oxford and Cardiff.

The Medical Council on Alcoholism is a scientific body with medical interests and it sponsors research into alcoholism. It has responsibility for a publication directed at general medical practitioners entitled *The Journal of Alcoholism,* which is published three times a year.

Alcoholics Anonymous has many branches and local meetings which provide information on alcoholism and which help alcoholics to sobriety. Al-Anon is an association of the wives of alcoholics, and is associated with Alcoholics Anonymous.

There are several organisations which are concerned with promoting temperance and abstinence from alcohol. These include the Temperance Council of Christian Churches, the United Kingdom Alliance, the British National Temperance League and the National and London United Temperance Council. These organisations provide information for teaching about the dangers arising from alcohol and drug consumption.

The Salvation Army and the Church Army have long been concerned with the abuse of alcohol and have both information and other services available to alcoholics.

The Christian Economic and Social Research Foundation provides information about changing patterns in alcohol consumption and publishes an analysis on trends of advertising about alcohol (see Chapter 19).

These bodies, for the most part, organise conference to facilitate communications about the problems of alcohol abuse, distribute posters, produce leaflets and other forms of information and publish several journals of limited and specialised circulation. The lack of co-ordination among the various services make it impossible to evaluate their efficacy

There are two centrally organised health education bodies in Scotland which are concerned with alcoholism, the Scottish Health Education Unit, which is a part of the Government's Scottish Office, and a voluntary body, the Scottish Council for Health Education.

Health education on alcohol dependence is of two varieties. The first is said to contribute to 'primary prevention' and is concerned with personal and social attitudes to alcoholism and sobriety and to drinking patterns generally. In some way, as yet undefined, these attitudes together with such factors as legal and fiscal policy are said to contribute to the level of alcoholism in the community. The Scottish Health Education Unit is concerned in the promotion of research in this field. The research, which is now underway, and which is expected to take a minimum period of two years, is designed to study the formation of attitudes to the use of alcohol amongst school children and young people. There is no other primary prevention orientated activity conducted in Scotland at the moment.

The second variety of health education is concerned with 'secondary prevention'; it is designed to deal with potential and actual alcoholics. Most of the efforts of the Health Education Unit and the Council for Health Education have concentrated on this area. Their professed aims have been:

a) to increase awareness in the general public of the nature of alcoholism to promote the notion that it is a disease with grave socio-medical consequences and that it can be arrested;

b) that influential members of the public should be encouraged to accept the seriousness of alcoholism as a problem, and that financial and other resources must be made available to combat it;

c) to increase the understanding of the problem in the medical, nursing and social work professions as well as professions like the police, etc. whose work brings them into daily contact with alcoholics;

d) that the alcoholic, his family, friends, employers, and colleagues should be led to the conviction that the disease can be arrested and that care should be sought.

In attempting to implement these proposals, the two agencies have carried out a poster campaign in 1968–69 (costing £3100) aimed at the general public and informing them that one in four male patients admitted to mental hospitals in Scotland is an alcoholic. This effort was widespread but its impact was limited. In 1969–70, the sum of £1700 was spent on newspaper advertising campaigns carried out during March, 1970, including some ten advertisements carried in the daily press. Evaluation of these advertisements suggests that approximately 7% of the readership of over one million persons saw and recalled this advertisement. In 1970–71 the two agencies proposed to move from simply informing the general public to informing the alcoholic or his relatives and friends that the disease can be arrested and, therefore, treatment should be sought. The sum of £7000 has been made available for a campaign towards the end of 1970, this may well be the largest such exercise in this field carried out in Great Britain.

In addition, conferences are organised by relevant organisations to discuss the problem of alcoholism with councillors, magistrates, ministers, employers and trade unionists. The Scottish Council of Health Education also holds one-day courses for hospital employees, teachers and others concerned with the need for education about alcohol dependence.

During 1968 and 1969 a review of what had been done in the field of health education, both nationally and internationally, was carried by an educationalist working in the Scottish Health Education Unit. This review is now being published in the Scottish Health Services Study series, and should shortly be available.

National and Local Organisations concerned with Public Education on Drug Abuse

The Association for the Prevention of Addiction is a national voluntary body which exists to help drug addicts and their parents, as well as to provide educational material to the public about drug addiction. The Association has a head office in London and local branches throughout Great Britain. The Association provides a variety of services, including the organisation of conferences, advisory centres, referral centres and educational projects.

The Society for the Study of Addiction is a scientific body with international membership, having for its objects the systematic study of dependence on alcohol and other drugs and the investigation of all forms of addiction. The Society holds a variety of meetings and is responsible for the publication of the British Journal of Addiction.

The Drug Dependency Discussion Group was set up under the auspices of the King's Fund Hospital Centre in May, 1968 and has general meetings attended by doctors, nurses and social workers concerned with the management of drug addiction.

The Womens' Group on Public Welfare prepared a report in 1967 on information gathered in 63 geographic areas of Great Britain. Preventative education on drug abuse seems to be underway in over half of these areas with local bodies arranging talks and conferences. Information has been collected and disseminated for the education of youth leaders and youth club members, as well as for educationalists, medical officers, probation officers and/or police. The report points out that the education of the general public has largely been in the hands of voluntary bodies, including Council of Social Services, community councils, associations for mental health, branches of the British Medical Association, religious organisations and womens' organisations generally, especially the Women's Royal Voluntary Society.

A number of communities have set up co-ordination and liaison committees consisting of individuals and members of professional bodies who are concerned with drug misuse and its control. Bradford, Birmingham, Leicester, Cambridge, and Wolverhampton are among the communities with groups existing for the containment of drug addiction. These groups all provide channels of communication for the many services dealing with drug addicts and undertake, in various ways, an advisory service to parents, teachers, general practitioners and others concerned with any aspect of drug addiction.

The National Association of Youth Clubs and the National Addiction Research Centre (Chelsea) have organised three experimental educational programmes. These included lectures, films, tape-recordings, pamphlets and group discussions on drugs for young people. An attempt was made to evaluate the effectiveness of these programmes and a detailed analysis of these results is continuing.

In general, there is widespread interest in the problems of drug abuse, and local communities are attempting to provide information for the public in the ways that would seem most suitable to their particular areas.

EDUCATION AND DRUNKEN DRIVING CAMPAIGNS

Towards the end of 1964 there took place the largest Road Safety Campaign ever conducted in this country. Television, press, outdoor and other media were used in order to urge people not to drink before driving and not to offer drinks to those who were about to drive. This campaign followed recent changes in the law relating to drinking and driving. The publicity also had an informative character, and stress was laid on medical evidence concerning the effect of small amounts of alcohol and on the high number of fatal accidents (half of which were known to have involved someone who had been drinking recently), during Christmas 1963 (Road Research Laboratory, 1965–1968).

The Road Research Laboratory of the Ministry of Transport commissioned an independent market research bureau to assess the effects of this campaign on people's behaviour and beliefs. This survey was conducted by means of a detailed questionnaire completed during personal interviews with a probability sample of just over 1000 men who held a full or provisional driving licence at that time and were interviewed immediately prior to the publicity campaign. A second sample of an equal number of different individuals answered the same questions directly after, to find out the extent to which people had seen and understood the publicity, what they had thought about it and their individual driving habits its and experiences. The principal conclusions drawn from this particular report were as follows:

a) There was no evidence that the campaign led to any overall reduction in the proportion of men who sometimes have a drink before driving.

b) Drinking before driving appears to be more likely amongst young or inexperienced drivers, and among the middle-class.

c) Nearly everyone interviewed afterwards had seen something of the campaign publicity, and attitudes expressed were 'generally favourable'.

d) The campaign increased public knowledge of the effects on driving of comparatively small amounts of drink.

e) Increased support was found for most of the new penalties for driving under the influence of drink, after the campaign—though overall ignorance was widespread.

f) People were assessed as being more intolerant towards drinking and driving *after* the campaign than before it.

(Road Research Laboratory, 1967; British Market Research Bureau Limited, 1965).

The full results of this campaign were assessed by a series of reports which attempted to pick out the effects of the exhibitions, the press campaigns, the showing of a film, the Ministry of Transport leaflet on drinking and driving, and the actual survey amongst drivers (Road Research Laboratory, 1965–1968).

A further new law on drinking and driving (Road Safety Act, 1967) came into force on 9th October, 1967, following which the Ministry of Transport once more ran a large-scale publicity campaign (from 25th September until 31st December). The aim of the campaign was to inform the public about the new law, to explain that there was to be a limit set in terms of blood concentration of alcohol, that an initial assessment of this level would be made by means of breath tests conducted by the police and to provide information about the penalties involved. An attempt was also made to make the public aware of the dangers involved in drinking and driving.

Two surveys were in fact carried out, one just before and one just after the campaign with the data collected by an independent organisation (National Opinion Polls Limited) for the Ministry of Transport. The questionnaire used was based on that described above, though slightly shorter, the questions being framed to provide as much information as possible concerning changes in knowledge, attitude and behaviour. In this case the sample was one already drawn for a different 'omnibus survey', the periods of the survey being September 13th–18th, 1967 and January 24th–29th, 1968. In summary, the results of the second survey were as follows:

1. Drivers drank away from home as often as previously following the new law, but were less likely to drive after drinking.

2. Amongst drivers there was an increasing knowledge about the new law and what it meant for them; few people disapproving of police powers.

3. The majority of drivers thought they knew how much drink it was safe to take before reaching the limit, and the extent to which they were tolerant of drinking and driving seemed not to have changed.

(Road Research Laboratory, 1968–70).

An attempt was made to assess the extent to which changes resulted from changes in the law, from the effect of the campaign or from the free publicity obtained.

REFERENCES

ADVISORY COMMITTEE ON DRUG DEPENDENCE, 1970. *The Amphetamines and Lysergic Acid Diethylamide (LSD)*. H.M.S.O., London.

BIRDWOOD G., 1969. *The Willing Victim: a Parents' Guide to Drug Abuse*. Secker and Warburg, London.

BRITISH MARKET RESEARCH BUREAU LIMITED, 1965. *Drinking and Driving: Report on Two Surveys Before and After a Road Safety Campaign*. British Market Research Bureau, London.

COOK T., GATH D. and HENSMAN C. (Ed.), 1969. *The Drunkenness Offence*. Pergamon, London.

COON C. and HARRIS R., 1970. *The Release Report on Drug Offenders and the Law*. Sphere, London.

DAWTRY, F. (Ed.), 1968. *Social Problems of Drug Abuse*. Butterworths, London.

DEEDS W., 1970. *The Drugs Epidemic*. Tom Stacy, London.

DEPARTMENT OF EDUCATION AND SCIENCE, 1968. *A Handbook of Health Education*. H.M.S.O., London.

ELIOT, Daphne. *The Facts About Alcohol*. National Council on Alcoholism, London.

GLATT M.M., 1970. *The Alcoholic and the Help He Needs*. Priory Press, Royston.

GLATT M.M., PITTMAN D., GILLESPIE D. and HILLS D., 1967. *The Drug Scene in Great Britain—Journey into Loneliness*. Arnold, London.

JONES T., 1968. *Drugs and the Police*. Butterworths, London.

KEMP, Robert. *Drinking and Alcoholism*. Family Doctor Booklet. British Medical Association, London.

KESSEL N. and WALTON H., 1965. *Alcoholism*. Penguin, London.

LAURIE, Peter, 1967. *Drugs: Medical, Psychological and Social Facts*. Penguin, London.

LINGEMAN R., 1970. *Drugs from A to Z*. Allan Lane, The Penguin Press, London.

McALHONE, Beryl (Ed.), 1970. *WHERE on drugs: a parents' handbook*. Advisory Centre on Education, Cambridge.

MITCHELL A.R.K., 1969. *Drugs: The Parents' Dilema*. Priory Press, Royston.

MONCKTON H.A., 1969. *History of the English Public House*. Bodley Head, London.

MOSS M. and DAVIES, E. Beresford, 1967. *A Survey of Alcoholism in an English County*. Geigy, London.

NATIONAL COUNCIL FOR CIVIL LIBERTIES, 1969. *Drugs and the Law*. National Council for Civil Liberties, London.

NEWMARK, Peter, 1968. *Connexions—Out of your Mind?* Penguin, London.

OFFICE OF HEALTH ECONOMICS, 1967. *Drug Addiction*. Office of Health Economics, London.

OFFICE OF HEALTH ECONOMICS, 1970. *Alcohol Abuse*. Office of Health Economics, London.

PRYS-WILLIAMS G., 1965 (a). *Decade of Drunkenness*. National Council on Alcoholism, London.

PRYS-WILLIAMS G., 1965 (b). *Chronic Alcoholics*. National Council on Alcoholism, London.

RITSON B. and HASSALL C., 1969. *The Management of Alcoholism*. Livingstone, London.

ROAD RESEARCH LABORATORY, 1965–1968. *Technical Reports*. Road Research Laboratory, Crowthorne.

ROAD RESEARCH LABORATORY, 1968–1970. *Technical Reports*. Road Research Laboratory, Crowthorne.

ROAD SAFETY ACT, 1967. H.M.S.O., London.

SCHOFIELD A., JOYCE C.R.B., MITCHESON M., DOWNES D. and CHAPPLE P. *Behind the Drug Scene*. Family Doctor Booklet, British Medical Association, London.

SILBERMAN M., 1967. *Aspects of Drugs Addiction*. Royal London Prisoners' Aid Society, London.

STEINBERG, Hannah (Ed.), 1969. *The Scientific Basis of Drug Dependence*. Churchill, London.

WEINER R.S.P., 1970. *Drugs and School Children*. Longmans, London.

WILLIAMS, Lincoln, 1967. *Alcoholism Explained*. Evans, London.

WILLIS J., 1969. *Drug Addiction, A Study for Nurses and Social Workers*. Faber, London.

WILSON C.D.M., 1968. *The Pharmacological and Epidemiological Aspects of Adolescent Drug Dependence*. Pergamon, Oxford.

WOOD Anthony. *Drug Dependence*. Corporation of Bristol and Bristol Council of Social Science.

WOOD Anthony. *Pot or Not?* British Medical Association, London.

WRIGHT J.D. *About Drugs*. Health Department, Wolverhampton.

CHAPTER 18

PROFESSIONAL EDUCATION AND TRAINING
ON THE
PROBLEMS OF ALCOHOL AND DRUGS

TRAINING FOR TEACHERS

The initial training of teachers in Great Britain is the responsibility of various universities, Institutes of Education and teacher training colleges. A short questionnaire was prepared by the Addiction Research Unit (Blumberg, 1970) on the availability and adequacy of training on the problems of alcohol and drug dependence. This questionnaire was sent to Institutes of Education and teacher training colleges in Great Britain. The usual arrangement in these teacher training institutions is to have at least one staff member responsible for teaching health education, though usually this is a responsibility additional to a more sizeable teaching commitment. While the health education curriculum always includes general hygiene, it may or may not extend to cover aspects of alcohol and drug dependence. The educational establishments are responsible for the design of curriculum. Approximately one-third of the teacher training colleges replied that they had no specified training for teachers on problems of alcohol or drug dependence. Just over one-third indicated that they required one or two lectures on the problem in a compulsory course. Just under one-third of the institutions reported a more intensive treatment of alcohol and drug dependence in either a compulsory or optional course.

Educational programmes and in-service training of teachers are the responsibility of over 150 Local Authorities. The Local Education Authorities have a wide variety of programmes for practising teachers. It is possible only to make general observations on the arrangements for imparting knowledge on alcohol and/or other drugs. Much will depend upon the individual headmasters and teachers, who may relate information to pupils or may be assisted by lecturers from outside, possibly provided by Local Medical Officers of Health, doctors, voluntary agencies, or other bodies. Questionnaires sent to the Local Education Authorities (Blumberg, 1970) yielded the following response:-

Out of 98 replies, 53 authorities indicated they had no clearly formulated policy, except that relevant publications and other information may be provided to head-teachers, or that there may be occasional talks by persons knowledgeable in the field.

Sixteen replies emphasised the in-service training of Medical Officers of Health within a school service. These medical officers would presumably be responsible for communicating their specialist knowledge.

Fourteen replies indicated some in-service training of teachers or some consideration being given to specific programmes in schools.

Sixteen replies indicated the availability of voluntary seminars and symposia for teachers.

(Blumberg, 1970).

In addition, the Health Education Council provides programme material on alcohol and drug dependence and in-service training for teachers, medical officers and school nurses.

TRAINING IN UNDERGRADUATE PROGRAMMES FOR MEDICINE

Medical students are not required to have any special practical experience of alcoholics or drug addicts beyond what they may encounter in the course of their clinical clerkships. It is likely that theoretical instruction on these topics would be limited to one or two lectures within the context of a series on psychiatry. The lecturers responsible would not necessarily be regarded as specialists in the field of addiction. Questionnaires on the training of medical students were sent to 34 medical schools by Blumberg (1970). Of the 22 replies received, all the schools indicated some relevant training. The minimum training consisted of one or two lectures, usually in the Department of Psychiatry and/or Pharmacology with the content related to standard text books in those fields. The amount of time as a whole devoted to psychiatry in the course of medical training hardly permits very specialist concentration on the problems of addiction. However, a few of the medical schools replying to the questionnaire did offer particularly comprehensive programmes, including additional training for those who wished it. Roughly equal teaching was indicated for drug and alcohol dependence.

The published syllabuses for the qualifying examinations of the Conjoint Board of the Royal College of Physicians (London) and the Royal College of Surgeons (England), and for various postgraduate diploma examinations make no specific references to alcohol or drugs use. Questions on dependence are frequently set for the Diploma in Medical Jurisprudence (Apothecaries).

Following the Todd Report (Royal Commission on Medical Education, 1968) substantial re-thinking and re-planning are likely to occur as regards the content and nature of undergraduate medical courses. It has been recommended that more attention be devoted to psychiatry in general medical training. However, it will be several years before these recommendations can be implemented.

TRAINING IN POSTGRADUATE PROGRAMMES FOR MEDICINE

At the postgraduate level, only doctors holding psychiatric appointments are likely to have specialist experience in the field of addiction. Most regional hospital boards and some teaching hospitals have special units for the treatment of alcoholism and other units for drug addiction (see Chapters 15 and 16). Junior medical posts in such units offer practical experience in the field of addiction, but it is still exceptional for such posts to be exclusively concerned with addiction.

Doctors specialising in Public Health are likely to have had a small number of lectures on the subjects of alcohol and drugs in the context of a wider course. Some may be able to have more specialist knowledge during their training through an elective course.

General medical practitioners are not likely to have had any special instruction in addiction, although some recent courses for trainee grades organised by the Royal College of General Practitioners have devoted one or two half days to this topic. There are also courses for general practitioners in most branches of medicine organised through local Deans who are linked with the British Postgraduate Medical Federation. It is rare to have special courses in alcoholism and drug addiction, though, say, one half-day out of a five-day course in psychiatry is arranged at some centres. The Federation does, however, recognise facilities for general practitioners available at the Summer School on Alcoholism (see below).

NURSING

Alcoholism and drug addiction feature in the syllabus for the training of nurses, especially psychiatric nurses and again it is likely that one or two lectures at the most are provided. There is no requirement actually to have nursed such patients or to have spent time in a specialised unit. Post-certificate courses do exist and any special practical experience would have to be obtained by working in a drug or alcohol unit. Such a post would be specially advertised.

PROBATION OFFICERS AND POLICE

Probation officers and police seem to have no special arrangement for acquiring expert knowledge in dealing with alcoholics and drug offenders. Police training takes place during three months of the outset of the career. In this training, special instructions on drugs and alcoholism play a very small part and seem to mainly consist of instruction in existing legislation. Police learn to deal with specific situations while on the job. Probation Officers are likely to get a brief general overview of addiction problems in the course of their training and, here again, experience is usually gained when dealing with individual cases.

SOCIAL WORK

There is no national syllabus for professional training in social work and syllabuses for diplomas and degrees in the social sciences, social administration and related subjects are laid down specifically by the university concerned. In addition to these preliminary diploma and degree courses, which are usually a pre-requisite to social work training courses, most universities offer a post-graduate social work course. Outside universities there exist other social work training courses promoted by the Council for the Training in Social Work, which are sited in Colleges of Further Education and Polytechnics. These courses combine social science and social administration teaching with social work training. Post-professional courses are offered by the National Institute of Social Work Training in London, where teaching is based on the contributions of students who are qualified senior social workers. Characteristic of all social work courses is flexibility of content which tends to change and develop yearly.

With some exceptions the basic social work training courses include at least some relevant lectures, usually equally divided between drug and alcohol use, and these are featured as topics of special interest or contemporary social problems. In 1968 7 of 26 Council for Training in Social Work Courses set questions specifically referring to drug addiction and misuse. Social workers most likely to deal with drug addicts or alcoholics are psychiatric social workers, medical social workers and probation officers. The social work courses which offer specialisation in one or more of these fields are likely to incorporate training related to alcohol and drug addiction. Information concerning the addictions is usually taught in the context of deviant behaviour and presented from a sociological point of view, as well as being included in a general series of lectures in clinical psychiatry. Applied social studies courses concentrate on the study of addictions as problems of individual behaviour and family relationships and consider methods of social work help on a case-work or small group basis. In addition to lectures, students can participate in case discussions, seminars, patient demonstrations and have first hand experience of clients misusing alcohol or drugs in field work placements, depending on their availability. The amount of training available for social workers depends on the extent of the problem in any particular geographic area and the number of facilities which are available for alcoholics and drug addicts.

THE SUMMER SCHOOL ON ALCOHOLISM

The inter-disciplinary nature of alcohol (and drug) dependence makes it difficult to co-ordinate specialised education. To meet this need, a Summer School on Alcoholism, under the aegis of the Camberwell Council on Alcoholism and supported by the Rowntree Social Services Trust, was inaugurated in 1969. The Summer School offers a whole week, once yearly, of specialised instruction in all aspects of alcoholism to representatives from all the professional groups involved—doctors, nurses, social workers, prison officers, police, probation officers and others. At the first two Schools some 200 members attended, and it was agreed that the Schools fulfilled a need for education in this field which had not previously been adequately met.

The staff is drawn from specialised professionals in the field of alcoholism working in universities, research institutions and alcohol units. The teaching methods include video-tape, group discussions and lecture.

Analysis of the professions of those attending the Summer School shows the disciplines involved and reflects the need for new types of specialised education in the fields of alcoholism and drug addiction.

Table 18—1.   **Summer School on Alcoholism: Members Attending (Cumulative total for 1969 and 1970).**

Psychiatrists	10	
Other doctors (whole or part-time)	31	41
Social Workers		40
Nurses		26
Probation Officers		21
Prison Staff (other than medical)		21
Mental (and other) Welfare Officers		14
Clergymen		12
Hostel Wardens		7
Psychologists		4
Police		1
Others		9
	Total:	196

Source: Personal Communication.

REFERENCES

BLUMBERG H., 1970. Unpublished Report. Addiction Research Unit, London.
ROYAL COMMISSION ON MEDICAL EDUCATION, 1968. H.M.S.O., London.

CHAPTER 19
ADVERTISING AND MASS MEDIA

ADVERTISING

Alcoholic drinks are widely advertised in Great Britain, especially in the press, on television and on outdoor posters. While household medicines can be advertised in the mass media, the bulk of marketing for pharmaceutical products is by advertisements in specialist medical journals, by promotional literature sent to doctors and by representatives of the pharmaceutical manufacturers. The patterns of advertising for alcohol and other drugs will be considered separately.

Advertising Alcohol

The total national advertising bill for alcoholic drinks in Great Britain in 1967 was £25.5 million. This figure represents 1.6% of the total national expenditure on drink in that year (£158.5 million). In the nine year period 1959–1967, the amount spent on advertising alcohol increased by more than 41% (see Table 19–1).

Table 19–1. Estimated Total Expenditure on Alcoholic Drink Advertising (£ million). 1959, 1962 and 1967.

	1959		1962		1967	
	£ million	%	£ million	%	£ million	%
Press	8.1	45.0	9.8	42.6	9.4	36.9
Television	2.4	13.3	4.4	19.1	6.5	25.5
Outdoor (posters, etc.)	3.1	17.2	3.7	16.1	4.1	16.1
Other	4.4	24.5	5.1	22.2	5.5	21.5
Total: (£ million)	18.0	100%	23.0	100%	25.5	100%

Source: Adapted from Christian Economic and Social Research Foundation. *Ten Years of Advertising Alcohol–A Study of Expenditure and Trends in the Sales Promotion of Alcoholic Drinks.* C.E.S.R.F., London. 1969.

The largest part of the advertising budget is spent on advertising in the newspapers and increasingly on the Independent Television networks (The British Broadcasting Corporation–B.B.C.–is not permitted to accept advertising). The remainder is spent on outdoor posters and hoardings, and on other varied publicity. Advertisements appear, for instance, in theatre and sports programmes, in airline literature, on beer mats, ash-trays, paper napkins and in short commercials at public cinemas.

Although advertisements in the newspapers and magazines are the most important medium for sales promotion of all alcoholic drinks taken together, television is becoming relatively more important. Between 1959 and 1967 television gained an additional 12.2% of alcohol advertising revenue while the press lost 8.1% (see Table 19–1). Outdoor and other advertising also received a relatively smaller share by 1967.

This trend from press to television advertising is most striking in the promotion of beer. In 1959, the beer industry spent £1.3 million on press display and £1.2 million on television. By 1967 only £912,000 was spent in the press and £3.7 million on television advertising.

The market for beer in the United Kingdom is complicated, and tastes are changing. Advertising took full account of these complexities. Lager, stout and other forms of the beverage such as light ale, canned, bottled and keg beers, each received tailor-made promotion. There was also a collective campaign by the brewers to encourage beer drinking generally, and also the habit of drinking in public houses, rather than at home.

The following may serve as illustrations of the type of presentation used:-

Lager represents a growth section of the beer market. The appeal used was initially to the young, and particularly to women, in the belief that they would be attracted to a light, chilled beer. Later the campaign emphasised the cosmopolitan connotation of lager drinking. Thus, one advertisement showed a girl drinking Skol with a caption tagged by the Italian flag which read:

'In tutto il mondo la freschezza di Skol'.
'Say Skol . . . and quench your thirst with the International lager brewed to the same high standards all round the world . . .'
(Christian Economic and Social Research Foundation, 1969).

Stout. The general trend of the market has been away from darker, sweeter beers, or drinks associated (as one advertising manager has put it) with char-ladies and labourers. The selling points have therefore been the gourmet aspect ('Guinness goes well with good food'), the alleged health-giving character of this beverage ('Not just because Mackeson looks good. Nor even because it tastes good. But because, as we've always said, by golly—it does you good'), and a direct appeal to women ('You should see me on a Friday, when I've done the weekend shopping—it's down with the shopping bags, feet up and a glass of Guinness. By the time the kids get back from school, I'm fighting fit again . . .').
(Christian Economic and Social Research Foundation, 1969).

Light Ales. These attracted three-fifths of all beer advertising in 1967 and the appeal was very wide-ranging. There was a straight appeal to men ('Red Barrel—for men who can handle a fistful of flavour'), but women also were aimed at, usually in a romantic or sociable setting. A man and a woman's hands on a double-handled glass was captioned: 'Ansells makes friends'. A couple at a party were captioned as saying: 'Gold Triangle Bass for both of us'.
(Christian Economic and Social Research Foundation, 1969).

The total expenditure on the advertising and sales promotion of alcoholic drinks other than beer in 1967 was £15 million (59% of total promotion). Television's share of this amount has not increased as it has for beer, mainly because of a voluntary agreement by manufacturers of spirits not to advertise on television.

However, the consumption of alcoholic drinks other than beer—spirits, wines and ciders—has been rising at a faster rate in Great Britain than that of beer itself over the last decade. This phenomenon apparently reflects rising incomes and the belief that drinking Beaujolais, for instance, rather than bitter beer, or gin rather than Guinness, is evidence of having attained a higher social standing. Sixty-seven per cent of public spending on alcohol other than beer, was on spirits (nearly half of this on whisky), 30% on wine, and the rest on cider, perry, etc.

The following are illustrations of how the mass media have handled the foregoing products:-

Whisky remains the most popular spirit, despite successive increases in the duty payable to the Exchequer (see Chapter 3). The stress in advertising has traditionally been placed on quality and the mystique of blending, but there have been regular efforts to associate whisky with outdoor activities (e.g. anglers, bathers, balloonists) and athletes (e.g. skiers and fencers). The female market is also amply catered for. ('Getting married? Brace yourself with a Black and White' and 'You don't have to be one of the boys to like J. and B. Rare Whisky . . .').

Wine has proved a rapidly expanding market. There is considerable stress on youth and sex appeal in advertisements. For example, one television commercial showed a host of young people at a party ('Cinzano makes fun go a long, long way!').

Table wines, on the other hand, were frequently presented as unpretentious, pleasant beverages for consumption with all kinds of meals. ('Och Aye! A tender young Haggis is all the better for a tassie of Blue Nun') and ('Nicolas is the French cuppa. When the French feel thirsty, they have a glass of vin ordinaire . . .').

Cider and Perry. The market was static from 1949 to 1964, and then expanded considerably. Advertisements aimed at upper income brackets have stressed the historical tradition of cider drinking, while brands vary their appeals with either male or mixed sex appeal. The well known Babycham copy and the associated symbol of a baby fawn have been primarily aimed at women and girls. ('Whenever beautiful girls get together, Babycham is the first choice—for its gay, sparkling personality').
(Christian Economic and Social Research Foundation, 1969).

Constraints Placed on Advertising Alcohol on Television

Certain constraints are placed on alcohol display on television for both direct advertising and indirect discussion affecting the use and 'image' of alcohol.

(a)   The *Independent Television Companies Association* permits, and is indeed financed by, advertising of a wide range of products, including alcoholic drinks. The following guidance is, however, issued to those responsible for the production of commercials relating to alcohol advertisements:-

1)   'Advertisement may not be transmitted in the commercial breaks immediately before, during or immediately after children's programmes.'

2)   'Advertisements may not directly encourage young people to drink alcohol. Actors and actresses appearing in advertisements should clearly be at least in their twenties. In relation to the advertising of the stronger types of drink, they may be required to be more mature still.'

3)   'Advertisements should not "dare" people to try a particular drink or imply that they will "prove" themselves in some way if they accept the challenge offered by the drink.'

4)   'It is advisable not to show children at all in advertisements for alcoholic drinks, but if they are used (for example, in family situations where it would be very natural for them to be present), it must be clearly established that they are not drinking the product.'

5)   'Advertisements should not be based on any theme emphasising the stimulant or sedative effects of the drink's alcoholic content. While advertisements may, of course, indicate that moderate drinking can help to make social occasions more cheerful and pleasant, the general impression should not be given that the product is being recommended mainly for its stimulant effect.'

6)   'Specific statements about the high alcoholic content of a drink are not acceptable.'

7)   'Nothing in an advertisement should associate drink with driving.'

8)   'There should be no encouragement towards over-indulgence or habitual drinking.'

9)   'The use of the term "tonic wine" is unacceptable in sound or vision.'

10)   'Claims that an alcoholic drink will be beneficial to health or general well-being must be approved by an I.T.C.A. medical consultant before acceptance.'

      Drinks of very low alcoholic strength which may be sold freely by unlicensed grocers, confectioners, etc. are normally accepted without any timing restriction. If, however, they can only be legally sold on licensed premises, the timing restrictions in paragraph 1 would apply. If any reference is made to spirits or other alcoholic drinks in advertisement for soda water, bitter lemon, tonic water, ginger ale, etc. this may, according to circumstances, require a timing restriction.'
      (Independent Television Companies' Association, 1969).

(b)   The British Broadcasting Corporation has no direct advertising of alcoholic drinks or any other product. However, there is occasional 'incidental advertising' when a brand name or product is mentioned on the air, or advertisements appear in the background of a television news programme or interview. Such occurrences are kept to a minimum.

Advertising Drugs

Household medicines, which can be bought freely without the need for a medical prescription, are advertised direct to the public. These drugs are not commonly abused although some can be harmful if taken in large quantities. The table below sets out the total advertising cost for common household remedies in 1969.

Table 19—2.   Cost of Advertising Household Medicines, Press and Television—1969. (£ thousands).

	Total Advertising	Television	Press
Analgesics, travel pills	1,832.5	974.4	858.1
Asthma, hay fever, catarrh remedies	136.3	–	136.3
Cold remedies	768.3	443.3	325.0
Cough remedies	949.1	691.2	257.9
Germicides and ointments	514.9	24.4	490.5
Indigestion remedies	1,388.4	913.3	475.1
Laxatives	765.8	597.0	168.8
Linaments and lotions	265.9	33.6	232.3
Slimming aids	1,131.8	123.5	1,008.3
Vitamins	1,232.9	344.5	888.4
Other	634.3	65.5	568.8
Total: (£ thousand)	9,620.2	4,210.7 (43.8%)	5,409.5 (56.2%)

Source: Derived from Media Expenditure Analysis, Limited. *Meal Monthly Digest of Advertising Expenditure*. London. 1970.

The advertising of medicines on the Independent Television Networks is guided by a code of Advertising Standards and Practice. Claims made about the efficacy of products, testimonials relating to the medicine, exaggerated copy and any appeals to fears that be unwarranted are controlled by the Code. Advertisements must not refer to any medicine or products that may be used for the treatment of illnesses (56 in all) specified in the Code, including arthritis, gallstones, kidney disorders, lazy eye, thrombosis, etc. (Independent Television Authority, 1969).

Of more crucial importance than the advertising of household medicines is the promotion of medicines available on prescription through the National Health Service. In 1968, sales to the National Health Service amounted to £127 million while sales of household medicines accounted for £45 million (see Chapters 3, 6). This promotion is not aimed at the general public, but rather at medical practitioners by the use of advertisements in professional and technical journals, promotional literature sent to doctors through the post, representatives of the pharmaceutical companies and other promotional activities. In 1965, the expenditure on promotion of National Health Service medicines totalled £15.4 million.

This expenditure of £15.4 million is aimed at general practitioners and hospital doctors (approximately 50,000 in Great Britain, 1965) who prescribe the pharmaceutical products. This would indicate that just over *£300* is spent on drug promotion per head of the target population. By comparison alcohol promotion in that same year represented about *65 pence* per head of its target population—40 million adults in Great Britain.

Journal advertising is the most obvious form of sales promotion and all widely read medical journals carry pharmaceutical advertisement. Accuracy in

Table 19—3.   Analysis of Expenditure on Promotion of N.H.S. Drug Sales in the United Kingdom—1965.

	£m.	Per cent
Representatives	7.0	45.5
Literature	2.6	16.9
Advertising in professional journals	1.6	10.4
Administration of sales promotion	1.8	11.7
Samples	1.3	8.4
Other promotional activities	1.1	7.1
	15.4	100.0

Source: *Report of the Committee of Enquiry into the Relationship of the Pharmaceutical Industry with the National Health Service, 1965—1967.* H.M.S.O., London. 1967.

advertisement is stressed by the code of marketing practice of the Association of the British Pharmaceutical Industry, and editors of principal journals have advertising copy vetted. However, Wade and Elmes (1963) in a study of 45 drug advertisements in a medical journal considered that 22 advertisements contained unwarranted claims and often serious side effects or disadvantages were not mentioned or glossed over.

Promotional literature is sent to doctors through the post and each general practitioner receives an average of seven items per day. These mailings usually relate to particular products and were either informative circulars containing the particulars of a drug, or 'reminders' which feature the name and uses of a drug, but not always the full details about it. The Committee of Enquiry into the Relationship of the Pharmaceutical Industry with the National Health Service (1967) states:

'The Royal College of General Practitioners described much of the literature as "bad—seemingly in the form of cheap publicity, with inaccurate claims, lack of contra-indications and good references, lack of price . . ." The British Medical Association told us that the main disadvantage to doctors was the absence of any "independent medical control or scrutiny over the literature" '.

Representatives are used by the pharmaceutical companies to inform the doctor of new medicines and to gather information about the use of the medicine in practice. However, the exact role that representatives play in promotion is not known.

The Committee of Enquiry into the Relationship of the Pharmaceutical Industry with the National Health Service (1967) felt it was essential to assess the impact of sales promotion, especially since a significant proportion of prescriptions are written for products that did not exist 15 years ago when many doctors were trained. The Committee commissioned a survey of some 500 general practitioners which is annexed to their Report. The main findings included:

'Clearly a large proportion of general practitioners look upon the industry's promotion as the best way of finding out about new products. This, of course, does not mean that the source which doctors tell an interviewer is, in their view, the best, is the one that actually influences them most in practice. For information about the efficacy of drugs, about 1 in 3 of general practitioners selected articles in journals as the best source, 1 in 4 recommendations from consultants and about 1 in 8 contacts with other doctors. It is perhaps significant that 1 doctor in 8 regarded representatives as the best source for finding out about the efficacy of medicines. The general practitioners were asked whether they considered that there was usually enough information in advertising literature to enable a doctor to decide whether to use a product. About 1 in 3 said that there was. Among doctors over 50, the proportion was 1 in 2. The doctors were also asked whether they felt that, on the whole, after seeing the representative, they would be able to decide whether to use the product. Almost 1 in 2 said they would.' (Committee of Enquiry into the Relationship of the Pharmaceutical Industry with the National Health Service, 1967).

MASS MEDIA

Aside from policies relating to advertising, the British Broadcasting Corporation (both television and radio), the Independent Television Authority and certain newspapers appear to have certain standards about the exposure of items dealing with drug and alcohol dependence.

The *British Broadcasting Corporation* (B.B.C.—television and radio). References to alcohol or alcoholism are left to the discretion of the producer for dramatic or fictional stories, as well as in documentaries. In addition, the B.B.C. recognises the growing interest, debate and concern over illicit drug use over the past few years. An internal guidance note issued to senior production staff in 1967 lists the illegal drugs and suggests that too hard and fast a distinction ought not to be drawn between addictive (and therefore dangerous), and non-addictive (and therefore supposedly less harmful) drugs. Both on legal and social grounds the Corporation should do nothing to condone the illegal use of drugs and particular care should be taken not to condone this drug use by default. For example, drug use should not be shown as a commonplace event or as a gratuitous background to some other television subject.

The B.B.C. deals with subjects of both drink and drugs in current affairs programmes on television and radio.

The *Independent Television Authority* seems to have no explicit policy towards alcohol or drug presentation although producers appear to exercise restraint and discretion. Programmes of current interest on alcohol and drugs are screened on the Independent Television network.

The Press

A short questionnaire was sent to ten national newspapers and two 'underground' publications asking if these papers had any editorial policies on alcoholism and/or drug dependence (Addiction Research Unit, 1970). Five national papers replied (three daily and two Sunday only) to the effect that the printing of articles on drugs depended on their news merit and that editorial policy was flexible depending on current information available. The prime consideration (the papers claimed) was to supply a clear appreciation of the social and medical problems inherent in the control and prevention of drug and alcohol dependence. One newspaper stated that editorially, drug addiction was regarded as an illness requiring treatment rather than with condemnation. Another paper expressed concern about police powers of arrest and search and supported the distinction between 'soft' and 'hard' drugs.

The two 'Underground' newspapers expressed tolerance of cannabis taking or active endeavour towards cannabis law reform. Regarding hard drugs, they have warnings to their readers on the dangers where they feel it necessary. The editors do not believe that the problems of alcoholism are fully relevant to the 'predominantly younger readership' involved.

In 1970, there was a total of more than 11,000 articles in the local and national press relating to drugs (Institute for the Study of Drug Dependence, 1970). A scientific analysis of newspaper content and information in relation to drugs and/or alcohol has not been carried out to date.

REFERENCE

ADDICTION RESEARCH UNIT, 1970. Unpublished report.

CHRISTIAN ECONOMIC AND SOCIAL RESEARCH FOUNDATION, 1969. *Ten Years of Advertising Alcohol: A Study of Expenditure and Trends in the Sales Promotion of Alcoholic Drinks.* C.E.S.R.F., London.

COMMITTEE OF ENQUIRY INTO THE RELATIONSHIP OF THE PHARMACEUTICAL INDUSTRY TO THE NATIONAL HEALTH SERVICE, 1965–1967. *Report.* H.M.S.O., London.

INDEPENDENT TELEVISION AUTHORITY, 1969. *The Independent Television Code of Advertising Standards and Practice.* I.T.A., London.

INDEPENDENT TELEVISION COMPANIES' ASSOCIATION, 1969. *Notes of Guidance: Advertising of Alcoholic Drinks.* I.T.C.A., London.

INSTITUTE FOR THE STUDY OF DRUG DEPENDENCE, 1970. Personal Communication.

MEDIA EXPENDITURE ANALYSIS LIMITED, 1970. *Meal Monthly Digest of Advertising Expenditure–December, 1969.* M.E.A.L., London.

CHAPTER 20
PREVENTION OF
DRUG AND ALCOHOL DEPENDENCE

The preceding nineteen chapters of this book have shown that drug and alcohol dependence is a complex and many-faceted problem. There is no such thing as 'the' problem of drug dependence or 'the' problem of alcoholism. There is, rather, a number of distinct problems involving different chemical substances being consumed in a wide variety of patterns by varied populations. Any programme of prevention of dependence problems is likely to be a long-term investment in changing cultural and sub-cultural attitudes towards drug and alcohol use. While it would be impossible in the context of this chapter to put forward a specific preventative programme, basic approaches to prevention in education, legislation and social change will be discussed.

EDUCATIONAL APPROACHES TO PREVENTION

The hope is frequently expressed that simple educational programmes disseminating factual information about the dangers of particular substances will be sufficient to prevent alcohol or drug dependence. However, there is little evidence that this is so. Knowledge in itself is not necessarily protective and sophisticated approaches to health education are needed to place drug and alcohol use in its proper perspective. Debate and discussion are often more appropriate than rigid lecture methods, and the credibility of the teacher must be considered. Credibility is likely to be enhanced by wide-ranging consideration of the society in which drugs are used.

Especially advanced techniques will be needed to influence groups in the population who might be particularly at risk, such as adolescents or children of alcoholics. These 'at risk' groups may include persons with delinquent or sociopathic tendencies who have already resisted attempts at formal education in other contexts. Unfounded scare or fear techniques tend only to discredit information and may therefore be more harmful than helpful. Even when material is chosen with care, persons particularly attracted by risk taking may be stimulated to try drugs, although many others might be deterred from their use.

Educational measures may be directed towards changing the attitudes of the community, not only towards the use of dependence producing drugs, but also towards the use of drugs in general. Emphasis on the therapeutic or relaxant value of drugs seems to have promoted the belief that for every illness or problem there is a pill or perhaps a drink that will bring relief. It is probably best that children be instructed about the proper use of chemical substances throughout their school careers rather than having particular risks emphasised by spotlight presentation.

LEGISLATION

Legislation may be directed at the manufacture, distribution, storage, prescription, sale, price, place or time of sale, or consumption of a chemical substance. Different substances clearly attract different elements of response according to a society's assessment of their inherent danger. Control may also be aimed at the user of the drug by curtailing his liberty or imposing other restraints upon him if he illegally possesses or uses the substance. The management of drug or alcohol dependence requires conditions which encourage the use of these drugs be brought under control. Although legal controls have been, and remain the most important and widespread approach to the management of dependence problems, their efficacy has rarely been tested. It would be useful to view changes in legislation as opportunities for public health experiments. For instance, if it is believed that an alteration in penalties would result in an altered prevalence or incidence of a particular problem, then data should be gathered, if possible, which can confirm or refute this expectation.

SOCIAL CHANGE

The misuse of drugs or alcohol involves a complex interaction of the drug, the person and his environment which includes the social, economic, cultural and political order in which he is living. When the use of alcohol or drugs becomes a widespread problem in a given culture, it can mean, at times, not only the disorder of certain individuals, but also disorder within the social conditions and structure of a society. While alcoholism for instance has at times seemed to be closely connected with gross poverty and consequent social disruption, this is not the whole answer. In Britain, where excessive drinking among the poor was once rife, the alcoholism of executives now gives rise to some concern. Similarly, with drug dependence the elimination of poverty or social injustice does not guarantee the eradication of dependence problems. Nonetheless, focused social action, perhaps most appropriately in local communities where specific needs can be investigated in depth, may certainly be useful in preventing the spread of dependence disorders.

Edwards (1970) has provided a classic example of a wide ranging approach to prevention in the field of alcohol dependence. A select committee reported on the 'extent, causes and consequences of the prevailing rise of intoxication among the labouring classes of the United Kingdom' in 1834. Some of their conclusions detailed below show the breadth necessary for an effective campaign of prevention.

'(1)   "Limitation of the number of liquor outlets, annual licensing, and the keepers of such houses to be subject to progressively increasing fines for disorderly conduct, and forfeiture of licence and closing up of the houses for repeated offences . . . the closing of all such houses at an earlier hour in the evening than at present . . . the making of all Retail Spirit Shops as open to public view as other shops where wholesome provisions are sold." '

'(2)   "The discontinuance of all issues of ardent spirits (except as medicine under the direction of the medical officers) to the Navy and the Army." '

'(3)   "The prohibition of the practice of paying the wages of workers at public houses . . . and payment of such wages to every individual his exact amount . . . so as to render it unnecessary for men to frequent the public houses, and spend a portion of their earnings to obtain change." '

'(4) "The payment of wages at or before the breakfast hour in the mornings of the principal market day in each town to enable to wives to lay out their earnings in necessary provisions at an early period of the market, instead of risking its dissipation at night in the public house." '

'(5) "The establishment of public walks, and gardens, or open spaces for athletic and healthy exercise in the open air, in the immediate vicinity of every town, of an extent and character adopted to its population; and of district and parish libraries, museums and reading rooms, accessible at the lowest rate of charge; so as to admit of one or the other being visited in any weather, and at any time; with rigid exclusion of all Intoxicating Drinks." '

'(6) "The reduction of the duty on tea, coffee and sugar, and all the healthy and unintoxicating articles of drink in ordinary use; so as to place within the reach of all classes the least injurious beverages on much cheaper terms than the most destructive." '

'(7) "The removal of all taxes on knowledge and the extending of every facility to the widest spread of useful information to the humblest of the community." '

(Edwards, 1970; Report of the Select Committee appointed to inquire into the Extent, Causes and Consequences of the Prevailing Vice of Intoxication among the Labouring Classes, 1834).

REFERENCES

EDWARDS G., 1970. Place of treatment professions in society's response to chemical abuse. *Brit.Med.J.* 2, 193.

REPORT OF THE SELECT COMMITTEE, 1834. *Report of the Select Committee Appointed to Inquire into the Extent, Causes, and Consequences of the Prevailing Vice of Intoxication Among the Labouring Classes.* Unpublished Source. Home Office Library, London.

CHAPTER 21
RESEARCH INTO DRUG AND ALCOHOL
DEPENDENCE IN GREAT BRITAIN

This chapter reviews the basic areas of research into drug and alcohol dependence and the relationship of this research to social policy. It is not within the scope of this book to provide an exhaustive listing of all research projects in these fields; however, the organizations carrying out, financing and co-ordinating research are reviewed.

Research into Drug and Alcohol Dependence

The Medical Research Council (1971a) has compiled a list of research projects on drug dependence which the Council supports, and added projects that were known to the Home Office in March, 1970. There were 109 projects, including work on biochemistry, pharmacology, assay techniques, genetics, pathology, animal studies, general clinical work, treatment, social-psychological studies and delinquency research. The work was carried out in 49 centres in England, Scotland and Wales under the aegis of hospitals, universities and/or research institutes. Among the centres engaged in drug research were the Clinical Psychiatry Unit (Chichester), the Addiction Research Unit (London), Oxford University Department of Pharmacology, Chelsea College of Science and Technology (London), Clinical Research and Drug Dependence Treatment Unit (Bethlem Royal and Maudsley Hospital, London), Department of Pharmacology (University of Dundee), and the National Addiction and Research Institute (London).

No comparable listing exists for research projects specifically concerned with alcohol dependence. Basic research into the biochemical and medical aspects of alcohol consumption is carried out at several hospitals and universities. Epidemiological studies of alcoholism have been done by research centres such as the Addiction Research Unit (London) and the Unit for Epidemiological Studies in Psychiatry (Edinburgh University). Clinical aspects of alcohol dependence are investigated to some extent by the specialised alcohol treatment units in hospitals such as St. Bernard's Hospital (London), Warlingham Park Hospital (Surrey), Mapperley Hospital (Nottingham), Whitchurch Hospital (Cardiff), Southern General Hospital (Glasgow) and Warneford Hospital (Oxford).

In addition, Government bodies with their own research units, such as the Home Office, Department of Health and Social Security, the Government Social Survey and the Road Research Laboratory (Ministry of Transport) have been concerned with aspects of drug and/or alcohol research.

Financing of Research

Many small research projects on alcohol or drug dependence are financed by the research worker's hospital or university department. However, the Department of Health and Social Security, the Home Office and the Ministry of Transport have commissioned larger scale research. The Medical Research Council, an independent body with a large Government grant, sponsors a number of biochemical, pharmacological and epidemiological studies of drug and/or alcohol dependence.

In addition to these public organizations, a large number of foundations and charitable organisation sponsor individual research projects. Similarly, independent bodies such as the Medical Council on Alcoholism, the Christian Economic and Social Research Foundation and the Institute for the Study of Drug Dependence have financed research on alcohol or drugs.

The Dissemination and Evaluation of Research Results.

The Home Office has its Standing Advisory Committee on Drug Dependence, which reviews research and makes recommendations dealing with drug abuse (see Chapters 4, 10, 11, 12, 14) and the Home Office Working Party on the Habitual Drunkenness Offender surveys research in that field (see Chapter 8).

The British Medical Association convened working parties concerned with particular drugs and its panel on alcohol, other drugs and road accidents is involved in assessment of research reports.

The Medical Research Council established three expert working parties in 1969 to examine aspects of drug dependence, namely biochemistry and pharmacology, epidemiology, and treatment.

The Working Party on the Biochemical and Pharmacological Aspects of Drug Dependence concentrated on methods available for detecting drugs of dependence in the body. They considered that objective assessment of drugs that had been taken is essential and knowledge of the precise mechanisms of drug action will only be gained once it is known how much of a drug is present in the tissues and blood, and in what form.

After examining the state of knowledge in relation to specific drug groups (opiates, amphetamines, barbiturates, cannabis and LSD), the Working Party concludes:

'The main deficiency in our present knowledge in this area is our inability to detect certain drugs in urine, blood or tissues either because the most advanced techniques (gas-liquid chromatography combined with mass-spectrometry) have not yet been applied, or because the studies with radio-actively labelled substances needed to identify the bio-transformations which these drugs undergo, have not yet been undertaken. Once this knowledge is available, it should be applied not only to detection, but to the study of the effects of these drugs in man, under the wide variety of conditions that obtain in the drug users' world.' (Medical Research Council, 1971b).

The Working Party on the Epidemiology of Drug Dependence felt that no single hypothesis, such as rebellion, availability of drugs or poverty, could account for drug use in Great Britain and that only multi-factorial hypotheses would prove useful. The complexity of the phenomenon indicates that answers can only be achieved over a long period of time. The Working Party listed five broad aspects of the problem that needed detailed study and recommended how these might be tackled.

i. *The prevalence of drug taking.* It would be necessary to pursue studies of all
    types of drug abuse, including casual and soft drug use, in defined
    geographical areas and of certain groups in different areas. The situation in
    the community as a whole must be considered.

ii. *The dissemination of drugs.* More systematic work should be carried out to
    find out how and where drugs become available in the community.

iii. *The natural history of drug taking.* Wide ranging prospective studies dealing
    with the process of initiation of drug use, its continuance and treatment
    should be carried out. Appropriate control groups will be necessary in these
    studies.

iv. *Central data collection and monitoring of trends.* Full use should be made of
    data from the Home Office, Department of Health and Social Security, the
    Scottish Home and Health Department, the National Health Service Pricing
    Bureaux and other sources.

v. *Methodology.* Refinement of techniques in field surveys and establishing
    reliability and validity of instruments is essential. (Medical Research Council,
    1971b).

The Working Party on the Evaluation of Different Methods of Treatment of
Drug Dependence pointed out that most drug addicts do not consider themselves
ill and do not wish to be rid of their dependence, so that the concept of
maintenance must be included within the term 'treatment'.

The Working Party was aware of the considerable difficulties of research in this
area, but recommended that research should be carried out into the long term
outcome of treatment and the different types of after-care. A clinical trial of the
relative merits of methadone and heroin maintenance treatment should be
undertaken.

They felt that opportunities for research esist within the penal system and
should be exploited. The Working Party further recommended the evaluation of
special treatment regimes, such as psychotherapy and behaviour therapy, and
recommended that an attempt be made to evaluate existing treatment centres
(Medical Research Council, 1971b).

Journals Publishing Research on Drug and/or Alcohol Dependence

The only specialised journal for scientific research dealing with alcohol and
drug dependence is the *British Journal of the Addictions* (formerly known as the
British Journal of Inebriety). However, research reports on dependence are often
published in the medical journals, such as the *Lancet, British Medical Journal,
British Journal of Psychiatry* (formerly the Journal of Mental Science), and
The Practitioner, among other related publications.

RESEARCH AND POLICY

The first part of this chapter discussed certain facilities which exist for the
promotion, enactment and communication of research. It is equally important,
however, in any description of a nation's response to consider whether the research
these organisations promote and the results conveyed affect in any way the
formulation and enactment of policy. While it is perhaps an over-simplification
to suggest that in the physical sciences there is an automatic progression linking

theory, development and application, the fact that the results of research in the social and medical sciences are rarely seen as having economic implications means that the progression is even more tenuous in this area. That the abolition of the rum ration could have been advocated in 1838 for almost precisely the same reasons as were adduced in 1970 (Edwards and Jaffe, 1970) when eventually the ration was withdrawn, reveals something of the time scale affecting the application of research findings in this field. Nevertheless, there is evidence of an increasing concern for the utilisation of social research (Social Science Research Council, 1969; Wootton, 1967; Watson, 1970, Cherns, 1967, 1968, 1969) and a dawning awareness of the essential wastefulness of a system of public support for research which neither precludes duplication nor guarantees the application of results once discovered.

For research to be related to the formulation of policy requires that there be some contact, if only vicariously through the published literature, between researchers and those responsible for the formulation of policy in this area. It is illustrative of society's present lop-sided response to the problem of drug and alcohol dependence that whereas there exists a single authoratitive forum for discussing drug dependence (Advisory Committee on Drug Dependence), no such forum exists for the discussion of government policy relating to alcohol dependence. The Advisory Committee will, if the provisions of the Misuse of Drugs Bill currently under review are adopted, be replaced by an Advisory Council on the Misuse of Drugs with responsibility to:-

(a)   'Keep under review the situation in the United Kingdom with respect to drugs which are being, or appear to them likely to be misused and of which the misuse is having or appears to them capable of having harmful effects sufficient to constitute a social problem, and to advise the ministers on measures (whether or not involving alteration of the law) which in the opinion of the Council ought to be taken for preventing the misuse of such drugs or remedying the effects of their misuse.'

(b)   'Consider and advise the ministers, Secretary of State or the Minister of Home Affairs for Northern Ireland on any matter relating to drug dependence or the misuse of drugs . . .'
        (Misuse of Drugs Bill, 1970).

In addition, the Advisory Council may 'refer to the expert committee any matter relating to drug dependence or the misuse of drugs, including any matter relating to the exercise by the Secretary of State of any power to make regulations or order conferred on him by this Act . . .' (Misuse of Drugs Bill, 1970).

Members of the Advisory Council, of whom there are to be not less than twenty, are to be appointed after consultation with the appropriate professional organisations so as to represent the relevant professions, and are to include some having 'wide and recent experience of social problems connected with the misuse of drugs'. In addition, the Advisory Council may appoint committes, which may in part include persons who are not members of the Council, to consider and report on any matter referred to them by the Council.

The membership of the Advisory Council, its wide terms of reference and direct access to the appropriate ministers, offers at least the possibility of a close liaison between those having experience of the problems posed by drug dependence and those with the responsibility and power to enact policy in this area.

The mere existence of such a body does not, however, guarantee that the liaison be close, nor does it remove all the problems of relating research and policy in this field. Indeed, there are a number of problems, some of which are inherent, which render the direct application of research to policy difficult. There is foremost, the absence of relevant information, a deficiency which derives in part from the rapid and recent escalation of the drug problem in the United Kingdom. It has been necessary in the face of this change and the degree of public concern contingent on it, to introduce legislative and administrative changes before all the appropriate information could be obtained and before provision could be made to monitor the effect of such changes once introduced. There is, in addition, the fact that the problem, once recognised, has assumed a bewildering variety of forms. Initially construed as a problem of heroin and cocaine misuse, it has become additionally a problem of methylamphetamine and barbiturate injection, and is now properly recognised as a problem of multiple drug misuse. The time scale over which these changes in the phenomena have occurred is infinitely shorter than that over which the appropriate legislative changes can be made, except that extremely wide ranging legislation is introduced in the first instance.

It is, of course, no simple matter to monitor these changes. While it may seem entirely appropriate to assess the effects of the heroin treatment policy by recording the number of new notifications of heroin dependence, any complementary increase in the number of persons injecting barbiturates obviously reflects on the efficacy of this policy. In other instances the effects of legislation may be belated, or else appear in a form which is not readily recognised. In some cases it may not be possible to predict the effect of legislation and so make appropriate observations. The inadequacies are not all on the side of the legislation however, the social sciences are still at a relatively early stage of development, and neither the theoretical models or methodological tools of these sciences are capable of accommodating all the contingencies involved in monitoring these changes.

Nor are all the obstacles theoretical or methodological, some at least derive from the different professional training and predilections of the parties involved. Those who formulate policy are necessarily sensitive to public pressures and so must act in ways which are politically expedient. They are motivated by different political persuasions and may occasionally act in ways at variance with what scientists would regard as objectively indicated.

By contrast, those engaged in research, usually members of academic departments or research institutes, owe their principal allegiance to that body of theory and fact making up their particular discipline. They are, in addition, extremely sensitive to any suggestion of political manipulation and instead cultivate an academic individualism which, while promoting their own careers, may lead them into spheres of endeavour which have no obvious relevance to contemporary events. To the extent that researchers disclaim that individual projects can be evaluated except in terms of their scientific merit, it is impossible to ensure the co-ordination of research or declare certain priorities. In fact, most bodies financing research come to some sort of compromise. They may entertain proposals from a wide variety of fields and even adopt a quota system in supporting each of these, while at the same time favouring either formally or informally, certain declared areas of scientific or economic importance.

One consequence of the researcher's individualism and resultant resistance to any attempt to organise him is a certain wastefulness. Projects of an essentially similar nature can be pursued concurrently and their duplication only revealed when they reach the stage of publication.

There is, however, an even more pressing need than the avoidance of redundancy which recommends greater co-ordination in drug addiction and alcoholism research. It can be argued that the nature of the phenomenon studied demands a multi-disciplinary approach and, moreover, willingness to accommodate a degree of complexity which few individual researchers can countenance. In the absence of such co-ordination one can expect a proliferation of individually conceived studies fraught by many of the same methodological limitations. A degree of co-ordination exists in the present framework of research sponsorship, in so far that the same people have membership on a number of grant giving or advisory committees. The Medical Research Council's recent appointment of a Working Group to consider further the implications of its three working party reports represents a more formal attempt to ensure the co-ordination of research in the areas of drug dependence.

Merely to pronounce scientific truths is not of course to ensure their acceptance. The resistance shown by cigarette smokers to the evidence of an association between lung cancer and smoking suggests that gaining acceptance of the facts requires that attention be given to attributes of the audience. In this connection it is of note that following the publication of the second Royal College of Physicians' report on Smoking and Health an organization for Action on Smoking and Health (A.S.H.) has been established by the Royal College of Physicians with the declared intention of provoking further discussion and research into the dangers of smoking.

Whatever the difficulties confronting any attempt to reconcile research and policy, few would doubt the value to be gained from a more systematic application of the results of research in the areas of drug addiction and alcoholism to the formulation and assessment of social policy, or question the fact that to some extent the continued pursuance of more and more research in the absence of any attempt to apply what is already known constitutes an extravagance which cannot be afforded.

REFERENCES

CHERNS A.B., 1967. Putting psychology to work. *Occupational Psychology*. 41, 77.

CHERNS A.B., 1968. The use of the social sciences. *Human Relations*. 21(4), 313.

CHERNS A.B., 1969. Social psychology and development. *Bull.Brit.Psychol.Soc.* 22, 93.

EDWARDS G. and JAFFE J.H., 1970. *Working Paper prepared for the World Health Organisations Expert Committee on Drug Dependence*. W.H.O., Geneva.

MEDICAL RESEARCH COUNCIL, 1971a. *List of Research Projects in Drug Dependence*. Medical Research Council, London.

MEDICAL RESEARCH COUNCIL, 1971b. *Press Notice–Research into Drug Dependence: Review by M.R.C. Working Parties*. Medical Research Council, London.

MISUSE OF DRUGS BILL. H.M.S.O., London.

SOCIAL SCIENCE RESEARCH COUNCIL, 1969. Research and government. *Social Science Research Council Newsletter*. No. 7.

WATSON P., 1970. Social sciences: research priorities. *New Society*. 13th August.

WOOTTON B., 1967. *In a World I Never Made*. Allen and Unwin, London.

SECTION 6
TOBACCO AND THE NATION'S HEALTH*

Chapter 22 examines the prevalence of smoking in Britain in 1968 and the changes that have occurred in the 1960's. Possible influences on these changing patterns of consumption are considered. The annual health cost of smoking is reviewed and suggestions are made for combating the widespread use of tobacco in Britain.

*This section was written by Dr. M.A. Hamilton Russell.

CHAPTER 22
TOBACCO AND THE NATION'S HEALTH

The Situation in 1968

In the United Kingdom in 1968 there were some 23 million adult tobacco smokers of whom over 21 million were smokers of cigarettes. Thus 57% of the population aged 16 years and over were current smokers, 55% being cigarette smokers, each smoking an average of about 16 cigarettes a day (Tobacco Research Council, 1969). Over 5% of the expenditure of the average British household is spent on tobacco (Department of Employment and Productivity, 1970). As a nation of smokers Britain, with a consumption of about 6 lbs. of tobacco per adult per year, falls about midway among the developed countries (see Table 22–1).

Table 22–1. Annual Tobacco Consumption Per Adult in Each Country 1966–67.

Country	Year of Estimate	Consumption per adult per year (lbs.)	Country	Year of Estimate	Consumption per adult per year (lbs.)
Canada	1966	10.2	Japan	1966	5.4
U.S.A.	1967	10.1	France	1966	5.3
Netherlands	1967	8.7	Austria	1966	5.0
Denmark	1966	8.5	Greece	1966	5.0
New Zealand	1966	8.1	Norway	1966	4.9
Iceland	1967	7.7	Sweden	1966	4.8
Switzerland	1966	7.5	Spain	1966	4.6
Belgium	1967	7.4	Turkey	1966	4.6
Australia	1967	7.0	Finland	1966	4.5
Ireland	1967	6.6	South Africa	1966	4.5
West Germany	1966	6.4	Argentine	1966	4.2
U.K.	1967	6.1	Italy	1967	3.9

Source: Tobacco Research Council. Tobacco consumption in various countries. (Ed. D.H. Beese). London. 1968.

Figure 22–2. Daily Cigarette Consumption of Men and Women Smokers in 1968.

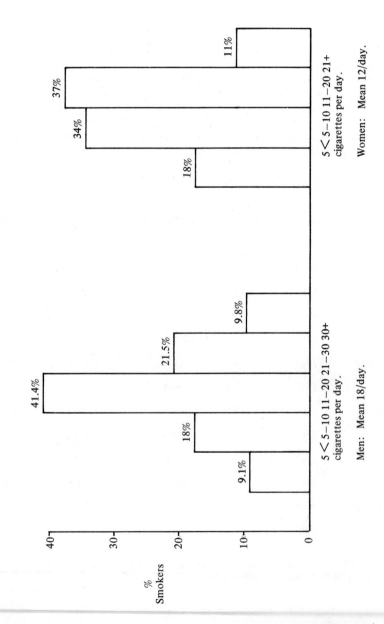

Source: Tobacco Research Council. *Statistics of smoking in the United Kingdom.* (Ed. G.F. Todd). London. 1969.

Per capita consumption of tobacco is, however, a crude estimate of how much is actually taken into the lungs. The relatively high cost of tobacco makes the British smoker reluctant to discard a long butt; it also leads to the manufacture of ever-lengthening filters to keep costs down. Both these tendencies mean that the British smoker may waste less and therefore smoke more tobacco than smokers in some other countries with a similar or even greater per capita tobacco consumption.

Smoking is commoner in men than women: 68.6% vs. 43.2% in 1968 (Tables 22–4 and 22–5, 22–6). Men also smoke more heavily—averaging 18 cigarettes a day compared with 12 a day for women (Tables 22–2, 22–3). The onset of smoking is now a phenomenon of adolescence and occurs on average just over a year earlier in boys than in girls (Table 22–4). Most recruitment occurs before the age of twenty but a few do take it up in their twenties and thirties. After the age of twenty a small proportion of smokers give up the habit without formal intervention. This so-called natural discontinuance tends to increase with age especially after the age of sixty (Table 22–4). The average daily cigarette consumption also tends to drop quite sharply after the age of sixty (Tobacco Research Council, 1969). Natural discontinuance just about balances the number of new recruits so that in men the prevalence of active smoking rises very little after the age of twenty and tends to drop after the age of 60 (Table 22–4).

This simplified cross-sectional view of smoking in Britain in 1968 conceals many complex trends. Examination of Table 22–3 will show the relative recency of female smoking of any magnitude. Strong cohort effects make interpretation of the relationship between age trends, consumption, prevalence rates and assessment of various anti-smoking influences even more difficult in women than it is in men. For example, the low prevalence of smoking in women over 60 shown in Table 22–4 is a legacy of 30–40 years ago when smoking in women altogether was less common than now. As these older women die over the next ten years and are replaced by younger ones who smoke more, there will be a tendency for the overall smoking rate for women to rise independently of any ongoing social influences. It is beyond the scope of this outline to cover this intricate field. For a more detailed analysis specialist readers are referred to a comprehensive Government Social Survey (McKennell and Thomas, 1967) and to a recent review (Russell, 1971).

Changes between 1958 and 1968

Over this eleven year period there have been a number of influences with potential for changing the pattern of smoking within the nation. The most obvious of these are:-

(a)   The increasing general awareness of the health hazards of smoking; the outstanding landmark of this field being the publication on 7th March, 1962 of the Royal College of Physicians' Report on *Smoking and Health*.

(b)   The various increases in tobacco duty and consequent rises in the price of tobacco products (see Table 22–7).

(c)   The ban imposed in August, 1965 on the advertising of cigarettes on commercial television.

To facilitate evaluation, these influences have been laid alongside various parameters of smoking in Tables 22–5 and 22–6. Changes in some of these smoking variables between 1958 and 1968 will be briefly discussed with reference mainly to the data for men, as the female pattern is complicated by cohort effects mentioned previously.

Figure 22−3.   Annual Cigarette Consumption in Pounds Per Adult of Men and Women, 1890−1968.

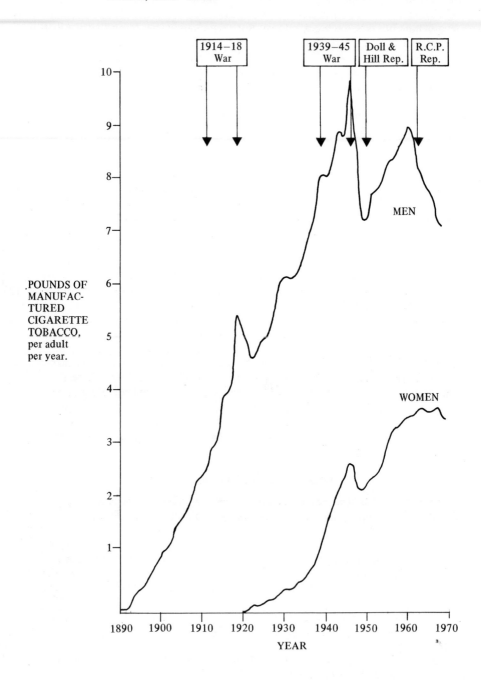

Note: An adult is a person aged 15 and over.

Source: Tobacco Research Council. *Statistics of smoking in the United Kingdom.*
(Ed. G.F. Todd). London. 1969.

Figure 22—4. Smoking Prevalence By Age in the United Kingdom, 1968.

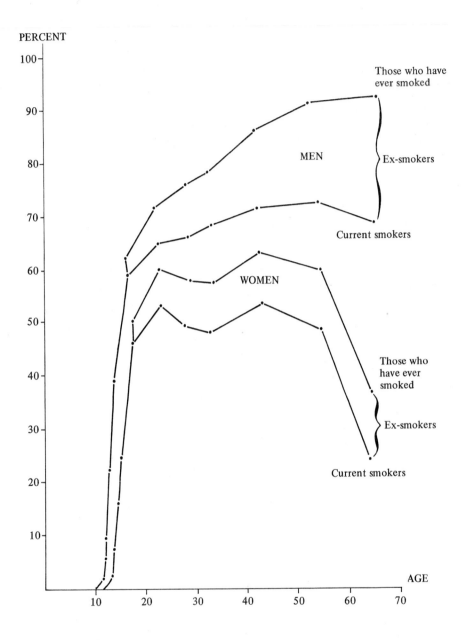

Note: Ages 10—16, page 98: A 'Smoker' is a person who smokes at least one cigarette a day.
Ages 16—60+, pages 26—27: A 'Smoker' is a person who by self-definition smokes
cigarettes, pipe or at least one cigar a week.
'Those who have ever smoked' are derived from the sum of 'current smokers' and
'ex-smokers'.

Source: Tobacco Research Council. *Statistics of Smoking in the United Kingdom.*
(Ed. G.F. Todd). London. 1969.

(i)   Changes in Smoking Prevalence:

The data (Tables 22–5 and 22–6) show that between 1958 and 1968 the prevalence of smoking among men (aged 16 and over) decreased by 3.4% (from 72% to 68.6%). Over the same period the percentage of women smokers increased by 3.6% (from 39.6% to 43.2%). The figures suggest a possible turning point between 1961 and 1963. The decrease in male smoking occurred at this point and at the same time a possible rising prevalence in women seems to have levelled off. It could be that the publication of the Royal College of Physicians' report in March, 1962 was largely responsible for this trend. Another possible factor was the rise in the price of cigarettes in July, 1961 from 4/1d. to 4/6d. for a packet of twenty; but the fact that the prevalence of smoking among men did not fall after equally swinging price rises in 1964 and 1965, suggests that the Royal College of Physicians' report was the dominant influence in the favourable turn between 1961 and 1963.

The decrease in male smoking seems to have been mainly accounted for by a reduction in the number of new smokers rather than a tendency for current smokers to give up, in that the proportion of men who had never smoked rose 3% between 1961 and 1963 whereas the proportion of ex-smokers increased only 0.9%.

Each increase in tobacco duty seems to have been associated with a rise in prevalence of men who have never smoked (Table 22–5). The overall rise was almost 4% (13.9% to 17.8%) between 1961 and 1966, a period which saw no less than three increases in tobacco duty. However, the major part of the rise (13.9% to 16.9%) occurred between 1961 and 1963, coinciding with the Royal College of Physicians' report.

The small rise in prevalence of ex-smokers was also associated with the Royal College of Physicians' report rather than the successive increases in tobacco duty. Indeed between 1963 and 1966 the prevalence of ex-smoking among men actually fell from 15.1% to 13.9% (see Table 22–5), despite increases in tobacco duty in 1964 and 1965.

The data therefore suggest that while the Royal College of Physicians' report seemed to act by influencing current smokers to stop as well as by reducing the recruitment of new smokers, the effect of a rise in the price of cigarettes was limited to reducing recruitment to smoking. It was, no doubt, the concurrence of these two influences that accounted for the major downturn in smoking prevalence between 1961 and 1963. The 1965 ban on the advertising of cigarettes on television seems to have had no effect on cigarette smoking prevalence.

Another interesting point is the relative transience of the small increase in ex-smokers achieved between 1961 and 1963. By 1966 the gain is lost. Indeed in the eleven years between 1958 and 1968 the prevalence of ex-smoking in men increased by only 1% (Table 22–5). On the other hand gains made in increasing the prevalence of those who have never smoked are largely maintained and account for most of the diminution in smoking prevalence over the eleven year period. This is contrary to the American experience where reduction in smoking prevalence over the past twelve years is due to a rise in incidence of ex-smoking rather than reduced recruitment to smoking (U.S. Dept. Health, Education and Welfare, 1970). It may be that emphasis on health risks by American anti-smoking propaganda is more effective with the middle-aged and elderly who form the bulk of potential ex-smokers, while the relatively greater emphasis on the expense of smoking given by high taxation in this country is more of a disincentive to the teenager about to start smoking. McKennell and Thomas (1967) have shown that health is the main motive for adults who stop or wish to stop smoking, while

Table 22–5.   Changes in Male Smoking Pattern in U.K. 1958–68, and Possible Influences

Year	Smoking prevalence in those aged 16 and over				Consumption per adult (aged 15 and over) per year		Consumption of manufactured cigs. smoked per week by persons aged 16 and over		Price of 20 standard and plain cigarettes	Possible influences
	All Products			Manufactured cigs.						
	Smoker %	Ex- %	Never %	Smoker %	All Tobacco lbs.	Manuf. Cigs. lbs.	Per person	Per cig. smoker		
1958	72.0	13.4	14.6	58.0	10.2	8.3	75	130	3/11d.	
1959					10.3	8.4			3/11d.	
1960					10.6	8.7			4/1d.	5th April Tobacco Duty + 2d./20 cigarettes
1961	71.9	14.2	13.9	58.6	10.4	8.6	78	132	4/6d.	26th July Tobacco Duty + 3½d./20 cigarettes
1962					9.9	8.0			4/6d.	7th March R.C.P. Report
1963	68.0	15.1	16.9	53.9	9.8	8.0	74	137	4/6d.	
1964					9.5	7.7			4/11d.	15th April Tobacco Duty + 4½d./20 cigarettes
1965	67.6	15.3	17.1	53.5	8.9	7.2	69	129	5/5d.	7th April Tobacco Duty + 5½d./20 cigarettes August: Ban on T.V. advertising of cigarettes
1966	68.3	13.9	17.8	54.4	8.7	7.1	69	128	5/5d.	
1967	67.9	14.5	17.5	54.1	8.8	7.1	70	130	5/5d.	
1968	68.6	14.5	16.9	54.9	8.8	7.1	70	128	5/7d. 6/1d.	20th March Tobacco Duty + 2d./20 cigarettes 23rd November Tobacco Duty + 5d./20 cigarettes

Source: 59th Report–Customs and Excise for the Year Ended 31st March, 1968. H.M.S.O., London. and *Statistics of Smoking in the United Kingdom*. (Ed. G.F. Todd.) Tobacco Research Council, London. 1969.

Table 22–6.   Changes in Female Smoking Patterns U.K. 1958–68 and Possible Influences

Year	Smoking prevalence in those aged 16 and over — All Products			Manufactured cigs.	Consumption per adult (aged 15 and over) per year		Consumption of manufactured cigs. smoked per week by 1 persons aged 16 and over		Price of 20 standard and plain cigarettes	Possible influences
	Smoker %	Ex- %	Never %	Smoker %	All Tobacco lbs.	Manuf. Cigs. lbs.	Per person	Per cig. smoker		
1958	39.6	6.7	53.7	39.5		3.3	31	78	3/11d.	
1959						3.4			3/11d.	
1960						3.5			4/1d.	5th April Tobacco Duty + 2d./20 cigarettes
1961	43.7	6.9	49.4	43.3		3.6	33	76	4/6d.	26th July Tobacco Duty + 3½d./20 cigarettes
1962						3.5			4/6d.	7th March R.C.P. Report
1963	43.0	7.5	49.5	42.7		3.7	36	86	4/6d.	
1964						3.6			4/11d.	15th April Tobacco Duty + 4½d./20 cigarettes
1965	42.6	7.8	49.5	42.3		3.6	36	85	5/5d.	7th April Tobacco Duty + 5½d./20 cigarettes August: Ban on T.V. advertising of cigarettes
1966	45.0	7.7	47.3	45.0		3.7	38	86	5/5d.	
1967	43.5	8.5	48.1	43.6		3.6	38	87	5/5d.	
1968	43.2	9.2	47.6	42.8		3.5	37	87	5/7d. 6/1d.	20th March Tobacco Duty + 2d./20 cigarettes 23rd November Tobacco Duty + 5d./20 cigarettes

Source: *59th Report–Customs and Excise for the Year Ended 31st March, 1968.* H.M.S.O., London. and *Statistics of Smoking in the United Kingdom.* (Ed. G.F. Todd.) Tobacco Research Council, London. 1969.

expense is more important to adolescents. However, Bynner (1969) has shown that
the health risks are of some importance in discouraging schoolboys from smoking.

(ii)   Changes in Consumption:

A detailed analysis of all the trends is not contemplated as it would involve
taking account of many complex influences such as the increased use of filter
cigarettes and the tendency of the tobacco companies to counter rises in tobacco
tax by increasing filter length and reducing the amount of tobacco in each cigarette.

Despite the evidence linking smoking with lung cancer (Doll and Hill, 1950),
cigarette consumption increased steadily between 1950 and 1960 (Table 22–3),
but since 1961 consumption has, with the exception of cigars, tended to diminish
(Tables 22–3, 22–5, 22–7). In men, the consumption per adult started falling in
1961, prior to the Royal College of Physicians' report. However, in 1962 total
cigarette and tobacco consumption showed the first down-turn for several years
(Table 22–7) suggesting that the Royal College of Physicians' report was a major
influence. It is interesting that the number of cigarettes smoked per adult male
smoker per week actually increased between 1961 and 1963 (Table 22–5). This
may be because it was the lighter smokers who were more likely to stop in response
to the report. Lynch (1963) showed that 9.2% of a sample of university staff
reduced or stopped smoking cigarettes in response to the Royal College of
Physicians' report, and that it was indeed the lighter smokers who were more
successful.

The data suggest that rises in tobacco tax do produce a substantial fall in
consumption whether this be in terms of total tobacco consumption, total
consumption of manufactured cigarettes (Table 22–7) or consumption per adult
(Table 22–5). All these parameters of consumption showed unusually large
annual decreases following the increases in tobacco duty in 1960–61 and
1964–65.

As with the prevalence figures, there is no evidence that the 1965 ban of
cigarette advertising on television did anything to reduce the consumption of
cigarettes. However, the tobacco companies did counter this legislation with
alternative promotional activity, most notably in the form of a massive proliferation
of gift coupon schemes.

The Health Cost of Smoking

Whether or not the smoking of cigarettes is harmful to health is no longer at
issue. The emphasis has now shifted to assessing the extent of this damage. What
is the price we in Britain pay in terms of national economy and individual suffering
for our continued smoking? At first look the figures are so astounding that they are
hard to believe. Many dismiss them as exaggerated and alarmist. They are, however,
based on sober appraisal of the facts (Fletcher and Horn, 1970; Lowe, 1970;
Royal College of Physicians', 1971). The situation has been well put by the Chief
Medical Officer of the Ministry of Health in successive Annual Reports and
summarised in a recent lecture (Godber, 1968, 1969, 1970a, 1970b). Part of the
price Britain pays for smoking is as follows:-

(i)   It has been claimed by the Chief Medical Officer of Health that nearly
100,000 people in Britain die each year before their time as a result of
smoking (Godber, 1970a). If this estimate is correct, smoking kills almost
as many British people each year as the total number of civilians killed by
enemy action during the whole of the last war 106,927 (Central Statistical
Office, 1951), 60,595 (O'Brien, 1955). A more modest but nevertheless

Table 22–7.   Changes in Total Sale of Tobacco Goods (In Weight) to the Public in the U.K. 1958–68.

Year	Million lb. manufactured weight				Possible Influences
	Manufactured cigarettes	Pipe + Hand-rolled cigarettes	Cigars	Snuff	Total	
1958	225.1	33.6	1.3	0.7	260.7	
1959	230.3	33.7	1.5	0.6	266.1	
1960	239.2	33.2	1.6	0.6	274.6	5th April Tobacco Duty + 2d./20 cigarettes
1961	243.1	32.4	1.6	0.6	277.7	26th July Tobacco Duty + 3½d./20 cigarettes
1962	230.9	33.0	1.9	0.6	266.4	7th March R.C.P. Report
1963	237.8	32.8	2.1	0.5	273.2	
1964	230.8	32.5	2.7	0.5	266.5	15th April Tobacco Duty + 4½d./20 cigarettes
1965	220.7	30.7	2.9	0.5	254.8	7th April Tobacco Duty + 5½d./20 cigarettes August: Ban on T.V. advertising of cigarettes
1966	223.3	29.7	3.5	0.5	257.0	
1967	221.3	29.6	4.0	0.5	255.4	
1968	220.2	28.6	4.1	0.5	253.4	20th March Tobacco Duty + 2d./20 cigarettes 23rd November Tobacco Duty + 5d./20 cigarettes

Source: 59th Report–Customs and Excise for the Year Ended 31st March, 1968. H.M.S.O., London. and Statistics of Smoking in the United Kingdom. (Ed. G.F. Todd.) Tobacco Research Council, London. 1969.

alarmingly high estimate has been made by Professor Lowe (1970). Using the excess mortality figures of smokers in an American prospective study (Hammond, 1966) and applying them to the mortality data for England and Wales, he calculated that some 38,000 men (24,503 under 65) and 4,000 women (2,678 under 65) die prematurely each year as a result of smoking (see Tables 22–8 and 22–9). This is over five times the death rate due to road accidents and more than eight times the suicide rate—7,368 and 5,056 respectively in 1968. (Central Statistical Office, 1969). Lowe's figures are very similar to those given in the Royal College of Physicians' Second Report (1971) namely between 20,000 and 24,000 premature deaths a year in men aged 35 to 64 caused by cigarette smoking. These 'smoking deaths' are mainly due to lung cancer, chronic bronchitis and ischaemic heart disease. Smoking is probably responsible for nine out of ten lung cancer deaths, three out of four bronchitic deaths and one in four deaths due to heart attacks. At the individual level, continued smoking takes an average of four years off the life of a young man—seven years if he smokes over forty a day (Godber, 1970b; Lowe, 1970).

(ii)   Apart from the death rate there is the increased morbidity due to smoking. It has been estimated that the number of working days lost annually through illness directly attributable to smoking is more than twenty times the number lost through industrial disputes (Godber, 1969). Added to the personal suffering and financial cost to industry is the enormous extra burden on the Health Service for both in-patient and out-patient care of those who are ill as a result of smoking. Ball (1970) has estimated that between five and eight thousand hospital beds are occupied each day by smokers who are in hospital only because they smoke. He has, furthermore, pointed out that this almost equals the full complement of beds of the twelve London teaching hospitals. Besides having a shorter life, the smoker may lead much of it in a state of prolonged disablement.

(iii) It is not only that the smoker harms himself. Besides producing smaller babies, mothers who smoke almost double the chance of their pregnancies ending in spontaneous abortion, stillbirth or neonatal death (Russell et al, 1966).

National Response to the Smoking Problem

Smoking is not only harmful to health, but in Britain, taxation ensures that it is also expensive. How is it that despite these disincentives smoking remains so widespread? This is largely due to an interplay of two main factors.

(a)   *The dependence factor:* The nature of cigarette smoking as a dependence disorder results in the sad fact that it is difficult for the individual to stop. Thus while three out of four smokers wish to or have tried stopping in the past, less than one in four ever succeed (Russell, 1971).

(b)   *The favourable social climate:* Government apathy, vested interests and extensive commercial advertising not only encourage denial and distortion of the true facts but also subtly propagate false facts. The result is that the prevailing social climate in this country is one of approval and tolerance of smoking. There are not many places where smoking is not freely permitted. Cigarettes are perhaps the most readily available of all commodities.

Table 22—8.   Estimate of Deaths Attributable to Smoking. Males 35 Years and Over, England and Wales, 1967.

AGE

	35—44	45—54	55—64	65—74	75—84	Total 35—84
Number of deaths from all causes	7,118	20,981	56,632	81,430	68,428	234,589
Percentage attributable to smoking*	33%	38%	25%	13%	4%	16%
Number of deaths attributable to smoking	2,372	7,973	14,158	10,586	2,736	37,826

* Derived from Hammond, E.C., 1966.

Source: Lowe, C.R. The cost to health of addiction to tobacco. Paper presented at International Conference on Alcohol and Addictions. Cardiff. 1970.

Table 22—9.   Estimate of Deaths Attributable to Smoking. Males 35 Years and Over England and Wales, 1967.

AGE

	35—44	45—54	55—64	65—74	75—84	Total 35—84
Number of deaths from all causes	5,032	13,328	30,657	61,832	90,324	201,173
Percentage attributable to smoking*	5%	9%	4%	2%	0%	2%
Number of deaths attributable to smoking	252	1,200	1,226	1,237	0	3,915

* Derived from Hammond, E.C., 1966.

Source: Lowe, C.R. The cost to health of addiction to tobacco. Paper presented at International Conference on Alcohol and Addictions. Cardiff. 1970.

It is twenty years since attention in this country was first clearly drawn to the relationship between smoking and lung cancer (Doll and Hill, 1950). The problem this posed remained for many years virtually unacknowledged—with the reluctant nation clutching the straw of academic purism and trusting that the association though strong was not causal. The lack of official response was reflected in the steady rise in tobacco consumption between 1950 and 1960 (see Table 22—3). It was only with the publication of the first Royal College of Physicians' Report on 'Smoking and Health' in 1962 that the nation and indeed the world was shaken into the realisation that smoking created a health problem that could no longer be ignored. The careful and balanced assemblage of scientific facts and the prestige of the committee responsible for the report forced the nation and the world to stir and take action. There was support from a similar report in the U.S.A. two years later. The response was at first small and inadequate but the campaign to curb smoking is gradually gaining momentum with the Government being slowly dragged in to take more effective action.

Attempts to deal with the situation have been made on a number of fronts: treatment of the individual smoker, large-scale health education programmes, and social control.

(i)   Treatment

After the 1962 Royal College of Physicians' report some thirty anti-smoking clinics were opened by local authorities throughout Britain. With one exception they all closed within five years due to disheartening results and lack of Government support. A low success rate is common to smoking treatment clinics in other countries. The general experience is that of those attending such a clinic some 30–40% are able to stop smoking by the end of the course of treatment but by follow-up at one year the success rate dwindles to a range of 12 to 28% (Russell, 1970). Bearing in mind that the natural discontinuance of smoking within the British population at large is about 18% (Russell, 1971), it seems that the achievements of these clinics are very limited. It makes little difference whether 5-day plans or weekly group counselling sessions are used. Drugs of varying types. (e.g. amphetamines, lobeline, tranquillisers) are if anything less helpful than placebos. Hypnotism and a great variety of behaviour therapy techniques (including desensitisation, stimulus satiation and aversion therapy) though promising in isolated cases, have all proved disappointing when subjected to the rigours of controlled trial and adequately long follow-up. A comprehensive review of the world literature on anti-smoking treatment methods has recently been provided by Schwartz (1969). The prevailing state of therapeutic doldrums is reflected in the fact that there are no more than two or three smoking treatment clinics currently active in the whole United Kingdom.

These disappointing results are due partly to the limitations of the treatment procedures but another reason is that it is usually the most difficult cases who seek treatment. They tend to be not only highly dependent, but are frequently neurotic, depressed or beset by social problems that make it impossible for them to apply the necessary sustained effort to the task of withdrawal. A high relapse rate is one of the features of the failure of treatment. This is almost certainly related to the widespread social pressures to smoke that confront the individual as soon as he walks out of the treatment clinic. There is little doubt that treatment could be much more effective if the general social climate was changed to one less favourably disposed towards smoking.

(ii)   Anti-smoking Propaganda

Smoking is so widespread that Health Authorities have rightly been attracted to the potential efficacy of large scale anti-smoking propaganda programmes. These have been aimed in two directions—the persuasion of established smokers to stop and the prevention of children from starting. So far these attempts have met with discouragingly limited success. Straight-forward dissemination of information about the multiple health hazards of smoking seldom has the desired effect whether pitched at schools, communities or the population at large. A £4,350 community campaign in Edinburgh produced some change in attitude but no reduction in smoking (Cartwright, et al, 1960). Preventive propaganda in schools using films, posters and talks by health officials has been largely ineffective (Jeffreys et al, 1967; Holland and Elliott, 1968). At a national level there have been spasmodic radio and television programmes and periodic poster campaigns which were able to produce attitude change in some smokers (McKennell & Thomas, 1967). However, organised, co-ordinated anti-smoking effort of significant magnitude has not yet been attempted on a national scale in this country. Recent official health education programmes have been conspicuously parsimonious. £100,000 a year of Government funds to persuade people not to smoke is unlikely to achieve much in the face of the £17 million spent annually by the tobacco companies on advertising.

Lack of sufficient funds to pay for adequate and persistent exposure of propaganda messages on the mass media has not been the only deficiency in anti-smoking campaigns. They have also lacked sophistication. But lessons are being learnt. Behavioural scientists interested in smoking problems are taking note of the growing field of communication theory and in their work on smoking modification they are contributing to that theory. The bulk of this work is, however, going on in the U.S.A. There is in Britain virtually no active research in this area though it is obviously of great relevance to the health education field.

It is no longer expected that simple communication of facts will invariably induce appropriate changes in attitude or that a shift of attitude will lead to a corresponding modification of behaviour. The effect of a communication depends on an interplay of variables involving the nature of the informant, the type of message and certain characteristics of the recipient. This is not the place to go into all the complexities of communication theory but it is clearly of relevance if future anti-smoking propaganda is to be made more effective. Two useful reviews of the subject have recently come from America (Leventhal, 1968; Higbee, 1969).

In their outstanding survey of smoking habits and attitudes of adults and adolescents in England and Wales, McKennell and Thomas (1967) have suggested guidelines for improving future anti-smoking campaigns. They showed that over 90% of smokers are already aware of the association of smoking with lung cancer but that many are defensive and deny the relevance of these risks to themselves. For instance, many heavy smokers consider that lung cancer is a risk only to those who smoke over a hundred cigarettes a day. To attack these defences directly, they suggest would be too threatening and therefore counter-productive for the majority of defended smokers. They advise that more emphasis should be placed on minor health ailments such as cough and breathlessness, which many smokers are already experiencing. More prominence should also be given to the 'expense theme'.

Another possible reason for the relative failure of anti-smoking campaigns is that they may have placed too much emphasis on the rational, cognitive reasons for not smoking, while the dominating, and often unconscious, social and psychological motives that determine the onset of smoking have been largely overlooked. The lesson of commercial advertising should perhaps be heeded. Repeated association of smoking with maturity, success, toughness, attractiveness and sophistication, etc., appeals to both conscious and unconscious needs. Though we consciously know that smoking a certain brand of cigarette will not give us a strong hairy arm, a fast car or an attractive sexual partner, our need for such assets may still influence us to yield to these illogical associations. A recent survey (Bynner, 1969) has shown that schoolboys are indeed partly motivated to smoke by the image of toughness, sexiness, and precocity that smoking provides.

In summary, to be more successful, future anti-smoking campaigns should employ some of the methods of commercial advertising. This would be expensive as it would involve frequent, persistent and widespread exposure of propaganda messages as well as sophisticated application of the principles of communication theory. It would also involve continuous monitoring of public response to allow feed-back control and adjustment of both form and content of the propaganda message. The two recent comprehensive Government Social Surveys (McKennell and Thomas, 1967; Bynner, 1969) have provided information that could act as a starting point for such a campaign; they have also made useful suggestions as to the most fruitful first steps.

(iii)   **Social Control**

The prevailing social climate is one in which the pressure promotes smoking rather than discourages it. The favourable image and omnipresence of smokers and smoking is a major factor in the recruitment of young people into smoking, in detering established smokers from trying to stop and in seducing recent ex-smokers back to smoking. Reference has been made to the key role this favourable social climate shares with the fact that nicotine is a dependence-producing drug. We cannot as yet do anything to alter the pharmacological effect of nicotine; this leaves the engineering of a change of social climate as the only practical way of curbing smoking on a massive scale. Advocacy of such social engineering is most difficult on ethical grounds, for it involves direct legislative intervention in the control of sales and advertising, banning of smoking in public places, and use of discriminative taxation. It therefore trespasses on the rightly sensitive area of infringement of personal liberty. A number of different means of social control will be considered.

(a)   *Restriction of tobacco advertising.* As commercial advertising is largely responsible for maintaining the favourable social climate and image of smoking, to achieve a change its influence would need to be countered or curbed. Between 1955 and 1968 the expenditure on advertising of tobacco products in the United Kingdom increased from below £3 million to £17 million a year. In 1963 gift coupon schemes were introduced. In 1966 they overtook advertising as a form of promotion and by 1968 accounted for over £35 million a year. Thus the total expenditure on commercial promotion of tobacco products in 1968 was over £52 million (Royal College of Physicians, 1971). If the Government does not choose to pay the enormous sum that would be necessary to compete adequately with the tobacco companies, the alternative is to restrict or ban tobacco advertising. A start was made in August, 1965 when a ban was imposed on the advertising of cigarettes on commercial television. The tobacco industry responded with the massive proliferation of gift coupon schemes and there is no evidence (Tables 22—5, 22—6, 22—7) that this tentative step by the Government achieved any diminution in smoking prevalence, tobacco consumption or even cigarette consumption. For worthwhile results to be achieved it may well be necessary to ban all forms of cigarette advertising and to accompany this with extensive anti-smoking propaganda of a commercial advertising type and scale.

(b)   *The Role of Taxation.* The fact that Britain's per capita tobacco consumption (see Table 22—1) is about midway among the developed nations despite the high taxation, would suggest that expense is not a strong deterrent. However, increases in tobacco duty in 1960—61 and again in 1964—5 (Table 22—10) were followed by and possibly contributed to unusually large decreases in per capita tobacco consumption in men—0.5 lbs. and 0.6 lbs. tobacco per head per year respectively (see

Table 22–5 and Table 22–3). There is also evidence, from Table 22–5, that over these periods there was a tendency for less new male smokers to be recruited (i.e. there was a rise in the percentage of those who had never smoked). There is, however, no corresponding indication that large numbers of established smokers were giving up smoking. The contribution of raised tobacco prices to the slight reduction in smoking prevalence over the past eleven years has been discussed earlier. Tobacco tax increases have, hitherto, been introduced primarily as a substantial source of revenue (see Table 22–10). The consequent reduction in tobacco consumption and smoking prevalence has been only incidental. Judicious tax increases with the specific purpose of curbing smoking would be likely to be highly effective though somewhat harsh. Selective tax increases to favour safer ways of smoking is also feasible. That this can be successful is amply demonstrated by the recent swing to the use of filter-tipped cigarettes.

(c)   *Other Legislative Measures.* Proposals have already been made in Parliament, for Britain to follow the American example in having nicotine and tar content as well as warnings of health hazards printed on all cigarette packets. There is lobbying for banning of smoking in certain public places and pressure for tighter control of sales outlets, for example, the banning of cigarette vending machines. This would help reduce children's access to cigarettes directly and it would also encourage tobacconists to pay more heed to the law that already forbids them from selling to children under sixteen years. All these measures would collectively contribute to making the public aware of the disadvantages of smoking as well as helping to undermine the favourable social climate. Surprisingly a majority of the smoking public and virtually all non-smokers would find many of these measures acceptable (McKennell and Thomas, 1967).

Suggestions for Future Anti-Smoking Strategy

To be too specific in offering suggestions for a task that has hitherto baffled so much skilled attention would be presumptuous indeed. Comprehensive tactical recommendations for future preventive measures have been set out in the Royal College of Physicians' second report (1971). Some suggestions for the broad outline and form of a future anti-smoking strategy are offered here.

In discussing the various approaches to the problem of curbing smoking, some attempt has been made, in preceding sections, to analyse the reasons for failure and to indicate how the situation might be improved. Whether we are primarily concerned with treatment of the individual case, with mass persuasion of the smoking population to stop or with prevention of young people from starting, for greater success we are always brought back to the interplay of two key factors *the favourable social climate* and *the dependence factor*. It is on these factors that future anti-smoking strategy should hinge. Any tactic or measure that can diminish the effect of either of these factors should also diminish smoking.

Of the two, the dependence factor is probably the most refractory owing to current lack of fundamental knowledge of the nature of dependence. Research in this area and into more effective treatment would be an important part of the wider strategy. About 50% of smokers acknowledge the disadvantages of smoking and wish to stop (McKennell and Thomas, 1967). If an effective 'smoking cure' were developed, these dissonant smokers would no doubt come swarming to get it. By virtue of their numerical strength alone current smokers contribute to maintaining

Table 22–10. Cigarette Prices, Tobacco Duty and its Contribution to Total Revenue from Central Government Taxation, 1956–1970.

Year	Retail price of 20 standard (full size, non-tipped) cigarettes	DUTY		Overall incidence of duty as a % of consumers' expenditure on cigarettes, pipe tobacco etc.	Tobacco Revenue per year	Total Customs & Excise (a) per year	Other Revenue (b) per year	Total Revenue per year	Tobacco Revenue as a percentage of Total Revenue
		Date of change	Approx. duty per packet 20 standard cigarettes						
	s. d.		s. d.	%	£ million	£ million	£ million	£ million	%
1956	3/10	18.4.56	2/10½	72.8	668.5	2,008.5	2,630.6	4,639.1	14.4
1957	3/11			72.3	701.8	2,108.4	2,811.9	4,920.3	14.3
1958	3/11			71.0	712.5	2,152.2	2,974.3	5,126.5	13.9
1959	3/11			71.9	736.2	2,188.5	3,119.1	5,307.6	13.9
1960	4/1	5.4.60	3/0½	71.3	788.5	2,282.6	3,094.8	5,377.4	14.7
1961	4/6	26.7.61	3/4	70.1	825.2	2,389.1	3,332.9	5,722.0	14.4
1962	4/6			70.4	869.2	2,581.9	3,781.1	6,363.0	13.7
1963	4/6			69.1	878.2	2,670.4	3,908.4	6,578.8	13.3
1964	4/11	15.4.64	3/8½	69.8	892.1	2,766.1	3,891.7	6,657.8	13.4
1965	5/5	7.4.65	4/2	69.7	983.7	3,171.4	4,261.5	7,432.9	13.2
1966	5/5			68.2	1,024.2	3,400.0	4,931.9	8,331.9	12.2
1967	5/5			68.7	1,024.6	3,539.7	5,842.4	9,382.1	10.9
1968	5/7	20.3.68	4/4	68.8	1,043.4	3,716.9	7,086.7	10,803.6	9.7
1969	6/1	23.11.68	4/9	68.9	1,103.6	4,611.2	8,310.2	12,921.4	8.5
1970	6/2		4/9	68.9	1,141.5	4,952.7	9,805.7	14,758.4	7.7

Source: *59th Report—Customs and Excise for the Year Ended 31st March, 1968.* H.M.S.O., London. Updated by personal communication with H.M. Customs and Excise Department.

the social climate favourable to smoking. By substantially reducing the number of smokers a more effective treatment of smoking would, therefore, have the bonus effect of helping to change the social climate away from acceptance of smoking.

Reference has been made in the preceding section to problems of communication. Effective communication is crucial to the engineering of a change of social climate from acceptance to disapproval of smoking. Previous discussion suggested that to be successful this would require a ban on all cigarette advertising and the launching of an extensive, persistent, sophisticated, advertising-type campaign to alter the image of smoking to one of general disfavour. Such a programme would need to be linked with social research including continuous evaluation and public reaction monitoring. It is likely that social research soundings would indicate that different sorts of message would be required for people of different ages. Possible ancilary tactics would include restriction of cigarette sales outlets, banning of smoking in certain public places, warnings printed on cigarette packets, etc. But each of these measures would require careful consideration and testing of public acceptability before introduction, for the essence of good communication is to avoid back-lash effects.

Just as successful treatment of large numbers of dependent smokers would contribute to changing the social climate, so would a change in social climate facilitate treatment. Once a change in social climate and the image of smoking was wrought, increasing numbers of mildly dependent smokers would stop and diminishing numbers of young people would adopt the habit. The initial phase of such a programme would be the most difficult, with later stages tending to be facilitated by a snow-ball effect.

The role of doctors would be of tactical relevance—as examplers they affect the image of smoking, as informants of high credibility it would help if they took every opportunity to advise and encourage their patients to stop smoking. The power of simple but firm advice against smoking, given by a doctor to his patients is such that it could well yield a success rate of up to 20% (Russell, 1971b). If each of the 20,000 general practitioners in England were to persuade only one patient a week to stop smoking, the yield would be over one million ex-smokers a year. To equal this it would require 10,000 anti-smoking clinics each having a 33% success rate with 300 subjects a year.

The role of doctors would be of tactical relevance—as examples they affect the a temporary expediency for those who are unable to stop. Hopes for a 'safe cigarette' are to some extent misguided. It would solve only part of the problem in that a completely safe cigarette would have to be nicotine-free and most heavy smokers could as easily give up altogether as transfer to nicotine-free cigarettes. However, if teenagers who smoke initially for psychosocial rather than pharmacological motives could be induced to use nicotine-free cigarettes, it is possible that the almost inevitable escalation to dependent smoking might be prevented. Selective taxation might be a useful measure to promote such use of nicotine-free cigarettes. It would also help if taxation favoured cigar and pipe smoking. It is possible that as social customs change and knowledge and experience is gained of the dangerous and early stages of dependence, the large majority of us may, as in the case with alcohol, learn to limit out smoking to an occasional pipe or cigar. Indeed many would consider this goal preferable to the abolition of all smoking.

Clearly the suggested strategy demands a co-ordinated, sustained and massive intervention on a national scale. It would require a multi-disciplinary organising committee closely backed by the Government with generous financial and, if necessary, legislative support. Drastic and expensive though this may be, it would be a pity if the Government allowed its reluctance to lose the £1,000 million-plus it annually derives from tobacco revenue to stand in the way of what is potentially the most important health measure that is likely to be open to us for the rest of this century.

REFERENCES

BALL K.P., 1970. Hospital beds and cigarette smoking. *Lancet.* ii, 48.

BYNNER J.M. (Government Social Survey), 1969. *The Young Smoker.* H.M.S.O., London.

CARTWRIGHT A., MARTIN F.M. and THOMSON J.E., 1960. Efficacy of an anti-smoking campaign. *Lancet.* i, 327.

CENTRAL STATISTICAL OFFICE, 1951. *Statistical Digest of the War.* H.M.S.O., London.

CENTRAL STATISTICAL OFFICE, 1969. *Annual Abstract of Statistics. No. 106.* H.M.S.O., London.

CUSTOMS AND EXCISE (H.M.), 1969. *59th Report–Customs and Excise for the Year Ended 31st March, 1968.* H.M.S.O., London.

DEPARTMENT OF EMPLOYMENT AND PRODUCTIVITY, 1970. *Family Expenditure Survey.* H.M.S.O., London.

DOLL R. and HILL A.B., 1950. Smoking and carcinoma of the lung. Preliminary report. *Brit.Med.J.* 2, 739.

FLETCHER C.M. and HORN D., 1970. Smoking and health. *W.H.O. Chronicle.* 24, 345.

GODBER G.E., 1968. *On the State of Public Health. The Annual Report of the Chief Medical Officer of the Ministry of Health for the Year, 1967.* H.M.S.O., London.

GODBER G.E., 1969. *On the State of the Public Health. The Annual Report of the Chief Medical Officer of the Ministry of Health for the Year, 1968.* H.M.S.O., London.

GODBER G.E. 1970a. *On the State of the Public Health. The Annual Report of the Chief Medical Officer of the Ministry of Health for the Year, 1969.* H.M.S.O., London.

GODBER G.E., 1970b. Smoking disease: a self-inflicted injury. *Amer.J.Pub.Hlth.* 60, 235.

HAMMOND E.C., 1966. Smoking in relation to the death rate of one million men and women. *J.Nat.Cancer Inst.* 19, 127.

HIGHBEE K.L. 1969. Fifteen years of fear arousal: research on threat appeals, 1953–1968. *Psychol.Bull.* 72, 426.

HOLLAND W.W. and ELIOTT A., 1968. Cigarette smoking, respiratory symptoms, and anti-smoking propaganda. *Lancet.* i, 41.

JEFFREYS M., NORMAN-TAYLOR W. and GRIFFITH G., 1967. Longer term results of an anti-smoking educational campaign. *Med.Offr.* 117, 93.

LEVENTHAL H., 1968. Experimental studies of anti-smoking communications. In E.E. Borgatta and R.R. Evans (Ed.). *Smoking, Health and Behaviour.* Aldine, Chicago.

LOWE C.R., 1970. The cost to health of addiction to tobacco. Paper prepared at the International Conference on Alcohol and Addictions. Cardiff.

LYNCH G.W., 1963. Smoking habits of medical and non-medical university staff: changes since the Royal College of Physicians' report. *Brit.Med.J.* 1, 852.

McKENNEL A.C. and THOMAS R.K. (Government Social Survey), 1967. *Adults' and Adolescents' Smoking Habits and Attitudes.* H.M.S.O., London.

O'BRIEN T.H., 1955. *Civil Defence.* H.M.S.O., London.

ROYAL COLLEGE OF PHYSICIANS, 1962. *Smoking and Health.* Pitman, London.

ROYAL COLLEGE OF PHYSICIANS, 1971. *Smoking and Health Now.* Pitman, London.

RUSSELL C.S., TAYLOR R. and MADISON R.N., 1966. Some effects of smoking in pregnancy. *J.Obster.Gynae.Brit.Cmwth.* 73, 742.

RUSSELL M.A.H., 1970. Effect of electric aversion on cigarette smoking. *Brit.Med.J.* 1, 82

RUSSELL M.A.H., 1971a. Cigarette smoking: natural history of a dependent disorder. *Brit.J.Med.Psychol.* In press.

RUSSELL M.A.H., 1971b. Cigarette dependence: the role of the doctor in the management. In press.

SCHWARTZ J.L., 1969. A critical review and evaluation of smoking control methods. *Public Health Reports.* 84, 483.

TOBACCO RESEARCH COUNCIL (Ed. D.H. Beese), 1968. *Tobacco Consumption in Various Countries.* Tobacco Research Council, London.

TOBACCO RESEARCH COUNCIL (Ed. G.F. Todd), 1969. *Statistics of Smoking in the United Kingdom.* Tobacco Research Council, London.

UNITED STATES DEPARTMENT OF HEALTH, EDUCATION AND WELFARE, 1970. *Changes in Cigarette Smoking Habits Between 1955 and 1966.* U.S. Government Printing Office, Washington.

INDEX